GDI+ Custom Controls with Visual C# 2005

A fast-paced example-driven tutorial to building custom controls using Visual C# 2005 Express Edition and .NET 2.0

Iulian Serban
Dragos Brezoi
Tiberiu Radu
Adam Ward

BIRMINGHAM - MUMBAI

GDI+ Custom Controls with Visual C# 2005

First published: July 2006

Production Reference: 1220706

Published by Packt Publishing Ltd.
32 Lincoln Road
Olton
Birmingham, B27 6PA, UK.

ISBN 1-904811-60-4

www.packtpub.com

Cover Image by www.visionwt.com

Credits

Authors
Iulian Serban
Dragos Brezoi
Tiberiu Radu
Adam Ward

Reviewer
Cosmin Oprea

Technical Editor
Mithil Kulkarni

Editorial Manager
Dipali Chittar

Development Editor
Cristian Darie

Indexer
Niranjan Jahagirdar

Proofreader
Chris Smith

Layouts and Illustrations
Shantanu Zagade

Cover Designer
Shantanu Zagade

About the Authors

Iulian Serban is a software architect who started programming at a very young age. He evolved through a lot of programming languages including Pascal, Delphi, C++ Builder, Visual C++ with MFC and finally .NET and C #. By the age of 17 he started working for Syncfusion, one of the largest .NET control builders in the US, writing code for professional custom controls. Nowadays he devotes most of his spare time to his own IT business, which is set to release significant software projects soon.

I'm using this opportunity to thank the Syncfusion team for their continued support, and for their professionalism.

Dragos Brezoi started programming to create an application for processing and adding extra effects to his guitar's sound. Several years after, he got a Masters Degree in Computer Science from the Politehnica University of Bucharest, and is now researching for a Ph.D. in Advanced Automatics. Dragos currently works as a programmer for Mikon Systems, developing industrial software. His skills cover a wide area of specialization from PLC and DSP programming to SCADA, OPC, and DCS solutions. At this moment he is creating professional human-machine interfaces, with a focus on developing advanced custom controls with C#.

My big thanks go to my son, Matei, who was a wonderful and cooperative baby and let me work on this book.

Tiberiu Radu has been working with computers for over 10 years now, programming in a wide range of languages including Pascal, C/C++, Visual Basic, Delphi, and C#. As a Microsoft Student Partner in the Microsoft Academic Program, he's devoting a lot of time to many .NET-related technologies. Tiberiu is in the last year of studies with the Automatic Control and Computers Faculty of the Politehnica University of Bucharest. While researching for his own IT security business, he developed skills in embedded programming and new web technologies, and is seeking new and innovating networking security solutions.

Adam Ward works for a communications technology company in Derby, England. Adam excels in experimental programming techniques and has a particular interest in high-speed algorithms and graphical methods. His professional work is based in a varied Research and Development environment and he thrives on tasks requiring innovation, skill, and fine-tuning. He has also been involved in experimental coding collaborations showcasing the power of C#. Away from work, Adam is turning his attentions to Linux systems and especially cross-platform programming under .NET-compatible systems.

About the Reviewer

Cosmin Oprea is a veteran in the software industry, having written code in languages ranging from C/C++ to VB6 and C#. His experience with GDI started when working with the Win32 API on Windows 95, and nowadays he's using GDI+ to give a final touch and better look and feel to his Windows Forms interfaces.

Cosmin is a big fan of agile methodologies (such as Extreme Programming), which he has successfully applied when developing various enterprise-class applications based on .NET technologies. Microsoft Romania has recently awarded Cosmin in recognition of his influence as a .NET evangelist, and for his contribution to the Romanian .NET User Association (RONUA).

Table of Contents

Preface

The amount of built-in functionality included in the .NET Framework is amazing. One could create complex applications with lots of functionality by simply assembling the pieces you're offered for free. Among those pieces you'll find lots of powerful, flexible, and configurable controls. Who would ever need to build their own controls, right?

While some can get away without ever needing to build a custom control, many don't, or don't want to. Sometimes building a custom control is a necessity, because what you want to achieve doesn't exist, or is too expensive to buy. This is particularly true for controls with customized shapes, which need to be drawn instead of reusing other existing controls.

In some other cases, developers build custom controls as part of their architecture, allowing them to reuse more efficiently common functionality (and code) that they trust and like. There are many circumstances where building a custom control can make a programmer's life easier.

Unfortunately, programmers frequently avoided learning how to build custom controls because learning all the complexities consume lots of time and energy. Comprehensive and advanced books on the subject well exceed 1,000 pages, and the excessive amount of information can indeed be intimidating.

This book takes a lighter approach, guiding you step by step into building your first custom controls, and writing quality code. You'll build a new example in each chapter, and in the end you'll build a completely functional custom control where you'll apply most of what you've learned in the book.

What This Book Covers

Chapter 1: *Introduction to Custom Controls* will be your introduction to the world of .NET custom controls. You'll learn what controls are, why they are useful, what they are made of, and towards the end of the chapter you'll also create a simple yet functional custom control called TinyNoiseMaker.

Chapter 2: *Introduction to GDI+* introduces you to the basics of drawing with GDI+. You will meet a few namespaces, classes, and events that form the foundations of drawing with .NET, and you'll see how to paint the surface of a custom control.

Chapter 3: *Basic Drawing* teaches you more about the coordinate system of GDI+, drawing lines and polygons using pens, brushes, and colors, and guides you to build a control named GradientLabel.

Chapter 4: *Drawing Complex Shapes and Using Transformations* teaches you how to use graphics paths, regions, and transformations to build complex shapes. You'll then use the theory to build a Clock control.

Chapter 5: *Drawing Control Parts, Borders, and Adornments* explores using the `ControlPaint` class to implement common functionality and adds finishing touches to your control. To demonstrate the theory you'll build a simple custom control named GradientButton.

Chapter 6: *Working with Images* covers common techniques for manipulating images. You'll build a control called ImageWarper that scales, skews, and rotates an image.

Chapter 7: *Printing* introduces this very important area of GDI+. In many circumstances you'll want to add printing support to your controls, and you'll see exactly how to do so by creating the PrintableRichTextBox control.

Chapter 8: *Collections* teaches more details about .NET collections, including the new .NET 2.0 generics. Collections are very useful when building custom controls, and as an example you'll build a Font Picker control.

Chapter 9: *Double Buffering* introduces this advanced technique that can make a big difference in improving the speed and responsiveness of your control. Scrolling is one such area where double buffering could make a difference, and you'll end the chapter by implementing a control that displays a scrolling text.

Chapter 10: *Handling Mouse Events* deals with a very important topic for any desktop application you'll ever write. Luckily enough, all controls that ship with .NET have integrated mouse support, but at times you'll need to customize the features. In this chapter, you'll implement two applications: one will allow you to drag an image inside a delimited area, and the second lets you drag pictures from your Windows system into your form.

Chapter 11: *Implementing Design-Time Support* shows you how to make your user controls designer friendly. This way, your control will be friendly not only to the end users working with it but also to developers as well.

Chapter 12: *Designing Intuitive Interfaces* is a high-level overview of some human interface aspects that, handled correctly, can help you build controls and applications that are easier and more fun to use.

Chapter 13: *The PieChart Control* is a comprehensive case study, showing you how to develop a complete custom control in several stages, each time adding features, fixing bugs, and improving functionality.

Appendix A: *Distributing Custom Controls* shows you how to compile a custom control into a separate DLL file, which can be reused later in other projects. You'll be shown how to do this with both Visual Studio 2005 and Visual C# 2005 Express Edition, which offers different built-in features.

Conventions

In this book, you will find a number of styles of text that distinguish between different kinds of information. Here are some examples of these styles, and an explanation of their meaning.

There are three styles for code. Code words in text are shown as follows: "We can include other contexts through the use of the `include` directive."

A block of code will be set as follows:

```
private void SetValues()
{
  totalCount = 0;
  if (mySlices != null)
  {
    foreach (Slice slice in mySlices)
    totalCount += slice.GetSliceRange();
  }
  // mySlicesPercent.Clear();
}
```

When we wish to draw your attention to a particular part of a code block, the relevant lines or items will be made bold:

```
private void SetValues()
{
  totalCount = 0;
  if (mySlices != null)
  {
    foreach (Slice slice in mySlices)
    totalCount += slice.GetSliceRange();
  }
  // mySlicesPercent.Clear();
}
```

New terms and **important words** are introduced in a bold-type font. Words that you see on the screen, in menus or dialog boxes for example, appear in our text like this: "clicking the Next button moves you to the next screen".

> Warnings or important notes appear in a box like this.

> Tips and tricks appear like this.

Reader Feedback

Feedback from our readers is always welcome. Let us know what you think about this book, what you liked or may have disliked. Reader feedback is important for us to develop titles that you really get the most out of.

To send us general feedback, simply drop an email to `feedback@packtpub.com`, making sure to mention the book title in the subject of your message.

If there is a book that you need and would like to see us publish, please send us a note in the SUGGEST A TITLE form on `www.packtpub.com` or email `suggest@packtpub.com`.

If there is a topic that you have expertise in and you are interested in either writing or contributing to a book, see our author guide on `www.packtpub.com/authors`.

Customer Support

Now that you are the proud owner of a Packt book, we have a number of things to help you to get the most from your purchase.

Downloading the Example Code for the Book

Visit `http://www.packtpub.com/support`, and select this book from the list of titles to download any example code or extra resources for this book. The files available for download will then be displayed.

> The downloadable files contain instructions on how to use them.

Errata

Although we have taken every care to ensure the accuracy of our contents, mistakes do happen. If you find a mistake in one of our books—maybe a mistake in text or code—we would be grateful if you would report this to us. By doing this you can save other readers from frustration, and help to improve subsequent versions of this book. If you find any errata, report them by visiting `http://www.packtpub.com/support`, selecting your book, clicking on the **Submit Errata** link, and entering the details of your errata. Once your errata have been verified, your submission will be accepted and the errata added to the list of existing errata. The existing errata can be viewed by selecting your title from `http://www.packtpub.com/support`.

Questions

You can contact us at `questions@packtpub.com` if you are having a problem with some aspect of the book, and we will do our best to address it

1

Introduction to Custom Controls

Welcome to the world of **Custom Controls**! This book will guide you through creating custom controls, from simple to complex ones. First, we will see what controls are, and how implementing custom controls helps saving time and money. After reading this book, you will know how to build different kinds of controls in a professional way.

This book not only presents the theory needed to understand how to build custom controls, but it also shows how to implement the theory in practice by creating functional custom controls. The theory is kept short and to the point because the purpose of the book is to teach building professional custom controls quickly and easily, through practice. After each block of theory, you'll be taken through an exercise that guides you to implement that theory in a functional control.

In this chapter, we'll have a quick overview of .NET custom controls, and also create a functional custom control towards the end of the chapter. Understanding their architecture is an important prerequisite before starting to create your own controls. More specifically, in this chapter you will:

- Learn what custom controls are, and why are they so useful
- Understand what custom controls are made of
- Build your first custom control using other controls and components

What Are Controls?

Controls are reusable pieces of user interface functionality. In the Windows world, controls represent the way the user interacts with the application. They allow the user to enter data and manipulate it, to perform certain actions on the application, input data, and display data in a way friendly to the human eye. An application's interface is made up of controls and its functionality is based on the interaction between these controls and the underlying code.

Let's take a look at the next few pictures and you will recognize some of today's most popular controls. You must be familiar with the ways in which using these controls makes programming much easier than it would have been to recreate the functionality by hand.

The Button

The Checkbox

The Label

The Progress Bar

The Radio Button

Every software application has an invisible part, which does the actual work, and a visible part, which provides the user interface. Controls are complete software elements that contain both: they are represented on the screen in a graphical way, and they contain code to sustain this interface.

Controls have two major functions:

- To listen to the user's commands and send them to the application
- To display the results from the application in a way that the user will understand

This way you can change the background color by using a *color picker control*, you can execute a certain operation just by pressing a button, or you can see the playing status of a movie just by looking at a *progress bar*. A particular kind of control is the **indicator**, which exposes data in a graphical way but doesn't let the user change that data. The label is the best example of such a control.

It's interesting to know that the whole idea of the controls has its roots in the development of personal computers. The developers had to emulate some real controls that offered a good look and feel to the application. Let's take the example of a common button. A real button has different forms and sizes and can be of multiple states, can be pushed and may revert if released, or can make a sound when pressed. In order to reproduce the characteristics of a real control many tricks have been used.

Back in the old days, it used to be harmony between the controls' look and feel, and the development of personal computers, operating systems, and development systems. Twenty years ago the common button had one color background, one single font text and when pressed, it didn't have a very inspiring animation (if it had one at all). Today, when you think about a button, you have in mind a rounded corner, gradient color border, bitmap, and multiple font and size animated button. Things have changed, and the requirements for building new controls have increased.

Introducing Custom Controls

The term *custom* is pretty expressive. While in many of your development tasks you can make use only of the default controls provided by your development environment (.NET in our case), in many other cases you'll need to build your own.

Custom-made controls are named, not very surprisingly, *custom controls.* A custom control is a control designed and programmed by you, and it may make use of other existing controls. Sometimes custom controls are called third-party controls, named by their origin.

Here are a few controls that we'll develop over the course of this book:

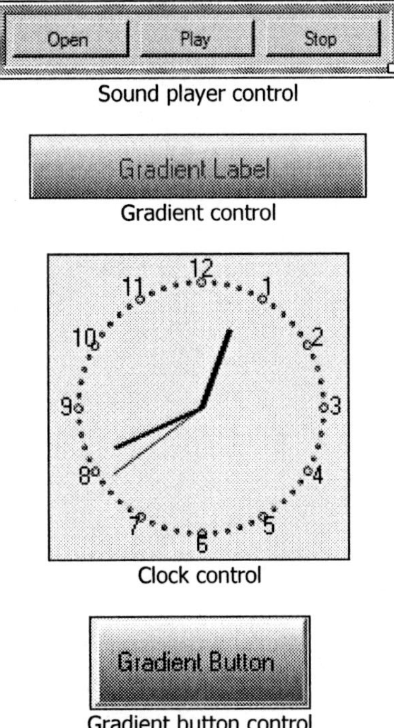

Sound player control

Gradient control

Clock control

Gradient button control

The case has been made: creating custom controls can be a necessity when the basic classes provided by the .NET Framework or the ones you can buy from third parties aren't enough, or are too expensive.

The improved coding efficiency you can gain by implementing functionality as a custom control, when it makes sense to do so, can be easily described using an example. If you have to use a pie chart with different elements in it in your application that will present some results in an elegant graphical way, there are two ways to implement this solution.

- **You can write the code directly in the form**. First, you will have to draw a pie chart with different elements in it, at a certain position. Second, you will have to override the mouse event handler of the form to get events for the chart. Third, assuming that this chart has some functionality, you will have to implement the desired model by attaching the code directly to the form code.

Now if you want to have multiple pie charts in an application, you need to follow the three steps mentioned above for each of them. Afterwards, even changing some simple functionality, such as moving a certain action from left button to right button, will need to be done three times. Your code will contain lots of duplicate functionality and will be hard to read, understand, debug, and extend. Not to mention that every time you modify the chart, you will have to rebuild your entire application.

- **You can build a custom control**. You will create a pie chart custom control that draws itself and has its own events and event handler mechanisms. It will expose different properties and methods necessary in the form. This custom control's position can then be easily changed inside the forms that use it by simply setting its coordinates. Also, once this custom control is created you will gain precious time, because the time you will spend making changes, adding extra features, and debugging the custom control will be shorter and code modification will happen in one place—the control code.

Packing functionality in the form of user controls brings a number of important benefits:

- Building custom controls facilitates code reusability because the same control can be used in any number of forms or tabs (or even other custom controls), without having to write the same code over and over again. This saves a lot of time in application development and untangles application code.
- It encourages functionality reusability, under OOP's "**black box**" principle. You don't need to know how the control works inside; all you need to know is the *public interface* it exposes. For example, think about one of the simplest controls available: the `Label` control. When working with labels in a Windows Forms project, you know that you need to set the label's `Text` property to the text you want displayed. You never care how the label works internally, and how it actually paints that text on the screen (it may not be obvious at the first sight, but work needs to be done even for such a simple task as painting some text on the form). Extrapolating from this simple example, you can get a feeling about how the black box concept applies to the more complex controls.
- It keeps application code simple. Let's say you need that your application, among other things, knows how to play sounds. Using a custom control to implement the functionality for playing sounds minimizes the code written in the application form. Instead of creating buttons and components, and adding and handling their events in the application code, you can simply create a custom control (such as the `TinyNoiseMaker` you'll build at the end of this chapter) that implements this functionality, and exposes it through a public interface that the application can use. Using custom controls keeps application code simple because the functionality is implemented inside the control and not in the application's form. In the extreme case, a form could be built exclusively of controls that are interacting with each other, and have no functionality implemented in it.

- Custom controls can be developed, compiled, packaged, and even sold separately, just like regular applications. This gives you a lot of flexibility in the way you develop and then use the controls.
- Building custom controls can make it easier to improve the appearance and usability of your application by implementing user-friendly code and design into the controls. If you want your application to look a certain way, setting the .NET Framework's controls' appearance properties isn't enough to create it. By creating custom controls with the appearance you want, your can greatly improve your application's look, feel, and functionality. This can be a fairly easy way to win more happy users on your side, because the user interface created specifically for the application can be much more user-friendly than one built with the built-in .NET controls.

Categories of User Controls

Depending on the way the control draws itself, there are three kinds of custom controls:

- **Non custom drawn**: These are controls that use other controls' user interfaces to cover their own interface. An example is a `Toolbar` control that uses toolbar buttons to cover its interface. You'll see a first example of such a control a bit later in this chapter.
- **Custom drawn**: These controls paint their user interface themselves according to input data, mouse and keyboard events, focus, and other variables. As an example, a PieChart control such as the one presented in Chapter 13 is custom drawn. To build this kind of controls you need to learn GDI+, and you'll meet the first example in Chapter 3.
- **Mixed**: The mixed controls use both of the above methods to cover their user interface. For example, a Chart control with scrollbars is in this category. You'll see lots of examples of these controls in this book. Of particular importance is the Pie Chart control, which is more complex and is presented in the final Chapter 13 of this book.

Preparing Your Environment

The examples in this book were tested with Visual C# 2005 Express Edition. This tool is freely downloadable from `http://msdn.microsoft.com/vstudio/express/visualcsharp/`.

Visual C# 2005 Express Edition offers all the functionality you need to build powerful Windows Forms applications with C# and .NET 2.0, and it includes support for building custom controls. Make sure this tool is properly installed before continuing, because you'll start using it later in this chapter, when building the `TinyNoiseMaker` control.

What Are Custom Controls Made Of?

To implement custom controls we need to understand how they and their component parts work. We will now learn about the visible and invisible parts of controls. Custom controls are made of two main parts. The first part is the "black box". This part is private to the control and holds the private data members and methods that build up the control's internal functionality. The second part is the control's public interface. This interface is made up of public **properties**, **events**, and

methods. They expose the control's functionality allowing the code that uses the control to manipulate the control programmatically.

Technically, a control is a class derived from the base `System.Windows.Forms.Control` class. It contains the basic functionality of any control, such as functionality for handling mouse events, keyboard events, focus and paint events, preset styles, and properties. The most basic definition of a custom control is as shown below:

```
public class MyControl:Control
{
}
```

In the following pages we will learn the basic components of a `Control` class. It is important to know and understand what these components are, and how to use them to implement control functionality as they will be present in any control we create. These components make up the body of the control's class, and represent the changes you implement into your custom control, on top of the base functionality you inherit from the base `Control` class. In other words, we inherit from the `Control` class some basic features, common for all controls, and we build custom functionality for our control by adding these components. We could also modify an existing control, to add an extra feature.

> This book assumes that you already have the foundation knowledge about Object-Oriented Programming principles, such as inheritance, encapsulation, and polymorphism. There is a free tutorial about these concepts and how they work with C# at `http://www.cristiandarie.ro/downloads/`.

Private Fields

A private field is, as its name suggests, a field that cannot be accessed from the outside. When building a custom control, the "outside" is the application that uses this control (it can also be another custom control that uses your control). Usually, for every public property of the control, there is at least one private field that stores the data exposed by it.

A good programming practice is to declare private class fields, and then expose them through public properties (explained next). The naming conventions we're using in this book specify that class names are named using Pascal casing (capitalizing the first letter of every word, such as in `ProgressBar`), and the fields are named using Camel casing (capitalizing the first letter of every word, except the first one, such as in `myProgressBar`).

Here's a code snippet that shows the definition of a control named `MyControl`, having four private fields:

```
public class MyControl : Control
{
  private Color backgroundColor;
  private Color foregroundColor;
  private int intemCount;
  private Brush backBrush;
}
```

Properties

When you select a control in the Form designer of Visual C# Express or Visual Studio, you can see the control's properties in the **Properties** window. A property is an attribute associated with a class or an object. For example, a common button has lots of properties: **name**, **text**, **font**, **size**, and many others. All these properties exposed by a common button are shown in the **Properties** window (if you're using Visual C# while reading this, you can open the **Properties** window by pressing *F4*).

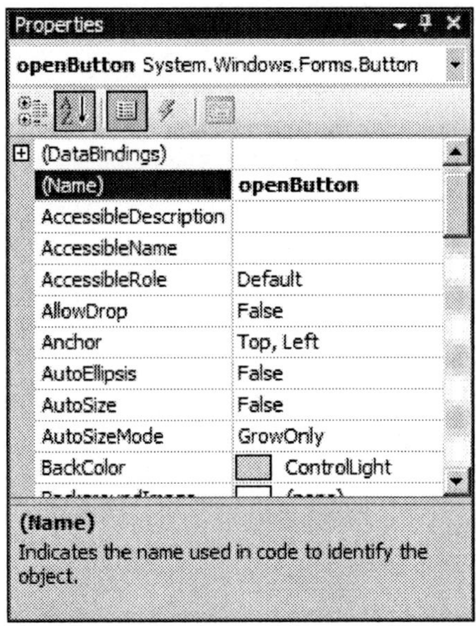

Properties are the key features of any control as they expose the control's settings and data. The public properties represent the way the user interacts with the settings of a control, by controlling the way the user gets or sets the private fields that hold the settings and data.

> Note that in this context, the user of a control is the *programmer* using the control in his or her applications. Controls can be used by *end users* only when included into an application, and they can't run standalone.

Properties contain code that filters the data that is read or set, in their `get` and `set` **accessors**. These accessors usually read or set the values of private members, which contain the actual data, on behalf of the property. By defining only the `get` accessor of a property you make it read-only, and by defining only the `set` accessor you make it write-only. Going back to the background color example, mentioned when explaining private fields, it is held in the control using a private field and is exposed outside of the control using a property that controls the way the private field is manipulated.

A property's default structure is:

```
public <type> <PropertyName>
{
  get
    {
      return <fieldName>;
    }
  set
    {
      <fieldName> = value;
    }
}
```

Here, `<type>` represents the data type of the property (such as `string`), `<PropertyName>` is the name of the property (such as `BackgroundColor`), and `<fieldName>` is the private field that stores the property data. Note that the property itself doesn't contain any data, and it's free to set or return any values in its `get` and `set` accessors.

Properties basically group together two methods that get and set the member value. They can also help instantiate null fields and perform actions when the value of a member changes, as you can see in the example below:

```
private Brush backBrush = null;
...
public Brush BackBrush
{
  get
  {
    if(backBrush == null)
    {
      backBrush = new SolidBrush(Color.Black);
    }
    return backBrush;
  }
  set
  {
    if(backBrush != value)
    {
      backBrush = value;
      Invalidate();
    }
  }
}
```

In the above code, in the `get` accessor, the first time a reference of the `backBrush` needs to be retrieved, the property initializes it to a default value and then returns it. If in the code trying to read the `BackBrush` property isn't enclosed in a `try/catch` block, a null reference exception may be fired.

Look at the code in the `set` accessor: When setting the `backBrush` field, if it is not different than the old value, nothing needs to happen. This helps optimize application code, so methods are not called when there is no need to do so.

It is best practice to implement properties this way as will be seen in the controls that we implement in this book.

Indexers

Let's say that you have a control, or data class that has a collection of items. Instead of exposing the collection by making it public through a property, it can be easier to add an **indexer** to the control. An indexer is a special type of property that makes the class be indexed as an array, so that its objects can be retrieved based on an index value.

For example, if an object called `list` has an indexer, you could get its collection items by reading `list[1]`, `list[2]`, and so on. Without an indexer, you would need to access its items as `list.Items[1]`, `list.Items[2]`, and so on. The difference between indexers and properties is that indexer accessors take parameters.

The default declaration of an indexer is:

```
public <type> this[int index]
{
  get
    {
      //return the object at the index;
    }
  set
    {
      //set the object at the index;
    }
}
```

Usually, the indexer returns an object held in a member array at the given index.

Let's take an example to understand the benefits of using indexers better. A color picker is a control that lets you choose a color. As an extra feature, the color picker can provide through an indexer some default colors, or the recently used colors. The objects in the array of colors are available by calling the `ColorPicker`'s indexer.

```
public class ColorPicker : Control
{
...
  private Color[] colors;
...
  public Color this[int index]
  {
    get
    {
      if(index >= 0 && index < colors.Length)
      {
        return colors[index];
      }
      else
      {
        return null;
      }
    }
    set
    {
      if(index >= 0 && index < colors.Length)
      {
        colors[index] = value;
      }
    }
  }
...
}
...
```

```
ColorPicker colorPicker1;
...
colorPicker1[0] = Color.Red;
```

The `get/set` syntax actually encourages you to validate the values you read or set. You can see a simple validation scheme in the sample code snippet.

Generally speaking you can use indexers when you can structure your data into an array; this means that the data must be numerable. For example, you will use a property to store the temperature in degrees, but you will use an indexer to store the day of the week.

Events and Delegates

Events and **delegates** are at the heart of programming for the Windows platform, because they are the main mechanisms by which the application interacts with the user (but they can be used for other purposes as well). Events and delegates allow a control (or any type of class, for that matter), to send a *signal* when something happens to it, and you can write a C# method to be executed automatically in response to that signal. The signal is the event itself, which is said to be *fired*. The delegate is a type of object that allows you to register the local C# method (which we'll call the *event handler*) to be executed when the event fires.

To explain with an example, let's say we have a form and a button on that form. We want to know when the button is clicked, so we can react to that action by executing some C# code. This link between the button and the form is done through an event. When the button is clicked, the `Click` event of the button is fired to notify that the button has been clicked. To react to the `Click` event, you create an event handler, which is a C# method that is executed when the `Click` event fires.

Events define actions that occur in a control. These actions can be caused by users interacting with the control, or by other implemented logic. A mouse click is an event, a key press is also an event fired by the control to notify that certain action has occurred in it. An event is fired by a sender and is captured by a receiver. A special type called a delegate does the link between the sender and the receiver.

Earlier we said that in response to an event being fired, we can register a local method to be executed automatically. While that helps you form an image of how the system works, in reality (and in C# code) nothing happens "automatically" if you don't write some code for it. When an event happens in a control, that control knows how to execute a method of the class using that control; in order for this to work, a *reference to the method* to be executed must be sent to the control. The delegate is such a method reference. A delegate is a data type that defines a method template, and a delegate instance is a reference to a particular method. Each event that can happen in a control knows how to execute a certain delegate type, which supports the parameters the event needs to send to its parent (these parameters contain the details of the event, which differ depending on the event).

Let's see how delegates are declared:

```
public delegate <return type> <delegate name> ( <parameter list> );
```

Example:

```
public delegate int myDelegate( int intValue );
```

This delegate represents the template for a method that takes as parameter an integer value, and also returns an integer. Multiple methods in other classes can be wired to this event if they match the event's delegate template. These methods are then called when the event is fired. Usually event delegates have the following layout:

```
public delegate void <myEventHandler>(object sender, <EventArgs> e);
```

Here, `<myEventHandler>` is the local method that executes when the event fires. A possible naming convention would be to use the event name appending "EventHandler," such as in ClickEventHandler, KeyDownEventHandler, and MouseOverEventHandler. The naming convention used by the Visual C# 2005 designer when generating event handlers is `<name of the control that fired the event>_<name of event>`, such as in `myButton_Click`.

When working with the built-in .NET controls, `<EventArgs>` is a class derived from the .NET Framework's `EventArgs` class. You can define your own events and delegates any way you want, but it is best practice to create them using the above layout.

Now let's see how events are defined. An event must be declared in the control that fires it, and the default declaration looks like this:

```
public event <myEventHandler> <Event_name>;
```

Example:

```
public event ClickEventHandler Click;
```

The receiver methods that are called when the event is fired are called event handlers. In other words, when creating a control that needs to notify the form or other controls when a certain action has happened, you need to add a public event to the control, and fire it when the action occurs. Then, any class that holds a reference to your control can subscribe to get notified by associating an event handler to the event. Let's see now how we can fire an event and how to handle it in another class.

Firing an event is usually done from a protected virtual method of the control that fires the event, declared like the one given below:

```
protected virtual void On<event name>(EventArgs e)
{
  if(<event name> != null)
  {
    <event name>(this,e);
  }
}
```

The fact that the method starts with "On" is not a requirement but a recommendation. For example, the `MouseOver` event would be fired by the `OnMouseOver` firing event method. This way the code is easier to read and understand.

The firing method is `virtual`, which means that you can override it when deriving from the control, if you need to change its default behavior.

The example overleaf raises the `BackgroundColorChanged` event when the value of the control's `backgroundColor` member is changed when setting the `BackgroundColor` property.

```
public class MyControl : Control
{
...
  private Color backgroundColor;
  public event EventHandler BackgroundColorChanged;
  public Color BackgroundColor
  {
    get
    {
      return backgroundColor;
    }
    set
    {
      if(backgroundColor != value)
      {
        backgroundColor = value;
        OnBackgroundColorChanged(EventArgs.Empty);
      }
    }
  }

  protected virtual void OnBackgroundColorChanged(EventArgs e)
  {
    if(BackgroundColorChanged != null)
    {
      BackgroundColorChanged(this,e);
    }
  }
...
}
```

The event variable is null when there is no event handler attached to it. This must be verified in the raising method or an exception will be fired if no event handlers are attached to the event.

Handling Events

To handle the event fired by the `MyControl` class above, you need to add an event handler to the class that uses the control. The event handler is a method that can be located in any class that wants to handle the event. The event is declared as `EventHandler`, which is the delegate used for notifying only, without passing any data with the event because the `EventArgs` class passed has no parameters. It is declared in the .NET Framework as:

```
public delegate void EventHandler(object sender,EventArgs e);
```

The event handler method must match the event's delegate signature:

```
MyControl myControl;
...
// Attaches the myControl_BackgroundColorChanged method to the event
myControl.BackgroundColorChanged += new
EventHandler(myControl_BackgroundColorChanged);
...
private void myControl_BackgroundColorChanged(object sender, EventArgs e)
{
  // Code that is executed when the BackgroundColorChanged event is fired.
}
```

The method `myControl_BackgroundColorChanged` will be called each time the `BackgroundColorChanged` event is fired in the `MyControl` class.

To implement more complex events that pass data to the event handlers, such as the control's state or other parameters (e.g. the `Click` event to pass the mouse coordinates), either use .NET events that are already implanted for certain situations (e.g. `ClickEventHandler`) or create your own events.

Collections

Some of the controls you'll write will need to store collections of items. For example, a `ListView` control has a collection of `ListViewItems` that hold information about its rows.

There are many kinds of structures that allow you store such data inside your controls. We'll have a quick look at some of the possibilities here, and we'll analyze them in greater detail in the next chapter.

The basic object that groups several elements is the `Array`. Storing items in arrays has the disadvantage of their fixed size, which limits the ways in which they can be used. You shouldn't use arrays to hold indexed data inside a control unless the number of items in the array is fixed (for example, an array of five colors).

```
Color[] colors = new Color[3];
```

The `ArrayList` is a .NET Framework class that stores any kind of items based on an index. Its main advantage over arrays is that it has dynamic size, and has the ability to add, insert, and remove items at a specified index. In building controls it's usually not a good practice to store indexed data in an `ArrayList` because type conversions are needed to obtain the object stored. Note that a `#using System.Collections` directive is required to use `ArrayLists`.

```
ArrayList aList = new ArrayList();
aList.Add(Color.Red);
aList.Add(Color.Green);
aList.Add(Color.Blue);
aList.RemoveAt(1);
// Conversion is needed because the arrayList indexer return type is object
Color col = (Color) aList[0];
```

`ArrayList` isn't the only class in the `System.Collections` namespace, and you'll learn about more of them in Chapter 8.

You can even create your own collection class by inheriting from `CollectionBase`. This way you can create customized collections for the type of object they're holding. The `ArrayList` class holds any kind of object, and its indexer's return type is `object`, while your collection's indexer return type is the type of the collection. By using a custom collection you can override the base class methods to implement additional functionality. For example, a `CollectionChanged` event can be added to notify the collection's parent class of its changes. Also, collections are of variable size and don't need to be created with a fixed number of elements as normal arrays do.

Collections are classes derived from the `CollectionBase` class. This class contains an inner array that can be used to store the items. For good practice collections are named by prefixing "Collection" with the type of object they're collecting with, such as in ColorCollection.

Let's see an example of building a collection. The code listing that follows is a console application that demonstrates some of the theory presented so far. If you try to build this in Visual C# Express as a console application, you may need to reference the `System.Drawing` assembly (by right-clicking the References entry in Solution Explorer), which contains the `System.Drawing` namespace.

```
using System;
using System.Collections;
using System.Drawing;

public class ColorCollection : CollectionBase
{
  //this event is fired when the collection's items have changed
  public event EventHandler Changed;
  //this is the constructor of the collection.
  public ColorCollection()
  {
  }

  //the indexer of the collection
  public Color this[int index]
  {
    get
    {
      return (Color)this.List[index];
    }
  }

  //this method fires the Changed event.
  protected virtual void OnChanged(EventArgs e)
  {
    if (Changed != null)
    {
      Changed(this, e);
    }
  }

  //returns the index of an item in the collection
  public int IndexOf(Color item)
  {
    return InnerList.IndexOf(item);
  }

  //adds an item to the collection
  public void Add(Color item)
  {
    this.List.Add(item);
    OnChanged(EventArgs.Empty);
  }

  //inserts an item in the collection at a specified index
  public void Insert(int index, Color item)
  {
    this.List.Insert(index, item);
    OnChanged(EventArgs.Empty);
  }

  //removes an item from the collection.
  public void Remove(Color item)
  {
    this.List.Remove(item);
    OnChanged(EventArgs.Empty);
  }
}

class Program
```

```
{
static void Main(string[] args)
  {
    // create a color collection
    ColorCollection colorCollection = new ColorCollection();
    // add two colors to the collection
    colorCollection.Add(Color.Red);
    colorCollection.Add(Color.Blue);
    // you can reference a color from the collection without making a cast
    Color color = colorCollection[0];
    // you can refer to collection items like any Color object
    Console.WriteLine(colorCollection[1].Name);
  }
}
```

The above template describes the basic implementation of a simple collection of `Color` objects. In the next chapter you'll learn even more about collections and related subjects, including a new feature in .NET 2.0 called **generics**.

Enums

Enums are user-defined value data types used to store a set of named constants that are all of the same data type. Enums can be used to define properties, which can receive a fixed set of values. For example, you can set the type of the border in a control by choosing from `None`, `2D`, and `3D`:

```
borderControl.Border = BorderType.Border3D;
```

The default declaration of an enum is:

```
public enum <Name>
{
  <value1>,
  <value2>,
  ...
  <valuen>
}
```

The declaration of the enum for the border example looks like:

```
public enum BorderType
{
  None, Border2D, Border3D
}
```

You can use this enum as a control property as shown in the following code snippet:

```
public class BorderControl : Control
{
  ...
  private void BorderType border;
  ...
  public BorderType Border
  {
    get
    {
      return border;
    }
    set
    {
      border = value;
    }
  }
}
```

Now, to set the property from another class is as simple as specifying the enum type and the chosen value:

```
BorderControl borderControl;
borderControl.Border = BorderType.Border3D;
```

Building TinyNoiseMaker

As we have learned about theory until now, let's play a little bit by creating a simple but functional custom control.

The first custom control we'll build in this book is a little sound player control called `TinyNoiseMaker`. Creating it will teach you the basic structure of a control: how to build the "black box" and then the public interface using events and properties. It demonstrates the use of two parts: the `OpenFileDialog` and the `SoundPlayer` controls.

The control plays a wave file loaded from the disk. Its interface is composed of three buttons that trigger the three main actions supported by the control: Load, Play, and Stop.

> The `SoundPlayer` component was introduced with .NET 2.0; so this example won't work with previous versions of the .NET Framework.

The following steps will guide you through creating the `TinyNoiseMaker`. You will start the project by creating a Windows Application called SoundPlayerTest, and inside this project you'll create the `TinyNoiseMaker` control.

Time for Action—Creating the TinyNoiseMaker Custom Control

1. Start Visual C# Express 2005 and create a new Visual C# Windows Application project named SoundPlayerTest, as shown in the following picture:

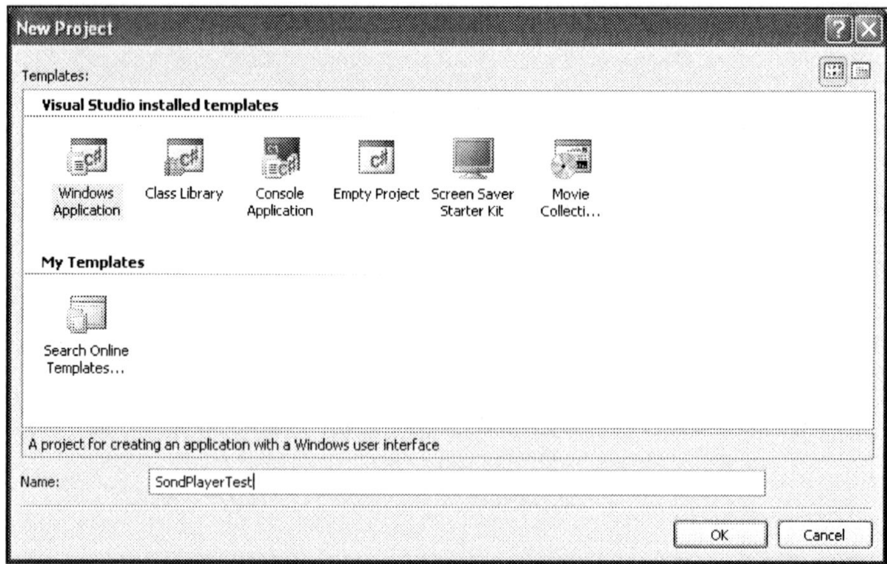

A typical requirement when building custom controls is to test them using a simple test application. In the case of .NET custom controls, that test application will be, most times, a simple Windows Forms Application. For this reason, through this book you'll usually start your projects as Windows Applications, then add a custom control to the project, and finally test it by adding it to the form Visual C# 2005 Express generated automatically when starting the project. In this exercise, SoundPlayerTest is the name of the Windows Application, and TinyNoiseMaker is the name of the control you're building.

2. Add a new control to the project. In Solution Explorer (View | Solution Explorer), right-click the project name (not the solution name) and click Add | User Control. Choose TinyNoiseMaker for the name of the control and click Add, as shown in figure below:

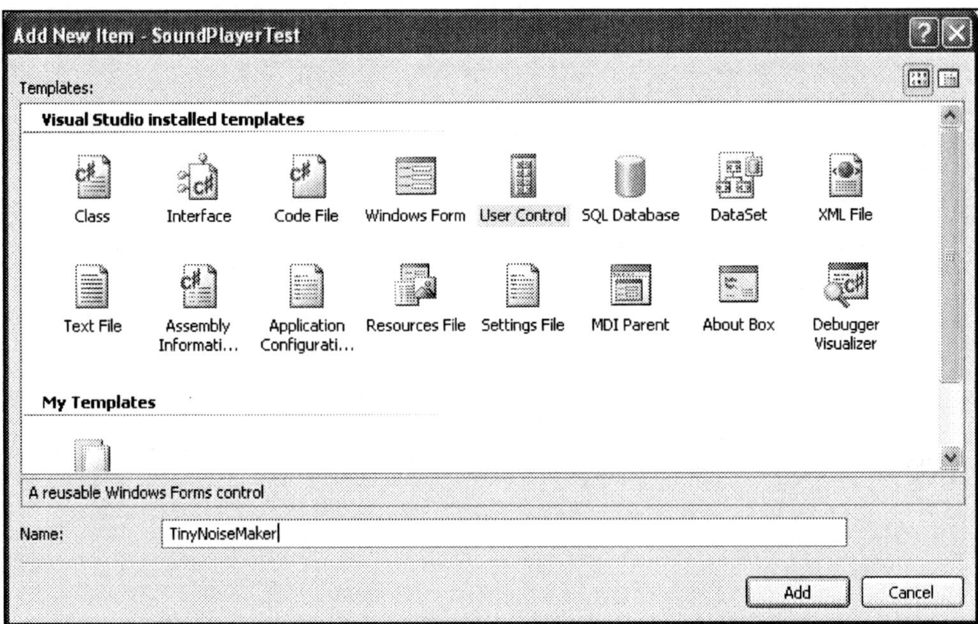

3. Let's add content to the control now. While TinyNoiseMaker is open in Design View, open the Toolbox (accessible through View | Toolbox), and add three Button controls from the Common Controls tab of the Toolbox, and one OpenFileDialog control from the Dialogs tab of the Toolbox, to the control's surface.

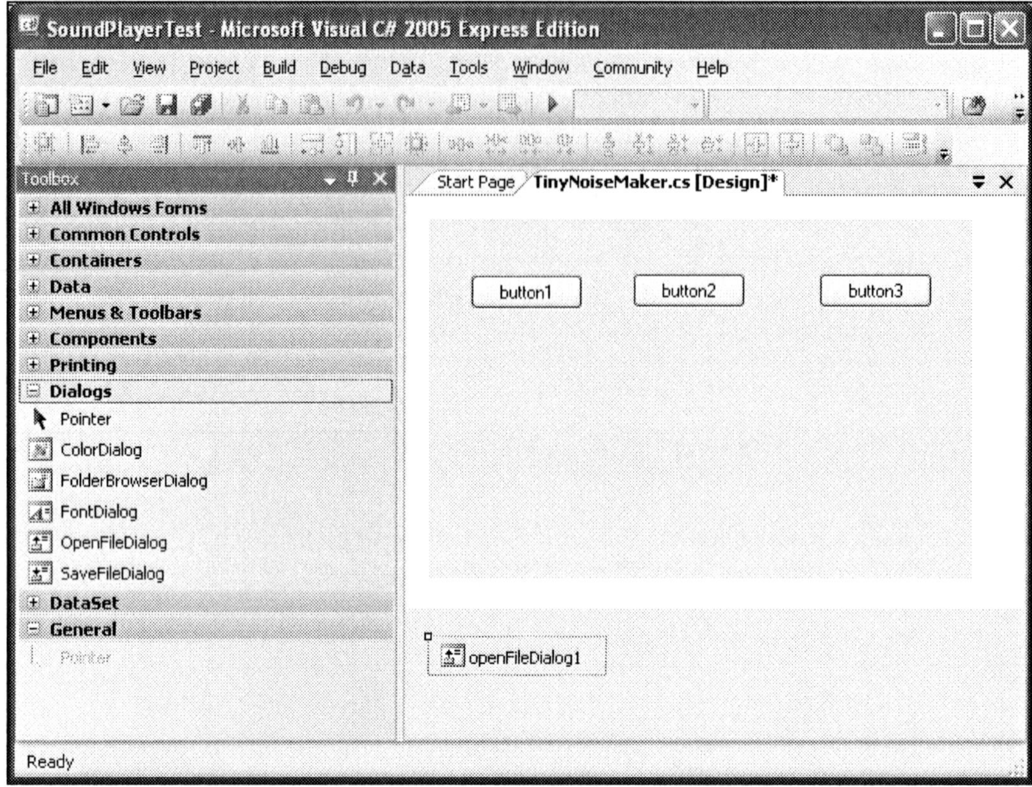

> Because `openFileDialog` doesn't have a visual interface, it'll appear in a special part of the designer, as you can see in the figure above.

4. Let's set some properties for our new controls. Use the Properties window (open it with *F4*) to set these properties:

Control Type	(Name)	Text	Location
`Button`	`openButton`	Open	4, 4
`Button`	`playButton`	Play	86, 4
`Button`	`stopButton`	Stop	168, 4
`OpenFileDialog`	`openFileDialog`	-	-

After setting these properties, your form will look like this:

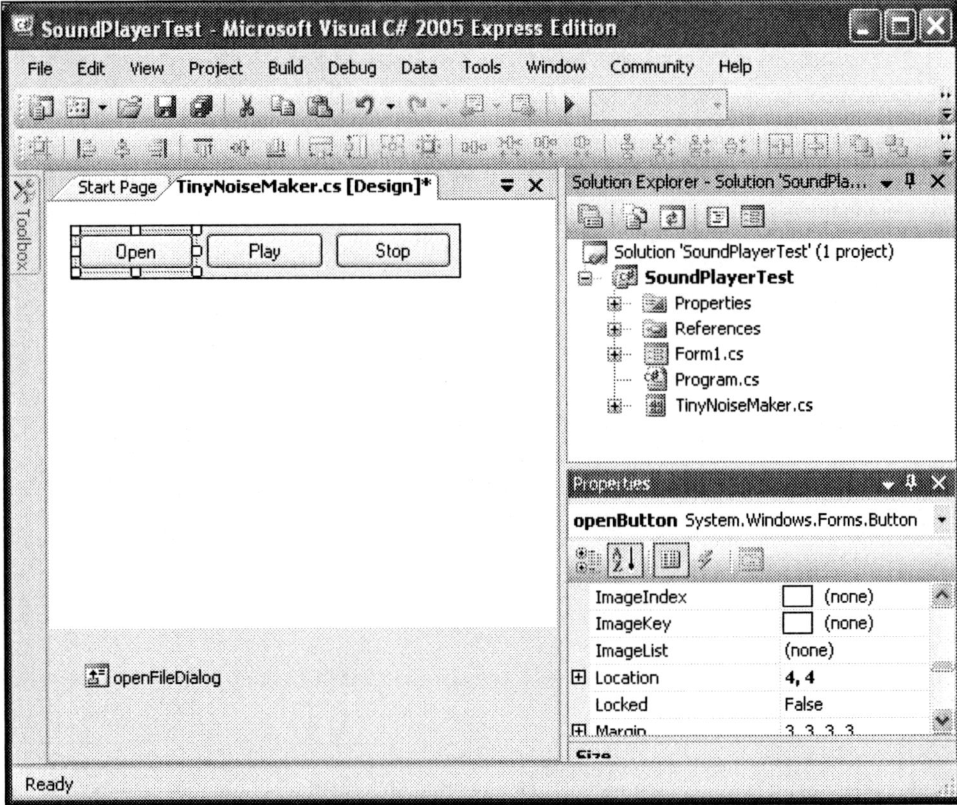

5. Select the control in the designer by clicking on an empty space, and set these properties:

Property Name	Property Value
Border Style	FixedSingle
Back Color	ControlLight
Size.Width	248
Size.Height	32

6. The result so far should be as in the screenshot shown below:

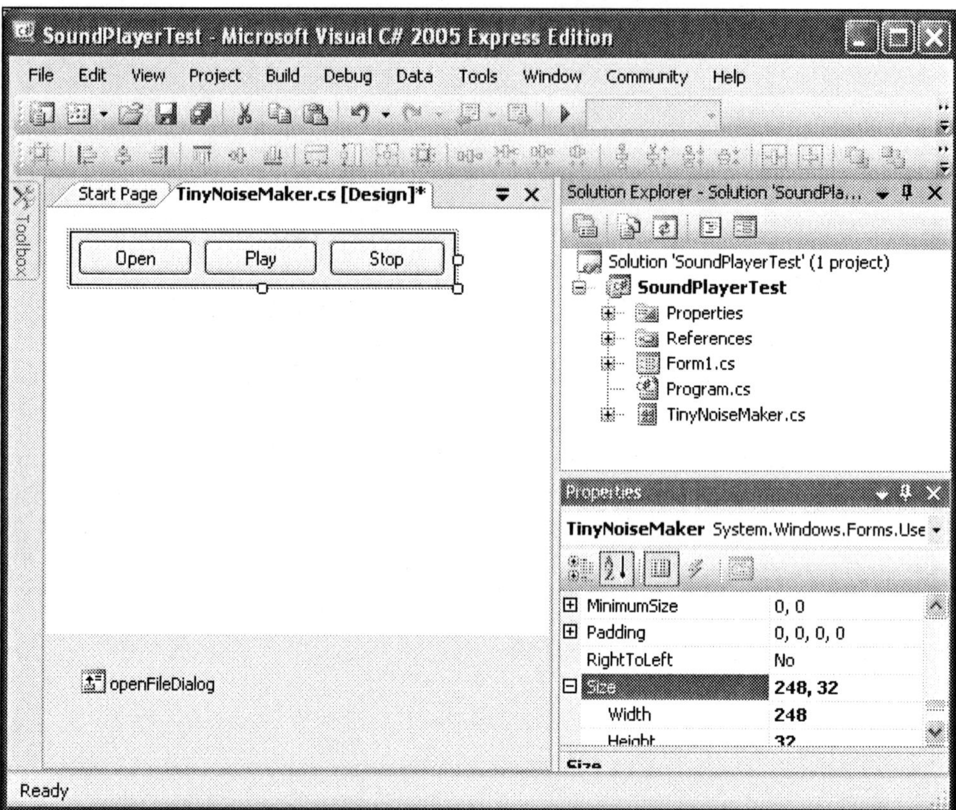

7. It's time to write some code. Switch to `TinyNoiseMaker.cs` to Code View (View | Code), and add the following lines to the `using` directives region:

```
using System.IO;
using System.Media;
```

8. Add a new member variable to the `TinyNoiseMaker` class, like this:

```
{
public partial class TinyNoiseMaker : UserControl
{
  private SoundPlayer soundPlayer;
```

9. Initialize the `soundPlayer` object in the constructor.

```
{
public TinyNoiseMaker();
{
  InitializeComponent();
  soundPlayer =  new SoundPlayer();
}
```

10. Switch to Design View, and double-click the Open button to have Visual C# Express 2005 automatically generate an event handler for the button's `Click` event. Then type the following in that method:

```
private void openButton_Click(object sender, EventArgs e)
{
  if (openFileDialog.ShowDialog() == DialogResult.OK)
    soundPlayer.Stream = new FileStream(openFileDialog.FileName,
                                        FileMode.Open,
                                        FileAccess.Read);
}
```

11. Switch again to Design View, double-click the Play button, and type the following code in the generated event handler:

```
private void playButton_Click(object sender, EventArgs e)
{
  soundPlayer.Play();
}
```

12. Repeat the step again for the Stop button and type in the code:

```
private void stopButton_Click(object sender, EventArgs e)
{
  soundPlayer.Stop();
}
```

13. TinyNoiseMaker is ready! Build the solution (Build | Build Solution) to make sure you didn't make any typing mistakes, and then open `Form1.cs` in Design View and drag TinyNoiseMaker from the Toolbox to Form1.

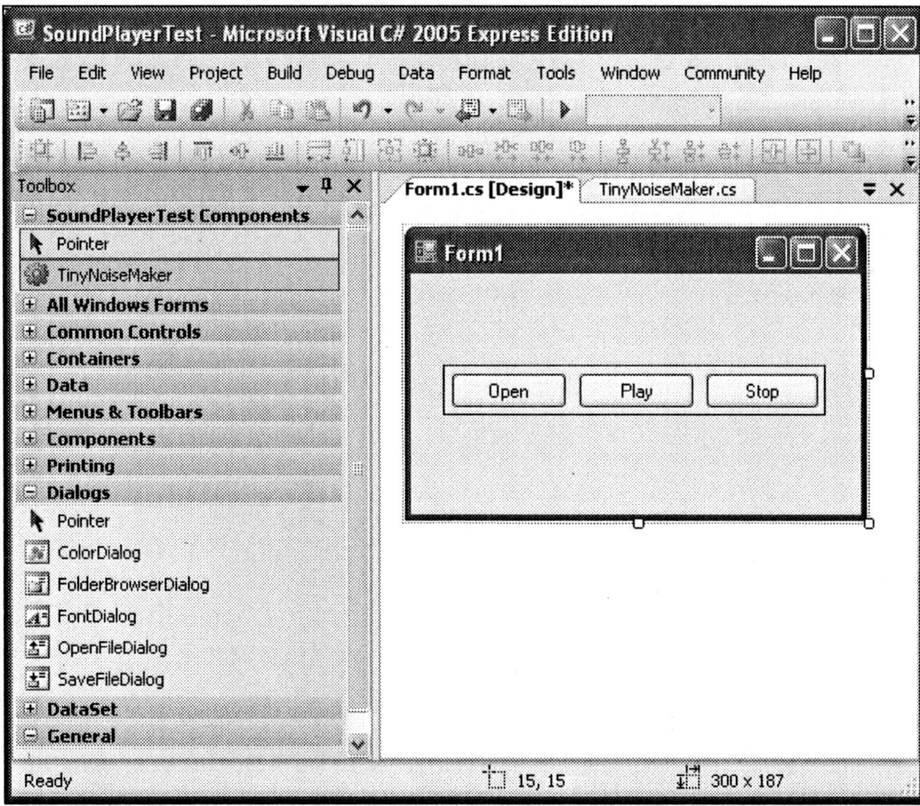

14. Run the application (*F5*), click the Open button, and select a valid `*.wav` file (you can try `C:\Windows\Media\tada.wav` file), click Play and enjoy the music or sound.

What Just Happened?

Congratulations on building your first control!

You started the project as a Windows Forms application, and added a new custom control afterwards. However, the `TinyNoiseMaker` control is independent from the rest of the application. At the end of the exercise, you just needed to add the control to your application's main form, and voilà, you had a working application!

The functionality of `TinyNoiseMaker` relies on the `SoundPlayer` component that you added as a private member of your control. `SoundPlayer` is a new control in .NET 2.0, and is located in the `System.Media` namespace, which explains why you needed to reference `System.Media` first. Analyzing the code in `openButton_Click`, `playButton_Click`, and `stopButton_Click` reveals how you can open a file from the disk, and play it using the `SoundPlayer`.

Trying to load an unsupported file type will throw an exception (see the figure below), and you need to consider implementing error-handling techniques in production code. You'll see more examples over the course of this book.

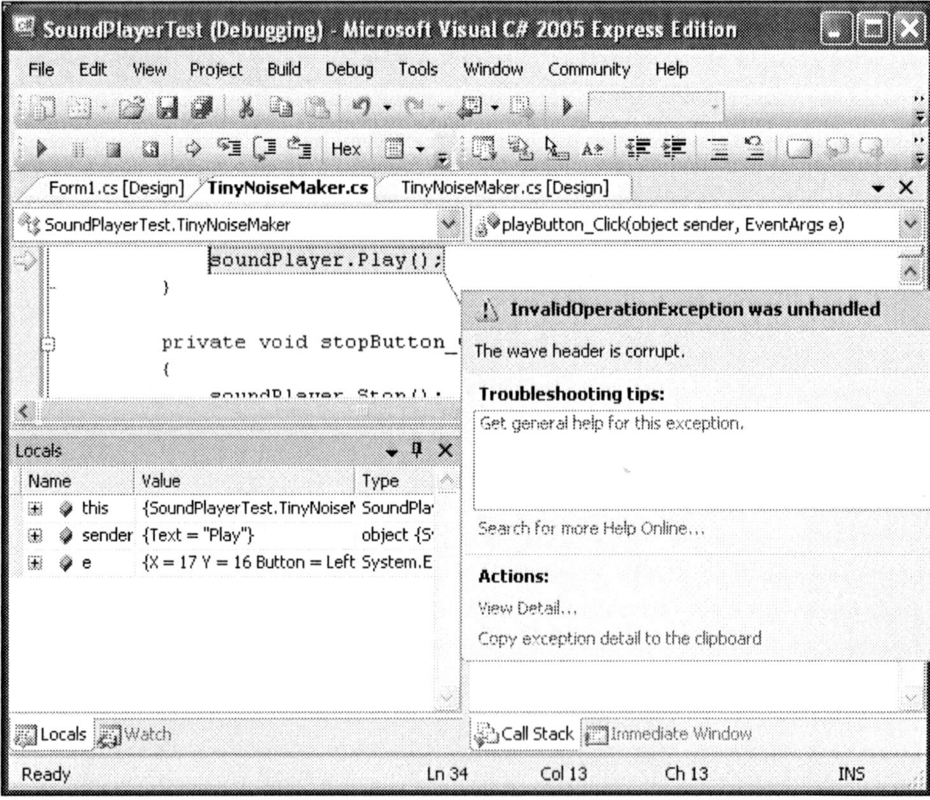

Now that your application is ready, it's also worth taking a look at the files that were built by Visual C# 2005 Express for you:

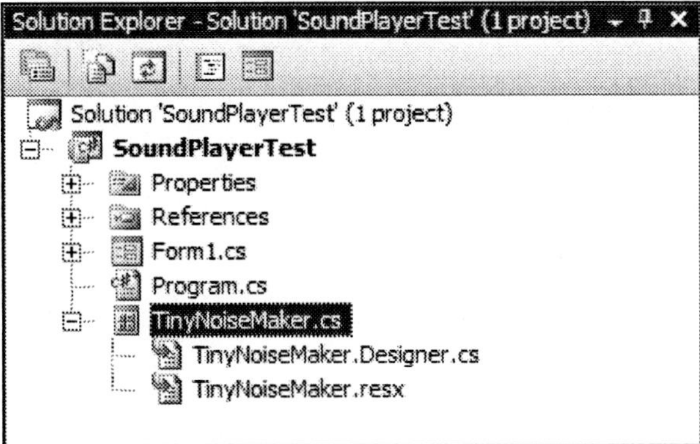

The files you're interested in are `TinyNoiseMaker.cs`, which contains your control's logic, and `TinyNoiseMaker.Designer.cs`, which contain the code that Visual C# 2005 built for generating the interface. Because these are standard files created in any Windows Application project, and familiarity with these kinds of projects is assumed, we won't labor this theory.

Extending TinyNoiseMaker

In this section you will be adding functionality to the control through public methods, properties, and events, in order to make its features programmatically accessible. The same result as pressing the buttons on the control's interface will be achievable through public methods called from anywhere. The public interface of the control will be formed by two public methods (`Play()`, `Stop()`), a property (`FileName`), and two events (`PlayStart`, `PlayStop`).

Time for Action—Adding Public Functionality

1. Open the `TinyNoiseMaker` control in Code View (View | Code), and add these two methods to the `TinyNoiseMaker` class:

```
public void Play()
{
  soundPlayer.Play();
}

public void Stop()
{
  soundPlayer.Stop();
}
```

2. Modify the `Play` and `Stop` event handlers so that they call these public methods. When the two buttons play and stop are pressed they call the `Play()` and `Stop()` methods that fire the desired events.

```
private void playButton_Click(object sender, EventArgs e)
    {
      Play();
```

```
}
private void stopButton_Click(object sender, EventArgs e)
{
  Stop();
}
```

3. At this moment the project can be compiled, so you can execute it again to make sure it still works. Let's continue by adding a property called `FileName`, which stores the file name in a private field called `fileName`. The goal is to make the functionality accessible to the control's clients programmatically, if they don't want to rely on the `Play`, `Open`, and `Stop` buttons of the control. Add this code to the `TinyNoiseMaker` class:

```
private string fileName;
public string FileName
{
  get
  {
    return fileName;
  }
  set
  {
    if (fileName != value)
    {
      fileName = value;
      soundPlayer.Stream = new FileStream(fileName, FileMode.Open,
                                          FileAccess.Read);
    }
  }
}
```

> It is good practice to check if the new value is different from the existing one, if this can avoid doing extra processing, as shown in this example.

4. Update the `openButton_Click()` method to make use of this new property:

```
private void openButton_Click(object sender, EventArgs e)
{
  if (openFileDialog.ShowDialog() == DialogResult.OK)
  {
    FileName = openFileDialog.FileName;
  }
}
```

5. Next, we will add the `PlayStart` and `PlayStop` events to the `TinyNoiseMaker` control. These events will be fired when the control starts playing or stops playing a file, to give the controls that use `TinyNoiseMaker` the possibility to react by performing certain actions when a file is being played. Add the events to the `TinyNoiseMaker` class:

```
public partial class TinyNoiseMaker : UserControl
{
  public event EventHandler PlayStart;
  public event EventHandler PlayStop;
```

6. Next we will add the methods that fire the `PlayStart` and `PlayStop` events. The new methods are named `OnPlayStart()` and `OnPlayStop()`, and they are `virtual`, meaning that they can be overridden by a potential control that would inherit from `TinyNoiseMaker`.

Methods such as `OnPlayStart()` and `OnPlayStop()` need to fire the events only if any methods (event handlers) are subscribed to them. Add these methods to the `TinyNoiseMaker` class, just after the two events you wrote earlier:

```
// fire the PlayStart event
protected virtual void OnPlayStart(EventArgs e)
{
  if (PlayStart != null)
  {
    PlayStart(this, e);
  }
}

// fire the PlayStop event
protected virtual void OnPlayStop(EventArgs e)
{
  if (PlayStop != null)
  {
    PlayStop(this, e);
  }
}
```

7. Now that you have set up the events and the methods that fire them, it's time to actually use them. Modify the `Play()` and `Stop()` methods that make the control play and stop playing to also fire the events.

```
public void Play()
{
  soundPlayer.Play();
  OnPlayStart(EventArgs.Empty);
}

public void Stop()
{
  soundPlayer.Stop();
  OnPlayStop(EventArgs.Empty);
}
```

8. Your control is now ready, packed with a new range of features. These new features can only be accessed programmatically, so if you execute the project now, you won't see anything new. For now, just execute the project and make sure it continues to work. Here's the complete listing of `TinyNoiseMaker.cs`, with some comments added, for your reference:

```
    using System;
    using System.Windows.Forms;
    using System.IO;
    using System.Media;

namespace SoundPlayerTest
{
  // the TinyNoiseMaker user control
  public partial class TinyNoiseMaker : UserControl
  {
    // private members
    private SoundPlayer soundPlayer;
    private string fileName;

    // public events
    public event EventHandler PlayStart;
    public event EventHandler PlayStop;

    // fire the PlayStart event
    protected virtual void OnPlayStart(EventArgs e)
```

```
{
  if (PlayStart != null)
  {
    PlayStart(this, e);
  }
}

// fire the PlayStop event
protected virtual void OnPlayStop(EventArgs e)
{
  if (PlayStop != null)
  {
    PlayStop(this, e);
  }
}

// public property stores the name of the file to be played
public string FileName
{
  get
  {
    return fileName;
  }
  set
  {
    if (fileName != value)
    {
      fileName = value;
      soundPlayer.Stream = new FileStream(fileName, FileMode.Open,
                                          FileAccess.Read);
    }
  }
}

// constructor initializes the SoundPlayer control
public TinyNoiseMaker()
{
  InitializeComponent();
  soundPlayer = new SoundPlayer();
}

// open the file to be played
private void openButton_Click(object sender, EventArgs e)
{
  if (openFileDialog.ShowDialog() == DialogResult.OK)
  {
    FileName = openFileDialog.FileName;
  }
}

// play the file when the Play button is clicked
private void playButton_Click(object sender, EventArgs e)
{
  Play();
}

// stop playing when the Stop button is clicked
private void stopButton_Click(object sender, EventArgs e)
{
  Stop();
}

// start playing the sound file
public void Play()
{
  // play the sound
  soundPlayer.Play();
```

```
            // fire the event
            OnPlayStart(EventArgs.Empty);
        }

        // stop playing the sound file
        public void Stop()
        {
            // stop playing the sound
            soundPlayer.Stop();
            // fire the event
            OnPlayStop(EventArgs.Empty);
        }

    }
}
```

What Just Happened?

Your control has now properties and events that enable code manipulation from another class. We added them because it's a common requirement to make functionality accessible programmatically, in case you (or your clients) want to use some functionality offered by your control without using its visual interface.

We'll see how to use the new public functionality in the sample that follows. After extending the control's functionality you will see how to use the `TinyNoiseMaker` control's public interface in a sample application. The new interface is formed by two public methods (`Play()`, `Stop()`), a property (`FileName`), and two events (`PlayStart`, `PlayStop`).

Time for Action—Using the Control's Public Interface

1. Open the Form1 form of your `SoundPlayerTest` project. Open Solution Explorer from View | Solution Explorer if it's not already open.
2. Select the TinyNoiseMaker control on the form, and click *F4* to open the Properties window. In the Properties window, you can see its new events by clicking the Events button (little yellow lightning symbol).

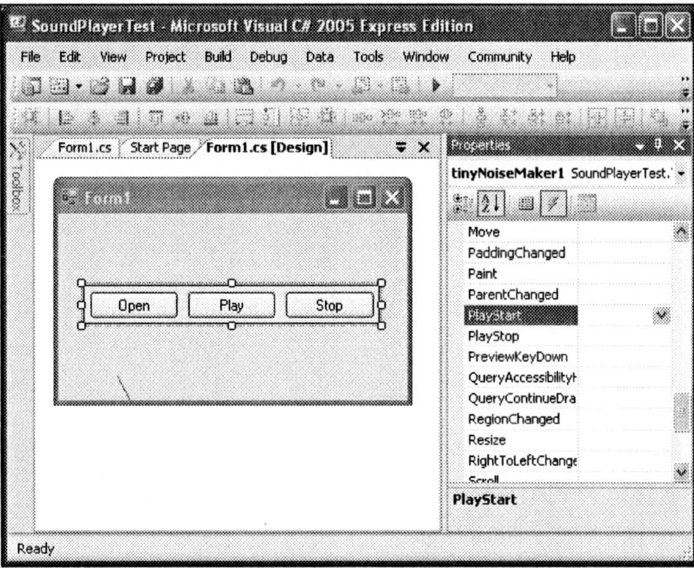

3. Double-click the PlayStart and PlayStop entries in the Properties window, add event handlers to the two events and add code to change the title of the form according to the action the control has performed:

```
private void tinyNoiseMaker1_PlayStart(object sender, EventArgs e)
{
  Text = "Play: " + tinyNoiseMaker1.FileName;
}

private void tinyNoiseMaker1_PlayStop(object sender, EventArgs e)
{
  Text = "Stop: " + tinyNoiseMaker1.FileName;
}
```

4. Execute the project again, open a file, and click the Play button. You'll receive feedback from the control, which is displayed in the title bar:

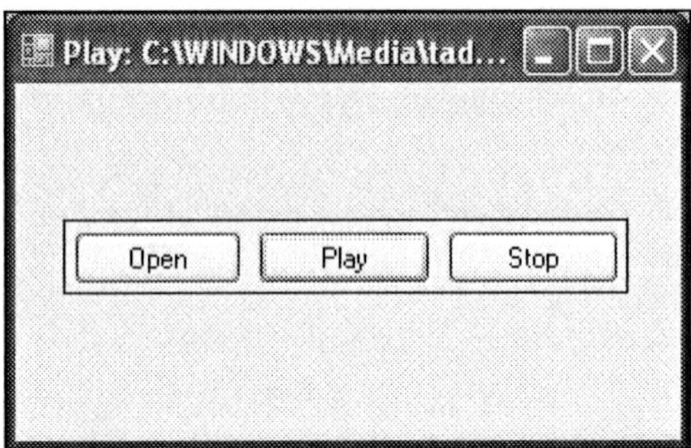

Let's now use the control's functionality that allows playing files without using the control's visual interface. Add a button on your application's form and set its name to playButton and its text property to Play My File. Then add an event handler to the button's `Click` event and write the following code. Replace the file path to a wave file located on your HDD:

```
private void playButton_Click(object sender, EventArgs e)
{
  tinyNoiseMaker1.FileName = "C:\\Windows\\Media\\tada.wav";;
  tinyNoiseMaker1.Play();
}
```

5. Execute the project, and click your new button. The result should resemble the following image:

6. Finally, let's save the solution. Go to File | Save All. Type SoundPlayerTest for the name, C:\CustomControlsBook\ (or another folder of your choice) for the location, and SoundPlayerTest for the solution name. Clear the Create directory for solution checkbox.

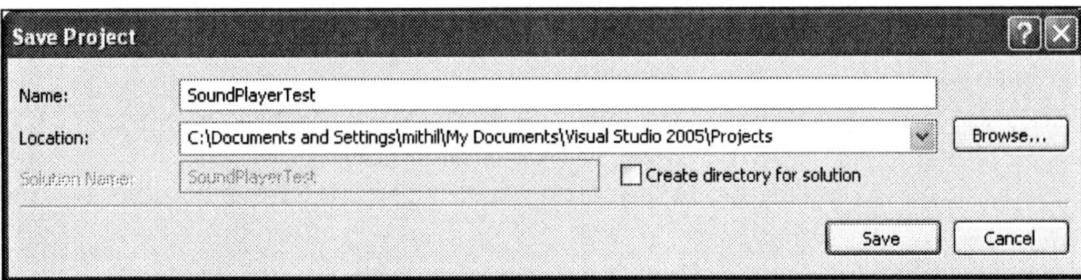

What Just Happened?

In this exercise you used the public functionality of the control to enable client programs to play sound files. Additionally, you handled the two events exposed by the control to inform the user about what the control is doing. These tasks are common when building custom controls, and you will meet similar functionality in the following chapters.

In this exercise you have learned how to build a simple non-custom-drawn control. Its interface is based on the interface of the `Button` controls, and its functionality is based on that of the `SoundPlayer` and the `OpenFileDialog` components. The usual practice is to make use of the control's visual elements, but as you can see, you are free to allow other programmers or programs to use your control's functionality programmatically by exposing that functionality through public methods, properties, and events.

Summary

In this chapter, you learned about the benefits custom controls can bring to your application. You took the first glance at building the basic structure of custom controls, and ended up creating a brand new, working custom control. In the following chapters you'll continue learning about the features you can implement in custom controls.

2
Introduction to GDI+

Some of the first design decisions you need to make when creating a new custom control are those related to its user interface. In Chapter 12 you'll learn a few usability guidelines related to building user-friendly interfaces, but here we'll focus on the technical side.

When building the user interface, sometimes you can use other controls, implicitly reusing their visual appearance. However, this is not always possible, so in many cases you need to draw on your control's surface, effectively building a custom-drawn control. Understanding how this can be done is critical for learning how to build powerful custom controls.

In this chapter you'll start learning the basics of creating custom-drawn controls. You will learn how to paint the surface of a control, and find out the tools needed to make it happen. More specifically in this chapter you will:

- Learn what control drawing is and how it works
- Learn what GDI+ is and how it helps rendering a custom control
- Understand the painting logic of any control
- Learn where to write the drawing code for different surfaces

Understanding Control Drawing

Did you ever want your application's controls to have a different border type or color, or even a different background, but you were limited to the few properties of the standard controls? Control drawing allows you to render anything on a control's surface.

A custom drawn control is a control whose appearance is changed by the programmer through code that draws patterns of pixels on the control's surface. These patterns can range from simple straight lines to very complex shapes, gradients, images, and standard control parts. You can choose to draw on top of another control's surface by inheriting its properties, or you can implement (and draw) everything from scratch.

When doing your own drawing, for starters you'll need a surface to draw on. The primary drawing surface is the screen surface on which the operating system draws the taskbar, paints the windows, and presents other visual elements. You are allowed to draw anything inside your own application's surface. The painting surfaces are hierarchically structured on the screen, some controls being the parents of child controls. This means that a control's surface is first painted by itself and then by its child controls.

The form is the root parent surface of an application. For example, if we have a form, a panel, and a button inside the panel, the form's surface will be rendered first, then the panel's surface, and then the button's surface. If these steps were processed in a different order, the results wouldn't be what you would expect; for example, if the button was drawn before the panel, the button wouldn't be visible. This hierarchical structure is based on the parent-child structure of forms. The panel is child to the form, and the button is child to the panel, and the parent elements are rendered before the child elements. This system is implemented automatically by the framework.

Understanding GDI+

The .NET Framework provides a graphical class library called **GDI+** which stands for **Graphical Device Interface Plus**. These classes offer you the means to implement your own drawing code. GDI+ supports drawing on three kinds of surfaces:

- **The Screen**. The ability to draw on the screen is arguably the most important feature when it comes to building custom controls' user interfaces. GDI+ makes it possible (and easy!) to draw complex shapes, text, and images on screen with great flexibility.
- **Images**. GDI+ also supports drawing on images, either loaded from a physical location (like the HDD), or images generated in the memory.
- **Printer**. Printing is also supported by GDI+, which makes the process very simple and straightforward.

GDI+ is organized in six namespaces, which reflect the three kinds of drawing GDI+ supports, and other general namespaces:

Namespace	Description
`System.Drawing`	Provides generic classes that apply to all drawing categories, providing support for colors, pens, brushes, fonts, and so on.
`System.Drawing.Drawing2D`	Provides support for drawing complex shapes and regions.
`System.Drawing.Imaging`	Provides functionality for rendering and manipulating images.
`System.Drawing.Printing`	Provides functionality for rendering on the printer, and print preview functionality. It also allows querying and altering printer settings.
`System.Drawing.Text`	Provides functionality for rendering and transforming text.
`System.Drawing.Design`	Provides functionality for implementing design-time support.

In the following sections you will learn how to initialize the drawing process on a control's surface with the help of GDI+.

The Graphics Object

The `Graphics` object is the core of GDI+. Every surface in an application has a `Graphics` object attached, which can be used to draw on that surface. Painting on the surface of a control involves obtaining a reference to its `Graphics` object. This can be done in two ways. The first way is to call `Control.CreateGraphics()`, which creates a `Graphics` object associated with the control.

However using the `Graphics` object obtained this way requires a bit more work on your side, and using this technique only makes sense under particular circumstances. You'll learn more about this in the later chapters.

The other way to obtain the `Graphics` object is by handling the `Paint` event, which provides the `Graphics` object as an argument. This method will be explained in the next section.

The Control.Paint Event

The base `Control` class exposes an event called `Paint`. When the control needs to refresh its surface, this event is raised, and by handling this event you can execute the necessary code that draws the control. This event is raised in circumstances such as when the form is made visible on the screen, when it is resized, and so on.

The `Paint` event's argument is a `PaintEventArgs` object that contains information about the boundaries of the control, and also provides the `Graphics` object attached to the control. This event is fired every time the control needs to refresh its appearance, so this is the ideal place to write rendering code of the control. You handle the `Paint` event in the event handler that looks like the code given below:

```
private void Form1_Paint(object sender, PaintEventArgs e)
..{
....//draw your form here
  }
```

Instead of handling the `Paint` event, you can override the `OnPaint()` method of the base class, which is used to fire the `Paint` event. When overriding the `OnPaint()` method you also need to call the `OnPaint()` method of the base class, to make sure that any code that it may implement gets executed.

```
protected override void OnPaint(PaintEventArgs e)
  {
    base.OnPaint(e);
    //draw your form here
  }
```

You'll generally call `base.OnPaint()` before writing your custom drawing code, to ensure that your drawing applies over the one implemented by the class you're inheriting. This extra level of flexibility and control can make overriding `OnPaint()` the preferred solution when building custom controls.

Invalidation

After rendering a control, its appearance remains unchanged until the control's surface is refreshed. The process of refreshing is called **invalidation** because regions in the control's visible area become invalid and need to be redrawn. The base class (`Control`) triggers automatic invalidation when the control is covered by another window and then is uncovered.

More complex controls can be invalidated programmatically when other events happen (e.g. a button when it's clicked). Invalidating a control is done by calling the `Control.Invalidate()` method. This calls the control's `Paint` event and the drawing code is executed again to render its appearance.

> It is possible to invalidate a small or specific region of a control, and not the whole control at the same time. The invalidated region is passed as parameter in the `Paint` event argument. The framework does this for you when causing automatic invalidation. To do this programmatically you need to pass the region you want to invalidate as argument of the `Invalidate()` method.

Let's see now how to draw on different surfaces.

Simple Drawing on a Form

It's time to see how actual drawing is done by following a few short exercises. We will start by drawing a text on a form's surface to see how basic drawing is implemented. First, we will draw inside a form by handling its `Paint` event, and then we'll draw inside a control's surface area by handling its `Paint` event, and by overriding the `OnPaint()` method.

In the first exercise you will paint a form's surface by handling its `Paint` event. The `Graphics` object will be used to render the text. Follow the steps to build the sample application.

Time for Action—Creating the Application

1. The first step is to create a new Windows Application project in Visual C# Express, just as you did in Chapter 1. The new project should be named PaintingTest.
2. Add an event handler to the Paint event of the form. To have Visual C# Express create the event handler for you, select the form in the designer, and open its Properties window. To see a list of the available events that can be handled, click the yellow lightning icon of the Properties window.

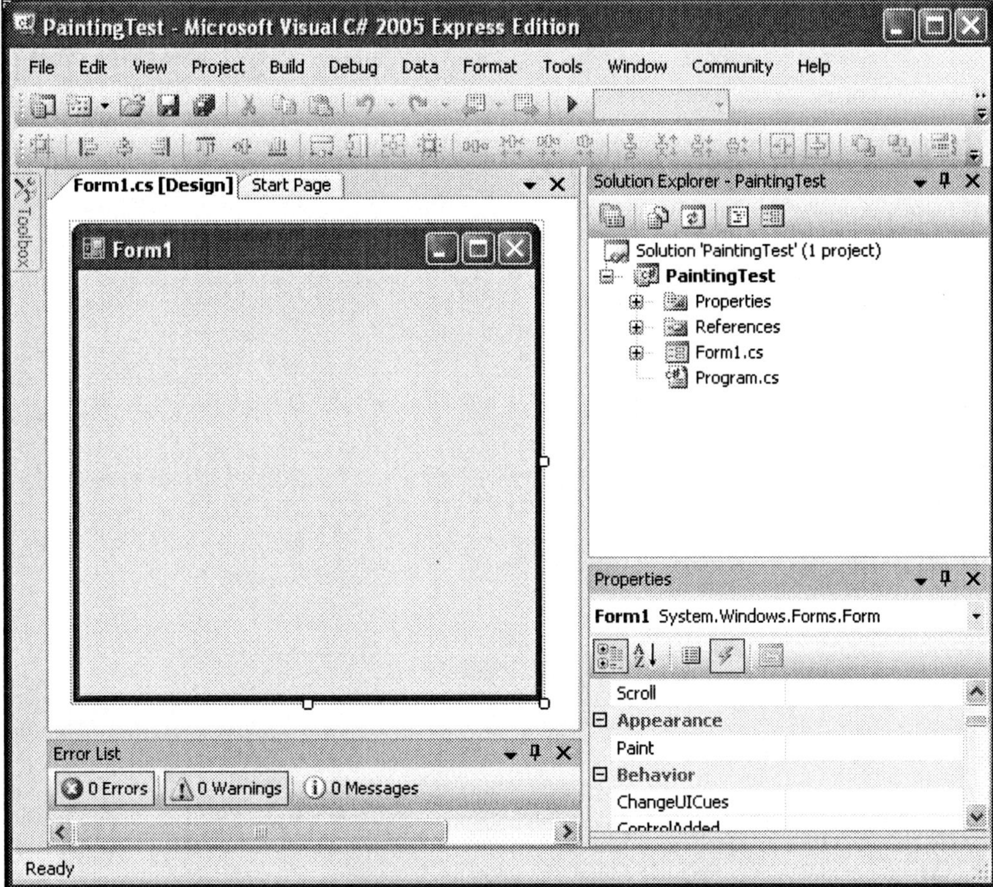

3. Double-click the Paint item in the list of events, and Visual C# Express will do the rest of the work for you. You will be presented with the code page of the form with the event handler wired to the event and ready to be changed:

```
private void Form1_Paint(object sender, PaintEventArgs e)
{

}
```

4. Add drawing code in the method as follows:

```
private void Form1_Paint(object sender, PaintEventArgs e)
{
  e.Graphics.DrawString("This text is rendered from the Paint event
  handler", Font, Brushes.Red, 0, 0);
}
```

5. Run the application, and you will notice the text is rendered on the form's surface.

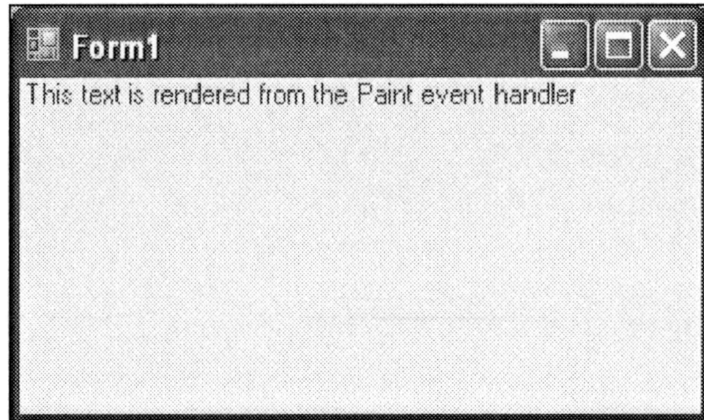

What Just Happened?

In this exercise you created a very simple application that only consists of a form. Here, the code to draw the text within the form area is inserted into the `Form1_Paint()` method. Notice that the area that can be drawn is smaller than the form and it does not contain the title bar. This area is called the *client area*. In this example you cannot redraw the scroll bars, the status bar, the menu, or the tool bars (which are not present in this example) by handling the form's `Paint` event.

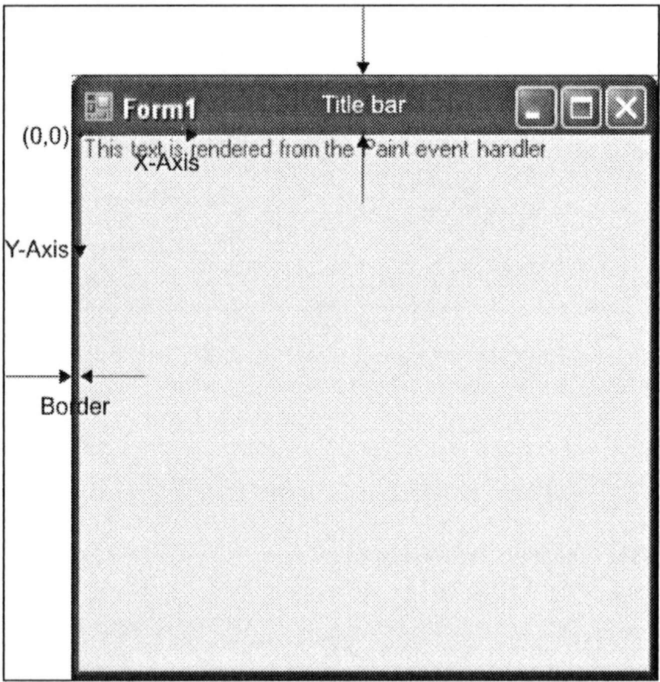

As you can see in the figure above, the (0,0) coordinate doesn't represent the upper-left corner of the form, but the upper-left corner of the client area, which is determined by excluding the borders and the title bar from the form area. To redraw the borders, the scroll bars, or the title bar you will have to override their `OnPaint()` methods.

Drawing Inside a Panel Object

In this example you paint on the surface of `Panel` control, by handling the panel's `Paint` event. The `Graphics` object will be used to render the text. This is close to control painting but it's not actually how it's done, because we still use a `Form` instead of building a control.

The following steps will guide you through creating the example.

Time for Action—Creating the Application

1. The first step is to open the `PaintingTest` application used in the previous exercise.
2. Drag a Panel control from the Toolbox onto the form surface and change its BackColor property to ControlLight to make the Panel's surface visible on the form's surface.
3. Add an event handler to the panel's Paint event just as you did for the Form in the previous exercise.

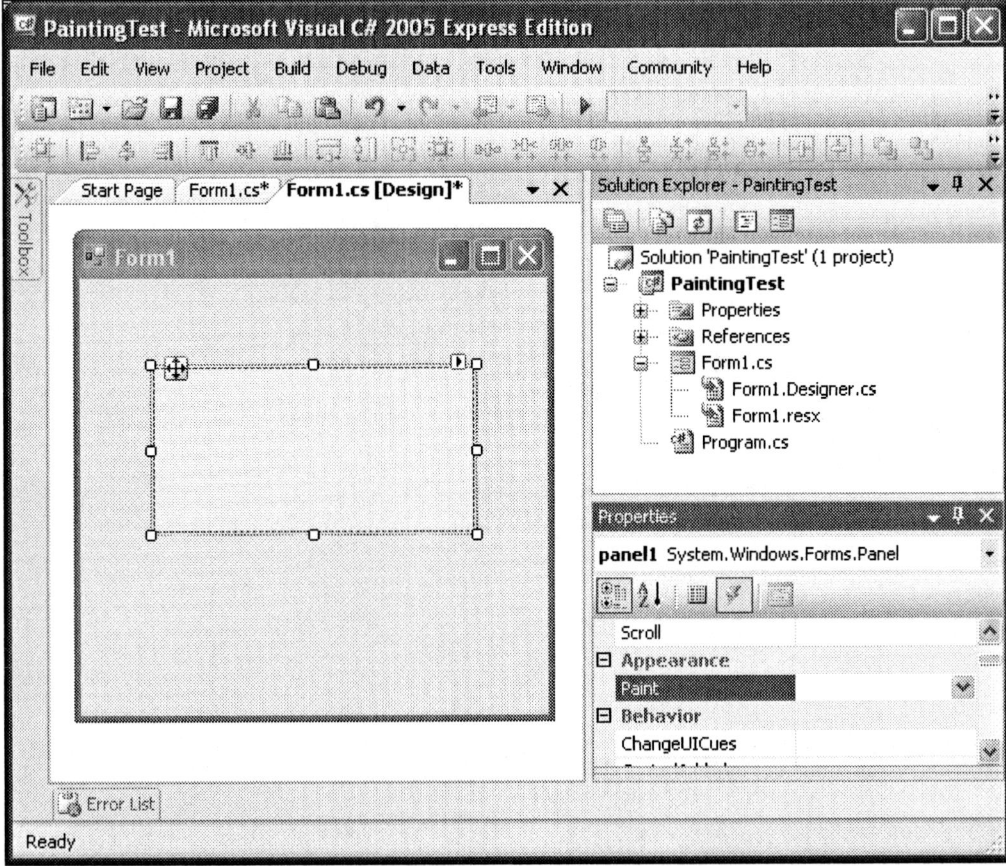

4. Edit the event handler generated for you by Visual C# Express as given below:

```
private void panel1_Paint(object sender, PaintEventArgs e)
{
```

```
e.Graphics.DrawString("This text is rendered in the Panel", panel1.Font,
Brushes.Red, 0, 0);
}
```

5. Run the application and you will notice the text is rendered on the panel's surface.

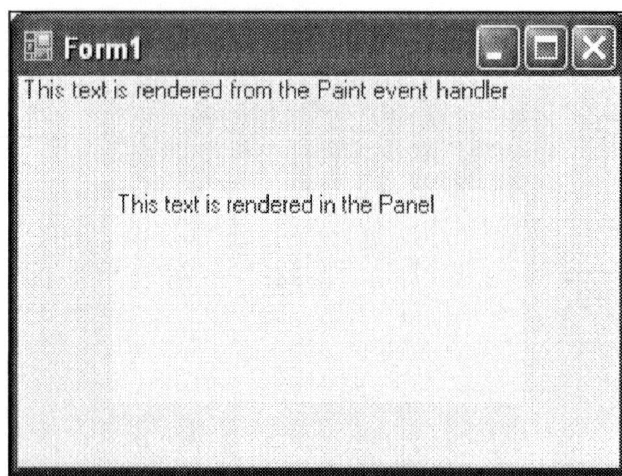

What Just Happened?

In this example you have learned to draw text into a `Panel`. The `Panel` itself has a client area, which can be drawn in the `panel1_Paint()` event handler. The (0,0) coordinate of the panel is shown in the following figure:

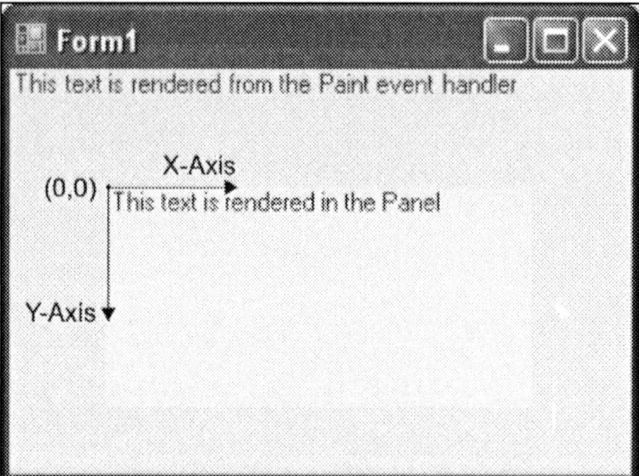

Drawing Inside a Control

Now you will see how control rendering is done by writing drawing code in the overridden `OnPaint()` method. The following drawing method will be used throughout the book and represents the standard way of rendering controls.

Time for Action—Creating the Application

1. The first step is to open the `PaintingTest` application used before.
2. Add a new control to the project. In Solution Explorer (View | Solution Explorer), right-click the project name (not the solution name) and click Add | User Control. Create a control named `PaintControl`. Then set its BackColor property to ControlDark so you can see its surface easily. Then you need to drag it on the form's surface. If the form needs resizing to fit the new control feel free to resize it.

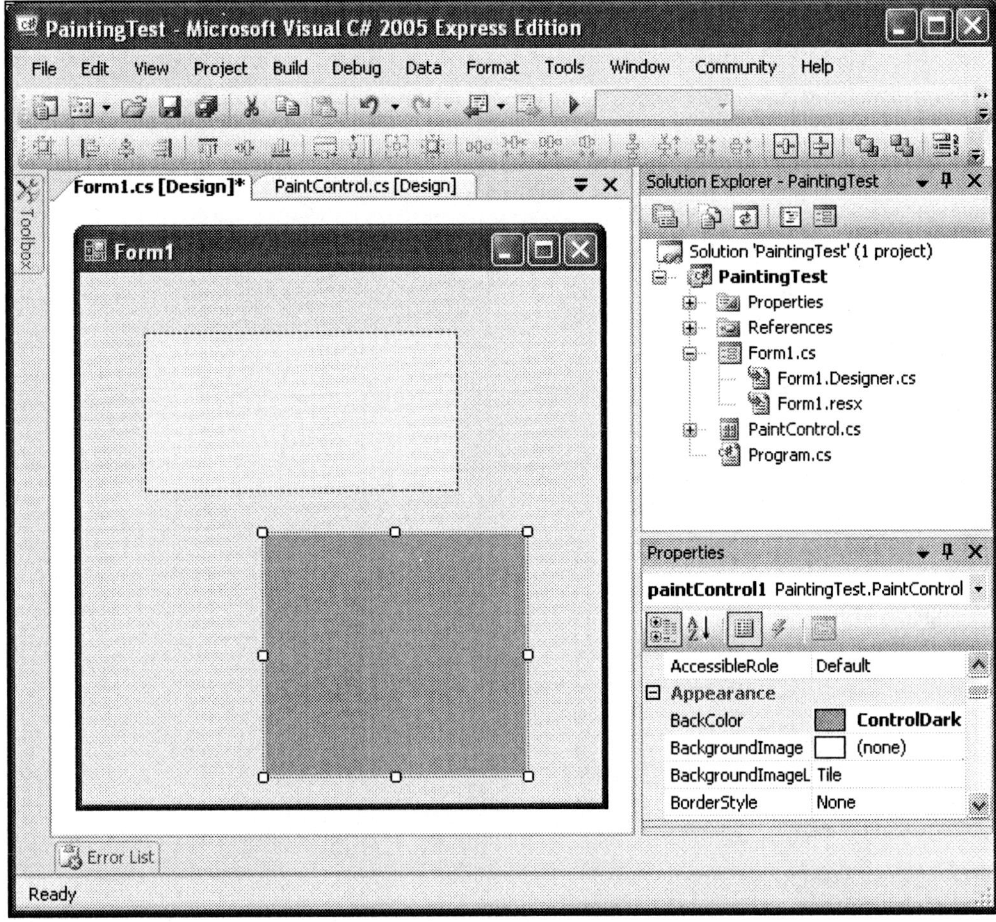

3. Override the control's `OnPaint()` method to add the drawing code. When overriding `OnPaint()` instead of handling the `Paint` event, you also need to call `base.OnPaint()` to enable the functionality provided by the base class.

```
protected override void OnPaint(PaintEventArgs e)
{
  base.OnPaint(e);
  e.Graphics.DrawString("This is control rendering", Font, Brushes.Blue,
  0, 0);
}
```

4. Run the application and you will notice the text is rendered inside the control.

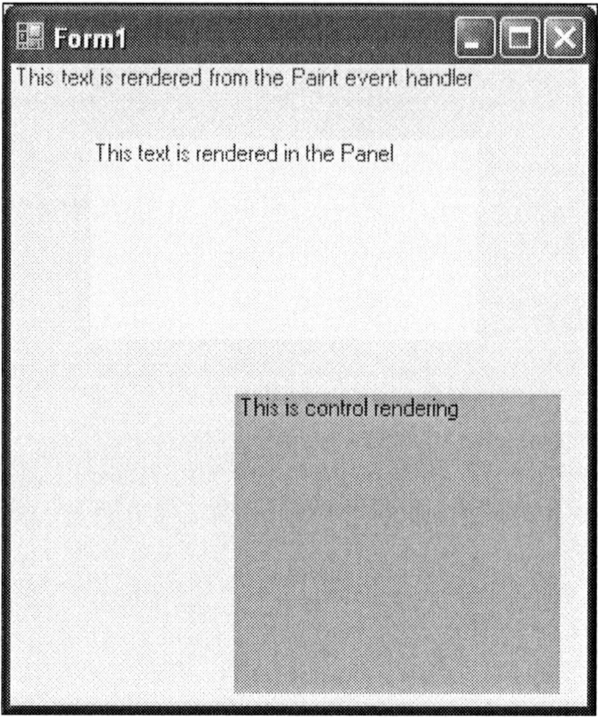

What Just Happened?

In this last example, you have drawn inside a control. Similarly to with the panel and the form, the control has a client area that can be drawn. This time we override the `OnPaint()` method instead of handling the `Paint` event, in which case we also needed to call the `OnPaint()` method of the base class.

In the end, you have an application that has a hierarchical surface painting. The form draws its client area and lets its children redraw themselves. The control is rendering its surface in overridden paint methods. All three surfaces have a (0,0) point and this is how you can easily draw without involving coordinates changing from screen to client or from client to screen. The (0,0) point is relative to the surface that is rendered and it is the axis origin. The following figure shows all three axis systems:

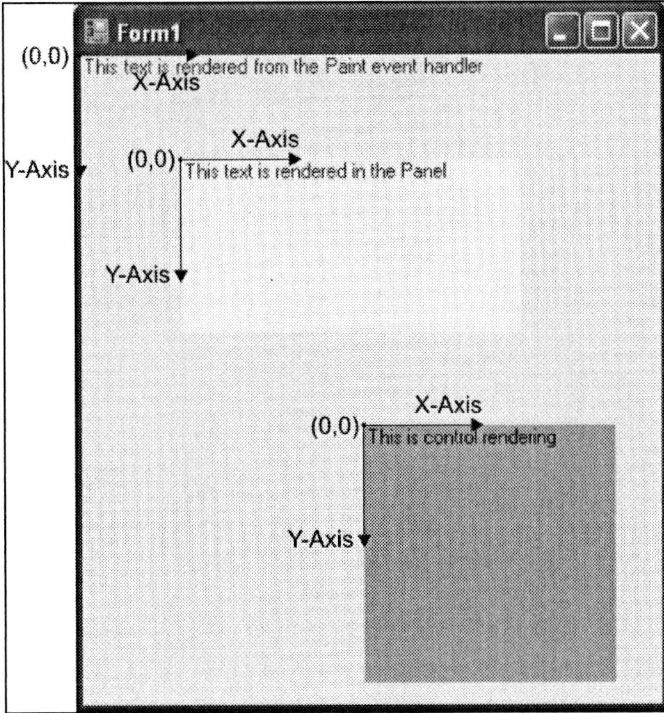

You will learn more on coordinates systems, and relative or absolute drawing in the next chapter.

Summary

In this chapter you have learned the very basics of how rendering a control works, and the tools needed to make it happen. In the exercises you have put the theory into practice to draw first inside a Form, then inside a Panel, and finally in a new control. This was a simple step, but an important one because it's critical to understand the basic principles. The next chapter will continue with a little bit more theory about drawing.

3
Basic Drawing

In this chapter you'll learn how to make drawings that are a bit more complex (and useful) than what you did in Chapter 2. While you're at it, you will:

- Understand drawing surfaces and the GDI+ coordinate systems
- Learn about the basic classes that are used in rendering controls
- See how to draw simple shapes and text

At the end of the chapter you'll build a new custom control called `GradientLabel`, where you'll put the new theory into practice.

The GDI+ Coordinate System

In order to do any real drawing, you need to know how to locate a point on the screen. If you want to draw a line between two points, you need to specify their locations.

The screen is divided into **pixels** arranged in rows and columns like a grid. The number of rows and columns are determined by the screen resolution. A pixel is the smallest division of the screen that can be set a color. One pixel can only have one color at any given time. We could look at the screen as a grid of colored pixels. The location and size of any window or control on the screen is by default measured in pixels.

Any pixel on the screen is identified by a pair of numbers, which represent its coordinates in the matrix. These coordinates are the row number and the column number that identify the pixel location. GDI+ uses a 2D rectangular (Cartesian) coordinate system. To properly define such a system, an origin and two axes must be specified. The origin of the system is the top left corner of the screen. The first axis, called the X axis, is the top margin of the screen and its direction is from left to right. The second axis, called the Y axis, is the left margin of the screen and its direction is from top to bottom. Any pixel has an X coordinate and a Y coordinate according to the axes that uniquely identify its location on screen. This is best illustrated by the following image:

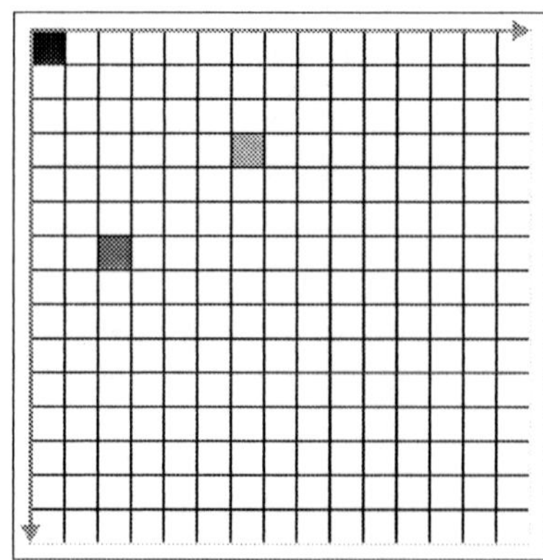

Pixel color	X coordinate	Y coordinate
Red	0	0
Green	6	3
Blue	2	6

Knowing how to locate pixel coordinates prepares you for the next step, which is understanding **surface boundaries**. As you already know, forms and controls have an area available to draw on, called the **client area**. The form's client area is the rectangle inside its borders (without the borders or the title bar above). The client area of controls is their whole rectangle by default (unless the control defines it otherwise).

The location of forms and controls represent their X and Y coordinates relative to an origin. This origin can be the origin of the screen or some other origin. For example, the form's location is relative to the screen origin. If a form's location is `X = 100` and `Y = 200`, this means that it is located 100 pixels to the right from the left side of the screen, and 200 pixels down from the top edge of the screen. Controls' locations are relative to the origin of the form's client area.

In theory the coordinates don't have to be integers, but in practice GDI+ will automatically round any non-integer coordinates to integers.

The .NET classes that hold information about locations and sizes are:

Class	Description
`Point`	Holds information about a location. Has X and Y integer properties.
`PointF`	The same as Point, but its properties are floats.
`Size`	Describes a size. Has width and height integer properties.
`SizeF`	The same as Size but its properties are floats.
`Rectangle`	Describes a rectangle. It is formed from a Point and a Size object.
`RectangleF`	The same as Rectangle but it's formed from PointF and SizeF.

These objects are used as parameters in the drawing methods of the `Graphics` class. The classes with float coordinates are used either when the coordinates result from a complex formula that returns non-integer coordinates, to spare conversions (e.g. when finding out the pixel coordinate at the middle of a control, the formula returns floats: `X = Width / 2f, Y = Height / 2f`), or when applying transformations (which will be explained in the next chapter when transformations are presented).

Forms and controls have properties that indicate location and size. This is shown in the following table:

Property	Type	Description
`Location`	`Point`	Indicates the location of the control in relation to the form's top left.
`Size`	`Size`	Indicates the control's width and height.
`ClientRectangle`	`Rectangle`	Indicates the control's client area. The rectangle's location is usually X = 0, Y = 0 and its size is usually the size of the control.
`Bounds`	`Rectangle`	Indicates the boundaries of the control. It's formed by the Location and Size.

When drawing a control using the `Graphics` object reference obtained for that control, its coordinate system's origin is the location of the control. When drawing a line from coordinates `X=0, Y=0` to coordinates `X= 50, Y= 50`, the line is drawn from the top left corner of the control diagonally down-right to the point with `X = 50, Y = 50`, relative to the control's top left corner. In other words, the `Graphics`' origin is offset to the top left of the control. This makes the control's location in the form and the form's location on the screen irrelevant for the rendering code of the control.

Drawing with GDI+

We will now pay our attention to the basic drawing tools GDI+ offers. We will take a look at the classes that hold information about colors, lines, fills, and the Graphics rendering methods that use them as their parameters. We'll learn about the following objects:

- `Color`
- `Pen`
- `Brush`
- `Font`

Using the Color Object

The `Color` object holds information about a color. It is given as parameter to everything that has a color (for example, brushes or pens) as will be seen in the next sections. A `Color` object can be created:

- From a collection of predefined opaque colors that are found as static members of the `Color` class. For system colors, the `SystemColors` static members are used.

```
Color color = Color.Red;
Color sysColor = SystemColors.ControlLight;
```

- From the basic three components of a color (Red, Green, Blue) with values from 0 to 255.

```
// Red
Color color = Color.FromArgb(255, 0, 0);
```

- From the basic three component colors and an Alpha parameter that indicates the transparency of the color also with values from 0 to 255 (255 being fully opaque).

```
// Half transparent Red
Color color = Color.FromArgb(128, 255, 0, 0);
```

Drawing Using the Pen Object

Drawing lines is one of the simplest things that can be done with GDI+. In many controls you see lines but probably never think about how they are rendered there. For example, to draw the dashed rectangle that appears around a control (such as a button) when it has focus, a line is rendered on the surface of the control. The button border is also composed of lines.

Usually the methods of the `Graphics` object that begin with `Draw` are used for rendering lines, or shape contours using lines.

Method	Description
`DrawArc`	Draws an arc (a section of an ellipse)
`DrawBezier`	Draw a Bezier spline
`DrawCurve`	Draw a cardinal spline through an array of points
`DrawEllipse`	Draw an ellipse
`DrawLine`	Draw a line between 2 points
`DrawPolygon`	Draw a polygon defined by an array of points

All these methods require a `Pen` object, which specifies the color, thickness, style, and other line characteristics.

A `Pen` object can be created using its constructor that takes as parameters the color and the thickness of the line. After the creation of the pen, the line style can be changed by altering its properties (for example `DashStyle`), or using static members as in the `Color` class.

```
Pen pen = new Pen(Color.Red, 3);
```

As with the `Color` object, pens can be created using a list of predefined objects:

```
Pen pen = Pens.Red;
```

> It is good practice to dispose the GDI+ objects after using them by calling their `Dispose()` method. This way you ensure the resources aren't locked for longer than necessary, because you don't rely on .NET's garbage collector to do the work for you. Otherwise the application can occasionally occupy more memory and run slower than it should. The helper classes include `Pen`, `Brush`, `Font`, and others.

Let's have a quick look at how to draw a line in a control's rendering method. To test this code you can use the `PaintControl` control from Chapter 2.

```
// Creates a half transparent red color
Color color = Color.FromArgb(128, 255, 0, 0);
// Creates a pen using the above color with a width of 3 pixels
Pen pen = new Pen(color, 3);
// Creates a blue pen with a width of 3 pixels
Pen pen2 = new Pen(Color.Blue, 3);
// Draws a diagonal line using the second pen
e.Graphics.DrawLine(pen2, 30, 30, 80, 80);
// Draws a diagonal line using the first transparent pen that overlaps the first
line
e.Graphics.DrawLine(pen, 0, 0, 50, 50);
// Disposes the two pens
pen.Dispose();
pen2.Dispose();
```

The code above renders on the surface of the control two diagonal lines, one using an opaque color, and the other using an alpha-blended (transparent) color.

Filling Surfaces Using the Brush Object

Filling surfaces makes it easy to cover wider areas, and it's commonly used for drawing backgrounds, filled shapes, and more. For example, a form's background is filled with its background color when it's rendered.

Filling surfaces is achieved in a similar way to drawing lines, but using the `Brush` object instead of `Pen`, and calling methods whose names start with Fill instead of the methods that start with Draw.

A technical difference between `Pen` and `Brush` is that the `Brush` class is *abstract*. This means that in practice you'll need to use specialized `Brush` classes (classes that derive from the `Brush` class), because abstract classes are not instantiable (you can't create objects with them). GDI+ ships with the following kinds of brushes:

Brush	Description
`SolidBrush`	Defines a brush that fills paths with a single color.
`HatchBrush`	Defines a brush having a hatch pattern, which can be set from a number of brushes through the `HatchStyle` property.
`LinearGradientBrush`	Defines a gradient brush. Many gradients types can be achieved with this brush (for example, different angles, and different color weights).
`PathGradientBrush`	Defines a brush that fills a path with a gradient.
`TextureBrush`	Defines a brush that fills a path using an image.

The `HatchBrush`, `LinearGradientBrush`, and `PathGradientBrush` objects are located in the `System.Drawing.Drawing2D namespace`. The next snippets assume that you've imported this namespace.

`Brush` objects can be created in the two ways:

- By using one of the predefined brushes:

```
Brush brush = Brushes.Red;
```

- By instantiating a specialized brush using its constructor:

```
SolidBrush sbrush = new SolidBrush(Color.Red);
LinearGradientBrush lbrush = new LinearGradientBrush(
                   new Point(0, 0),
                   new Point(50, 50),
                   Color.Red,
                   Color.Blue);
```

As with pens, it's good practice to dispose the brushes after using them.

Let's now take a look at how to draw using brushes. We will fill the `ClientRectangle` of a control with a diagonal gradient brush and then fill an ellipse inside with an inverted gradient brush. This can be tested using the `PaintControl` from Chapter 2.

```
LinearGradientBrush lbrush = new LinearGradientBrush(
                 new Point(0, 0),
                 new Point(Width, Height),
                 Color.LightSteelBlue,
                 Color.CornflowerBlue);
e.Graphics.FillRectangle(lbrush, ClientRectangle);
LinearGradientBrush lbrush2 = new LinearGradientBrush(
                 new Point(0, 0),
                 new Point(Width, Height),
                 Color.CornflowerBlue, Color.LightSteelBlue);
e.Graphics.FillEllipse(lbrush2, 25, 25, Width - 50, Height - 50);
lbrush.Dispose();
lbrush2.Dispose();
```

The results are obvious. Writing a small code snippet we were able to create a nice 3D effect using brushes:

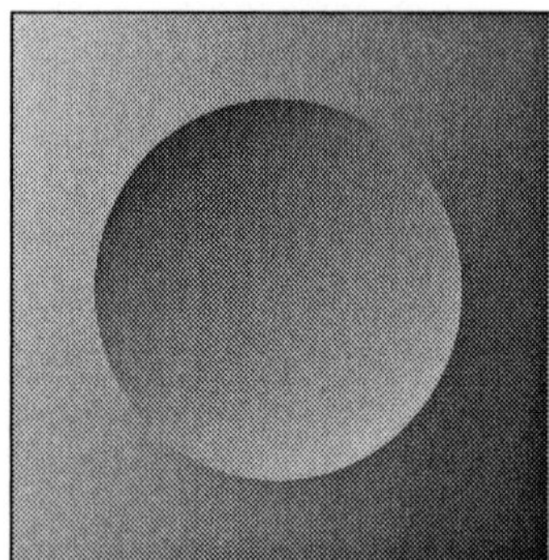

Drawing Text Using the Font Object

Rendering text is used (obviously) in controls that display text on their surface, such as labels, lists, and others. Rendering text is done using the `Graphics.DrawString()` method, which takes as parameters the string to display, a `Font` object, a `Brush` object, the coordinates, and other formatting objects.

The `Font` object holds font information, such as font family name, size, and style (e.g. bold, italic). A `Font` instance can be created using its constructor, but usually when building custom controls you don't need to create fonts this way. Forms and controls have a `Font` property in their base class. In the previous chapter you used the base class's `Font` property to render the text.

Also when rendering text, it's frequently required to know the size of the text to be rendered. To find out the size of a string, given a `Font`, the `Graphics.MeasureString()` method is used. This method returns a `SizeF` object that contains the size you're interested in:

```
SizeF fontSize = e.Graphics.MeasureString(Text,Font);
```

Let's see how we can render text in the middle of a control:

```
string text = "Middle String";
SizeF stringSize = e.Graphics.MeasureString(text, Font);
e.Graphics.DrawString(text, Font,
                     Brushes.Red,
                     (Width - stringSize.Width) / 2,
                     (Height - stringSize.Height) / 2);
```

Improving Drawing Quality

So far you have learned how to draw lines and how to use brushes. Now when you have this fresh in your mind we can examine how the GDI+ can offer varying levels of drawing quality. The default settings are normally quite coarse and can be a little clumsy at times. This clumsiness manifests itself as *jaggies*. If you look closely at a drawn line, you can see that angled lines seem jagged and *pixelated*. To solve this, GDI+ uses the `AntiAliasing` technique to make these *jaggies* appear smooth. This is done by adding blended colors at the edges of *jaggies* to fill in the area between two colors (line color and background color). To see this in action for yourself, type the following code into the paint event of an empty form:

```
private void form1_Paint(object sender, PaintEventArgs e)
{
  e.Graphics.DrawEllipse(new Pen(Color.Red, 10), 30, 30, 50, 50);
  e.Graphics.SmoothingMode = System.Drawing.Drawing2D.SmoothingMode.AntiAlias;
  e.Graphics.DrawEllipse(new Pen(Color.Blue, 10), 30, 100, 50, 50);
}
```

The first `e.Graphics` call will be familiar to you; it simply uses the `PaintEventArgs' Graphics` object to draw a circle on the form using a large red pen.

The next line is the interesting part. The `SmoothingMode` property of the `Graphics` class is assigned a new value, one that tells GDI+ that it should apply `AntiAliasing` to all subsequent drawing operations. Notice though, that this will not affect the circle that was drawn by the line above.

On the last line we draw another circle, this time in blue and just below the red circle. Take a very close look at the two circles; you will notice that the red circle has a "saw-toothed" edge to it and the blue one is much smoother. This is the effect that `AntiAliasing` has. Once again .NET has pulled another neat trick out of the bag in only handful of lines of code!

This high quality does come at a cost though. It takes a more complicated algorithm to fill in the missing pixels and this can slow down your program if you are doing some particularly complex drawing routines. You wouldn't normally notice this, as the `AntiAliasing` is quite efficient anyway. But the flexibility doesn't stop there, you can use the following in a similar manner.

The `Graphics` object's other rendering quality settings are as follows:

```
Graphics.SmoothingMode (see the above example)
Graphics.CompositingMode
Graphics.CompositingQuality
Graphics.InterpolationMode
Graphics.TextContrast
Graphics.TextRenderingHint
```

These other settings are subtler in their effects and they should be experimented with so that you can customize your drawing to your own purposes. Some really interesting effects can be created with GDI+ and these settings can add the finishing touches.

Building the GradientLabel Control

It's now time to put together what we've learned so far to implement a functional custom-drawn control. This control will put into practice most of the things learned so far. It is a label control with a gradient background and center-aligned text. It is very simple and easy-to-implement control that will demonstrate the drawing process.

Time for Action—Creating the GradientLabel Custom Control

1. The first step is to create a new Windows Application project in Visual C# Express named `GradientLabelTest`.
2. Then add a new control to the project. In Source Explorer, right-click on the project and click Add | UserControl and then name the control GradientLabel.
3. Set the Height of the control to 24, and edit the code so that the `GradientLabel` control derives from `Control`, not from `UserControl`. This exposes the Text property on the Properties tab.

> If you build the application at this moment you will get two errors. This is because the code generated automatically inserts two lines of code for auto scale. When changing the `GradientLabel` to derive from `Control` and not from `UserControl`, these two lines don't disappear automatically. You will have to delete them manually. Build the application; you will get the two errors. Double-click the errors; this will bring you to the `GradientLabel.Designer.cs`. Here you will delete the lines containing `AutoScale`.

4. In the `GradientLabelTest` form's designer, drag from the Toolbox a GradientLabel onto the form.
5. It's time to edit the control's code. Add a member data property that holds the second gradient color. For the first color we will use the control's `BackColor` property:

```
private Color backColor2 = SystemColors.ControlLight;
```

6. Now add the property that makes the member public:

```
public Color BackColor2
{
  get
  {
    return backColor2;
  }
  set
  {
    if (backColor2 != value)
    {
      backColor2 = value;
      Invalidate();
    }
  }
}
```

7. Finally, add the override `OnPaint()` method to write the rendering code. To be able to use the `LinearGradientBrush`, don't forget to add a `using System.Drawing.Drawing2D`.

```
protected override void OnPaint(PaintEventArgs e)
{
  base.OnPaint(e);
  LinearGradientBrush brush = new LinearGradientBrush(new Point(0, 0),
                              new
                              Point(0, Height), BackColor,
                                                 BackColor2);
  e.Graphics.FillRectangle(brush, ClientRectangle);
  Brush foreBrush = new SolidBrush(ForeColor);
  SizeF textSize = e.Graphics.MeasureString(Text, Font);
  e.Graphics.DrawString(Text, Font, foreBrush, (Width -
                        textSize.Width) /2,
                        (Height - textSize.Height) / 2);
  brush.Dispose();
  foreBrush.Dispose();
}
```

8. Play with the Text, BackColor, BackColor2, and ForeColor properties to change the appearance of the control. The result is:

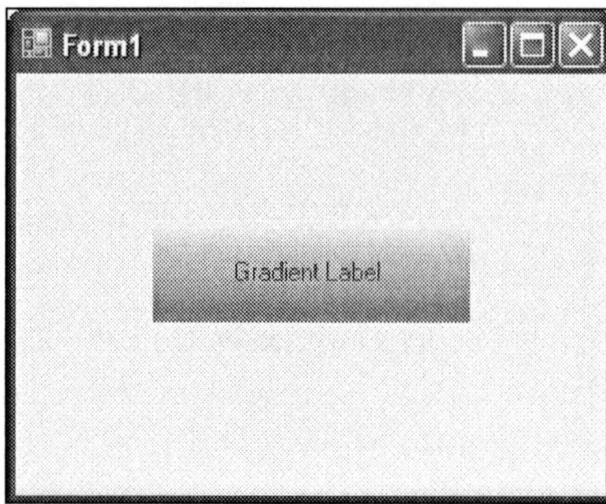

Congratulations, you have created the `GradientLabel` functional custom-drawn control!

What Just Happened?

In this exercise you have learned how to put into practice the drawing techniques learned so far. You have used a `LinearGradientBrush` to render the background of the control, and rendered the text in the middle of the control. You have created a functional `GradientLabel` control. This is just the beginning of GDI+ drawings. You can do a lot of tricks to improve your control's look, like: drawing text with different fonts and color, different sizes, bold, normal, and italic, underlined, strike out, or with the body drawn from a brush; but more important in my opinion is that you can draw text positioned on a curve. Also the background can be improved. With a little code and some skills you can develop a nice and fully functional custom-drawn control.

Summary

In this chapter you have learned the basics of rendering custom controls. More specifically you have learned how to draw lines, fill basic shapes with different colors and fills, render text, and draw using smoothing effects. All the techniques presented will be used in most custom drawn controls that we will create.

4

Drawing Complex Shapes and Using Transformations

Did you ever wonder how those non-rectangular windows and controls were implemented in applications? Do you want your application to have a special look by having a non-rectangular visual layout and have exactly the visual appearance you want? This chapter teaches you how you can achieve it. In the previous chapter, we learned how to do basic drawing, more specifically how to draw straight lines and how to fill polygons. We'll now explore most of what GDI+ has to offer in regard to drawing complex shapes and using transformations. This is useful if we want to create a non-rectangular control, or to draw curved figures on the surface of a control, which brings a friendly pleasant appearance to the application. We'll see how to:

- Render figures that include curved lines
- Create and fill any shape with any `Brush`
- Set drawing bounds
- Use `Graphics` transformations

At the end of the chapter, you'll put the theory into practice by building a `Clock` control.

Drawing Complex Shapes

When building custom controls, sometimes you are presented with a need to render non-straight lines, and to fill non-rectangular or curved surfaces. The .NET Framework has ways that facilitate the rendering of complex shapes and figures. In GDI+, shapes are stored in different data objects. We will next learn what these objects are and how to store paths and shapes in them by rendering the Visual Studio sign as an example:

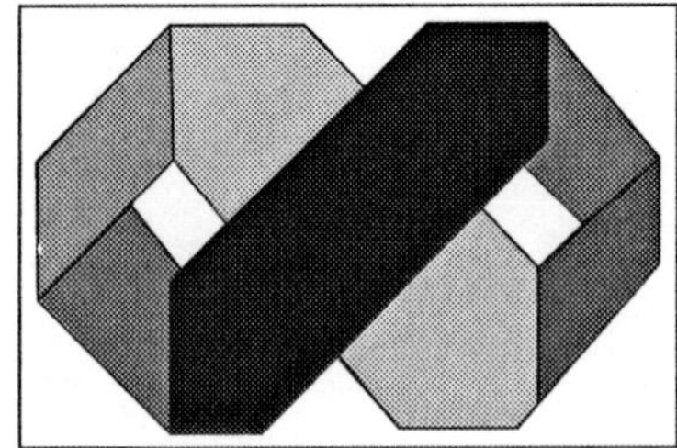

The GraphicsPath Object

The `GraphicsPath` object makes drawing complex shapes easy. Instead of using complex math formulas to render curved lines and paths, this class wraps up almost everything needed to create and store any kind of shape. We will next see how paths are created and stored in such an object.

A `GraphicsPath` object is composed of a collection of figures. A figure is a succession of connected lines of any type (straight or curved). A figure is closed when the last point's location is in the first point's location and is open otherwise. Almost any, if not any, shape can be obtained using the `GraphicsPath` object. When a `GraphicsPath` object is created, it has no figures. To add lines to the first figure, call the `Add()` method of the `GraphicsPath`, which will automatically start building the first figure. The methods will add different line types to the current figure one after another until you want the figure to be closed.

For example, the outer shape of the VS sign is created by concatenating a series of lines. Then if you want to start building another figure or close the current one, call the `GraphicsPath.CloseFigure()` method or the `GraphicsPath.CloseAllFigures()` method to close all the figures that are not closed.

Now let's have a quick look at the usage of the `GraphicsPath` object by drawing different shapes. The point coordinates are not the focus of this chapter; they were the result of testing coordinates against the original image. What we need to focus here is, the way paths are stored in the `GraphicsPath`, and how it is used as parameter in the `Draw()` methods of the `Graphics` class.

To demonstrate how easy it is to create a curved figure we will render a heart-shaped path:

```
//Create the GraphicsPath object
GraphicsPath gp = new GraphicsPath();
//Add the right side of the heart
gp.AddCurve(new Point[]{
  new Point(100,50),
  new Point(105,40),
  new Point(120,40),
  new Point(130,65),
  new Point(100,100)
  },0.5f);
//Add the left side of the heart
gp.AddCurve(new Point[]{
  new Point(100,100),
  new Point(70,65),
  new Point(80,40),
  new Point(95,40),
  new Point(100,50)
  }, 0.5f);
//Draw the path
e.Graphics.DrawPath(Pens.Red, gp);
```

The rendered path can be seen below. Notice how the line automatically curves around the specified points.

In the example above, the `AddCurve()` method was used to store the curved path. We will next see the methods in `GraphicsPath` that allow the addition of new lines and figures to create other shapes. These methods append a line or lines to the last unclosed figure of the path, and if the last figure is closed, they create a new figure with the specified lines.

Methods	Description
`AddArc`	Appends an arc from an ellipse. It takes as parameters the ellipse dimensions and the angles of the arc.
`AddBezier`	Appends a Bezier line. This method will be explained in an example a bit later.
`AddBeziers`	Appends a series of Bezier lines.
`AddClosedCurve`	Appends a closed curved line between given points based on a tension argument.
`AddCurve`	Appends a curve that is not automatically closed.
`AddElipse`	Appends an ellipse that fits inside a rectangle.
`AddLine`	Appends a line.
`AddLines`	Appends lines.
`AddPath`	Appends another `GraphicsPath`.
`AddPie`	Appends a pie slice.
`AddPolygon`	Appends a polygonal line.
`AddRectangle`	Appends a rectangle.
`AddString`	Appends the path of a given string.

Now, we'll have a look at how to use these methods by demonstrating the use of the `AddBezier()` method, and adding additional lines and points to see how the path is shaped by the specified points.

First, let's draw the Bezier line:

```
GraphicsPath gp = new GraphicsPath();
Point p1 = new Point(50, 100);
Point p2 = new Point(25, 75);
Point p3 = new Point(50, 50);
Point p4 = new Point(75, 50);
gp.AddBezier(p1,p2,p3,p4);
e.Graphics.DrawPath(Pens.Red, gp);
```

The result of this code is as follows:

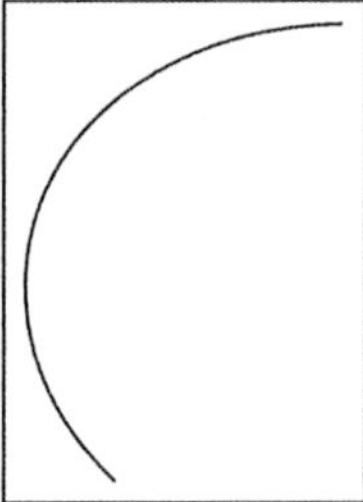

Now let's see how the line was formed by adding additional lines and rectangles. The first point in the AddBezier() line is the first point of the line. The second point forms a segment with the first point that represents the tangent to the curve in the starting point. The third point forms a segment with the last point that represents the tangent to the curve in the end point. So we will draw two lines from the first point to the second and from the third to the last. Then we will draw small rectangles centered in the specified points.

```
//Draw the tangents
e.Graphics.DrawLine(Pens.Black, p1, p2);
e.Graphics.DrawLine(Pens.Black, p3, p4);
//Offset the points so the rectangles are centered in the points
p1.Offset(-2, -2);
p2.Offset(-2, -2);
p3.Offset(-2, -2);
p4.Offset(-2, -2);
//The size of the rectangles
Size sz = new Size(4,4);
//Draw the rectangles that are centered in the points
e.Graphics.DrawRectangle(Pens.Black, new Rectangle(p1, sz));
e.Graphics.DrawRectangle(Pens.Black, new Rectangle(p2, sz));
e.Graphics.DrawRectangle(Pens.Black, new Rectangle(p3, sz));
e.Graphics.DrawRectangle(Pens.Black, new Rectangle(p4, sz));
```

The adornments show exactly how the line is formed. The two black lines represent the tangents to the curved line, and the black squares represent the points passed as parameters to the AddBezier() method:

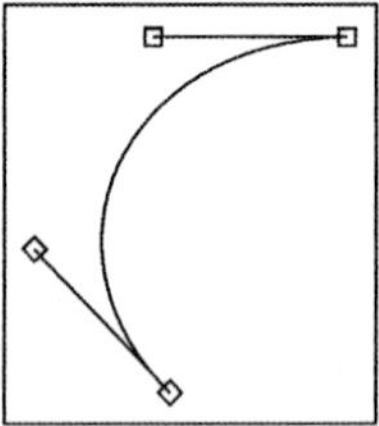

To continue to form the figure of the GraphicsPath call the Add() method. If the first point of the next line's location is different from the location of the last point of the previous line, the points will be joined by a straight line. If this is not the desired effect you should close the previous figure (with CloseFigure()) to start building a new one.

Let's now see how to create figures using the VS sign. We will create three figures corresponding to the outer shape, and the two inner holes.

```
GraphicsPath gp = new GraphicsPath();
gp.AddPolygon(new Point[]{
  new Point(0,30),
  new Point(30,0),
  new Point(60,0),
  new Point(73,15),
  new Point(88,0),
  new Point(115,0),
  new Point(140,30),
  new Point(140,53),
  new Point(108,90),
  new Point(82,90),
  new Point(67,73),
  new Point(50,90),
  new Point(30,90),
  new Point(0,60)
});
e.Graphics.DrawPath(Pens.Black, gp);
```

This renders the outer shape of the path. When calling the `AddPolygon()` method, a new figure is being created for the path, and automatically closes it, as a polygon is by definition a closed figure. We can build the same shape using the `AddLines()` method, but after calling the method we will have to call `GraphicsPath.CloseFigure()` to achieve the desired effect.

> Remember, the point coordinates are not important and are not the purpose of this exercise. Focus on the `Graphics` and `GraphicsPath` methods involved.

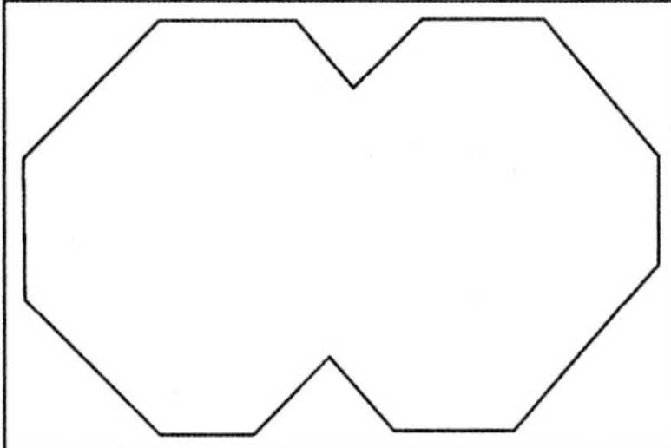

Now let's add two new figures corresponding to the interior parallelograms. Add this code before the graphics rendering method.

```
gp.AddPolygon(new Point[]{
  new Point(30,30),
  new Point(20,40),
  new Point(32,55),
  new Point(43,43)
});
gp.AddPolygon(new Point[]{
  new Point(110,30),
  new Point(125,45),
  new Point(115,55),
  new Point(100,40)
});
```

We now have the path of the sign as follows:

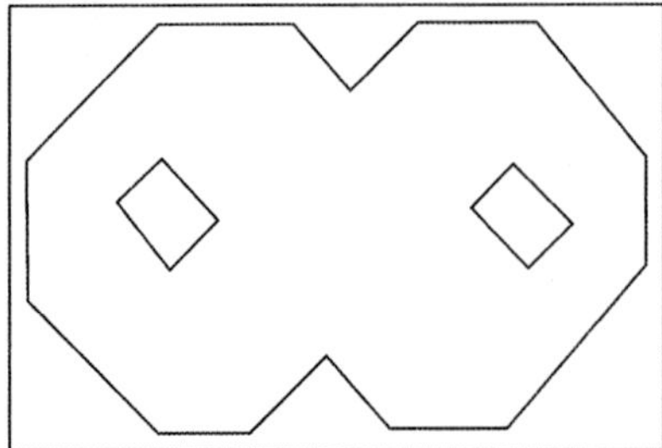

We will next learn how to fill complex shapes with different brushes. Usually we need to render filled shapes. The shapes are first created as paths, using the `GraphicsPath` class, and then are transformed into shapes using the `Region` class.

The Region Object

A `Region` object defines a surface bounded by a path. This surface can be created from a closed graphics path, or by performing different operations with other regions like union or intersection. The `Region` class is tightly related to the `GraphicsPath` class because most often it is created from closed `GraphicsPath` figures. The `GraphicsPath` is drawn using a `Pen` object and the `Region` is filled using a `Brush` object.

Let's see now how we can fill the VS sign using a region created from the `GraphicsPath` and a `GradientBrush`.

```
//Creates a new region from the path
Region rgn = new Region(gp);
LinearGradientBrush brush =
    new LinearGradientBrush(new Point(0, 0),
                            new Point(100, 100),
                            Color.LightSteelBlue,
                            Color.CornflowerBlue);
//Fills the region with the gradient brush
e.Graphics.FillRegion(brush,rgn);
brush.Dispose();
```

The result is:

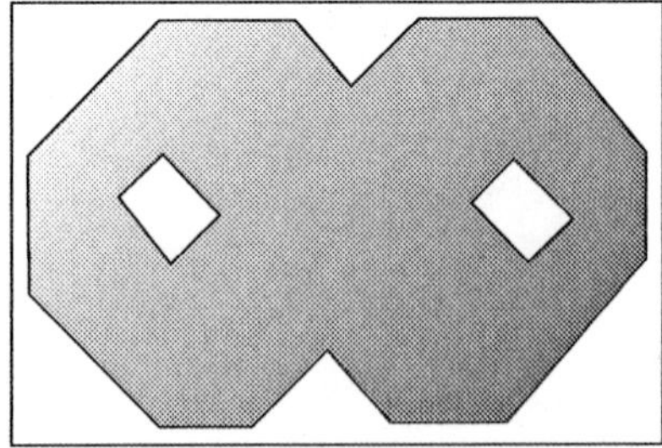

Now we have all the knowledge to render the VS sign. Each colored side will be assigned a `GraphicsPath`. Then each path will serve as boundary for a region that will be filled with a `GradientBrush`. In the next example we will see how to do this with the red region in the centre of the sign.

```
//Creates the path around the red region
      GraphicsPath gpr = new GraphicsPath();
      gpr.AddPolygon(new Point[]{
        new Point(88,0),
        new Point(115,0),
        new Point(115,25),
        new Point(50,90),
        new Point(30,90),
        new Point(30,55)
      });
```

Now replace the code that fills the sign shape with the `GradientBrush` with the following code:

```
LinearGradientBrush rBrush =
   new LinearGradientBrush(new Point(0, 0),
                           new Point(100, 100),
                           ControlPaint.LightLight(Color.Red),
                           Color.Red);
e.Graphics.FillRegion(rBrush, new Region(gpr));
rBrush.Dispose();
e.Graphics.DrawPath(Pens.Black, gp);
```

The VS sign is now starting to shape up:

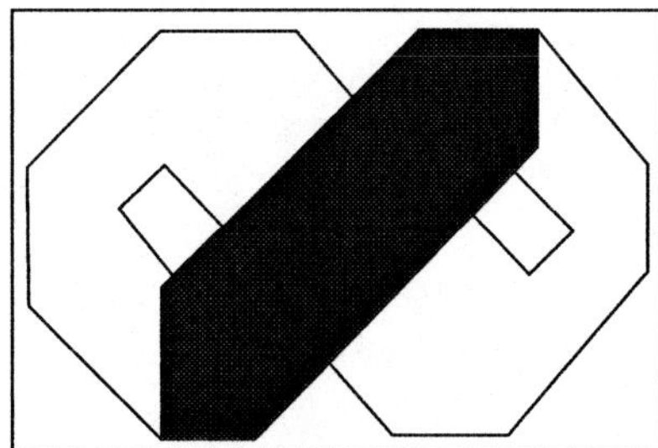

The same steps are repeated for each colored region to render the VS sign. (The full code is not presented here due to its length. It can be found on the Packt Publishing website, at `http://www.packtpub.com/support`.)

The result is:

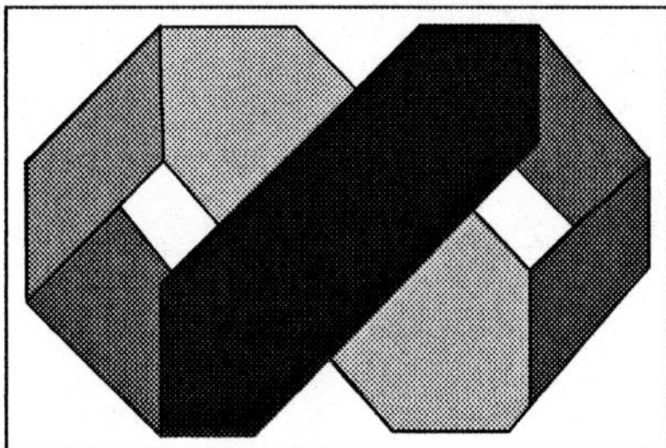

When rendering complex shapes, we sometimes need them to interact with each other. For example, we want two regions to be intersected, so we can render only the region that is common to both of them. Instead of trying to calculate their intersection, the `Region` class methods help ease this process.

We will now take a look at the `Region` methods that makes it interact with other regions or paths. They take another region, graphics path, or other shape as parameter (for example, a rectangle).

Method	Description
`Complement`	Makes the region contain the portion of the parameter's surface that does not intersect with it.
`Exclude`	Excludes the parameter's surface from the region.
`Intersect`	Makes the region contain only the surface common to its parameter and itself.
`Union`	Adds to the region the surface of its parameter.
`Xor`	Adds the surface of its parameter and excludes the intersection between the region and the parameter's surface.

Let's see it in action with an example. We have two circles that intersect in the middle. We will color the intersection differently.

```
GraphicsPath c1 = new GraphicsPath();
c1.AddEllipse(0, 0, 50, 50);
GraphicsPath c2 = new GraphicsPath();
c2.AddEllipse(30, 0, 50, 50);
Region r1 = new Region(c1);
Region r2 = new Region(c2);
e.Graphics.FillRegion(Brushes.Red, r1);
e.Graphics.FillRegion(Brushes.Blue, r2);
//r1 becomes the intersection between the two regions
r1.Intersect(r2);
e.Graphics.FillRegion(Brushes.Yellow, r1);
```

This is how we can obtain the intersection of two regions, which is also a region.

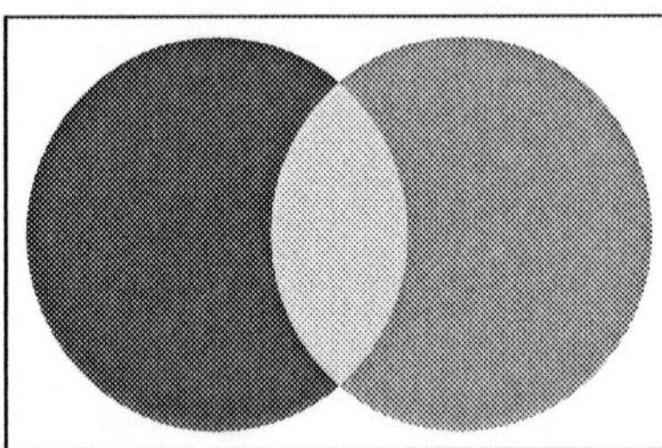

Or we could exclude the intersection before rendering as follows:

```
r1.Exclude(c2);
r2.Exclude(c1);
```

Resulting in the following:

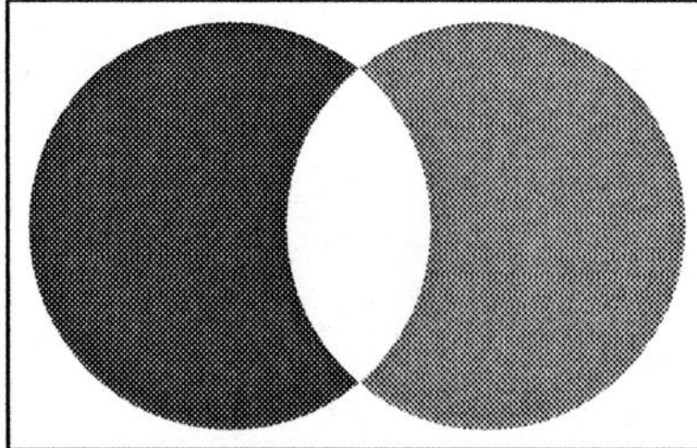

If we wanted to obtain this otherwise we would have to calculate the area in the center and create a graphics path that will be rendered differently. GDI+ makes it easy by using the `Region` methods.

Clipping Drawing Using Region Objects

When rendering custom controls, and creating complex drawing on their surface, it is often required to clip what we draw to a specific shape. Clipping drawing refers to the usage of a `Region` or closed `GraphicsPath` object as boundary for drawing. For example, if we set the clipping region to be a circle region, everything drawn outside that circle wouldn't be visible. Automatic clipping is done when drawing a control, in which case the clipping region is the control's client area. This way, you are prevented to draw outside the area provided by the `Graphics` object.

Clipping is useful when drawing custom controls if we want to avoid rendering outside a specified region. You might think that it is redundant to set boundaries for your own drawing. This is true for simple drawing with fixed coordinates, but when the coordinates are calculated using a formula and you don't know whether the resulting points will be in the specified area or not, it's best to set up a clipping region to make sure that nothing goes outside of it.

To set a clipping region, the `Graphics.SetClip()` method is used. It takes as parameters a `Region` and a `CombineMode` parameter that specifies how the given `Region` will be combined with the current set clipping `Region`. The given region can be combined in any way with the previous clipping region. The default clipping region is infinite. We will demonstrate its use in the next examples.

Keeping Drawing Inside a Region

We will first fill the surface of the control with a diagonal gradient brush, draw a diagonal line over a circle, and outline the circle region with a white line. Then we will add the clipping snippet to see the difference.

```
//Creates a new graphics path and adds a circle figure
GraphicsPath c1 = new GraphicsPath();
c1.AddEllipse(0, 0, 100, 100);
//Create the gradient brush
LinearGradientBrush brush =
    new LinearGradientBrush(new Point(0, 0), new Point(150, 120),
                            Color.Red, Color.Black);
//Fills the rectangle of the control with the given brush
e.Graphics.FillRectangle(brush, ClientRectangle);
//Draws a diagonal line over the circle
```

```
e.Graphics.DrawLine(Pens.Lime, 0, 0, 150, 120);
//Draws the circle to make it visible.
e.Graphics.DrawPath(Pens.White, c1);
brush.Dispose();
```

At this moment the rendering looks like this:

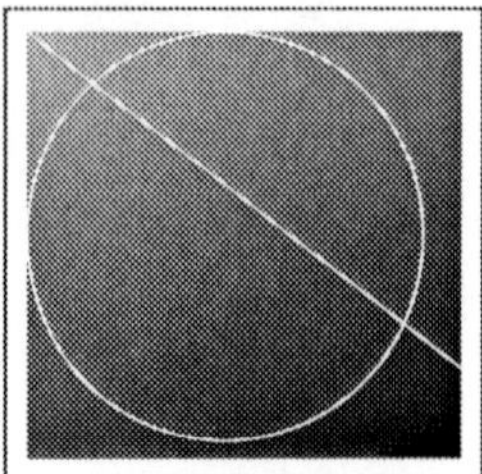

Adding the following code before drawing any line causes the rendering to be clipped to the region of the circle:

```
Region clip = new Region(c1);
//Replaces the current clipping region to the region of the circle
e.Graphics.SetClip(clip, CombineMode.Replace);
```

This represents the way to keep drawing inside a region.

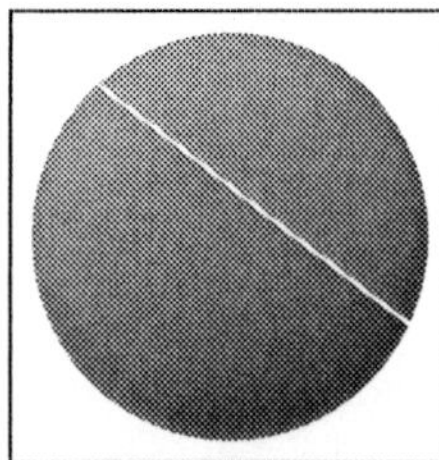

Keeping Drawing Outside a Region

When rendering controls that have complex rendering methods there is a need to keep some parts of the control "on top" of the others. This can be done in two ways. One is to render the top parts after everything else, and the other is to set up a clip region that excludes the regions of those parts. The second method is best if for any reason the position of the rendering code can't be changed. We will render a rectangle on top of a rendered region that is a xor operation of two ellipse regions, after setting the clipping region.

```
//Creates a new graphics path and adds a circle figure
GraphicsPath c1 = new GraphicsPath();
c1.AddEllipse(0, 0, 100, 100);
//Creates a new graphics path and adds a circle figure
GraphicsPath c2 = new GraphicsPath();
c2.AddEllipse(50, 0, 100, 100);
Region r1 = new Region(c1);
//Unions r1 with c2 and removes their intersection
r1.Xor(c2);
LinearGradientBrush brush =
    new LinearGradientBrush(new Point(0, 0), new Point(150, 120),
                            Color.Black, Color.Red);
```

```
//fills the ellipse xor region with the brush created above
e.Graphics.FillRegion(brush, r1);
//Clips the rendering area so it excludes r1
e.Graphics.SetClip(r1, CombineMode.Exclude);
LinearGradientBrush fillBrush =
    new LinearGradientBrush(new Point(0, 0),
                            new Point(150, 120),
                            Color.Red,
                            Color.Black);
//Fills the rectangle of the control with the given brush
e.Graphics.FillRectangle(fillBrush, ClientRectangle);
//Draws a diagonal line.
e.Graphics.DrawLine(Pens.Lime, 0, 0, 150, 120);
```

We first set up the region that will be "on top", meaning the eclipse regions xor and fill it with a diagonal brush. Then everything that was rendered apparently over that region (the rectangle and the line) was kept outside of the first region because we set the clipping region to exclude the first region.

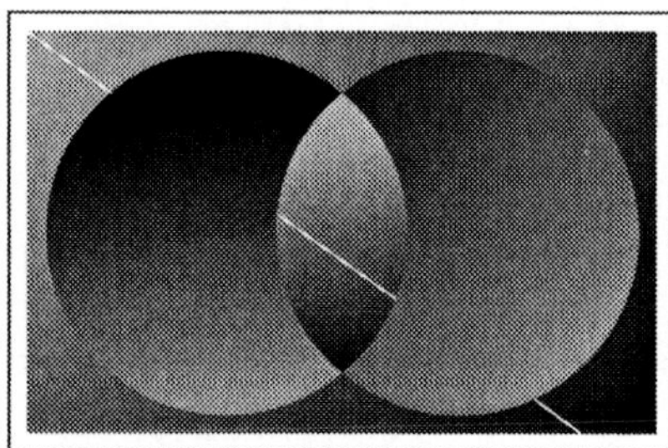

In this section you have learned how to create complex shapes using the `GraphicsPath`, how to fill them using the `Region`, and how to combine them using `Region` methods and clipping. We will now focus on making `Graphics` transformations.

Graphics Transformations

When creating controls that render complex figures with coordinates that are the result of calculations, involving common coordinate transformations, the `Graphics` class comes in handy to minimize the calculations involved. If you don't like using complex mathematical formulas to calculate coordinates, transformations can be used to facilitate control rendering that requires translations, rotations, scaling, and other types of transformations.

Transformations are operations done to the screen coordinate system to change the way shapes are drawn. Shapes can be translated, rotated, or scaled using these transformations. For example, if you wanted to draw a line at a 30 degree angle, you would have to calculate the end coordinates using mathematical formulas. Instead, using transformations you can specify that everything you draw from now on will be rotated at a 30 degree angle; then you just need to draw a horizontal line, which will appear on screen inclined at 30 degrees. Later in the chapter, you will see exactly how to use transformations by modifying the `Clock` control built using formulas. Let's have a look at how transformations are possible.

The screen coordinate system is composed of an origin and two axes. Each axis is composed of a line and a vector that has the length of 1. The transformations are achieved by changing these components of the coordinate system. For example, to translate a figure, the origin of the coordinate system is translated. When this is done, everything drawn will be translated accordingly.

These transformations are implemented in the `Graphics` class by calling the transformation methods. After a transformation has been specified to a `Graphics` object, everything drawn subsequently will be transformed using that transformation. The transformations can be combined to obtain different effects. Transformations are applied until the `Graphics.ResetTransform()` method is called.

Now let's have a look at the different transformation types and how to implement them.

Translation

The translation transformation offsets the origin of the coordinate system. Everything rendered after this transformation will be offset by the amount the origin was offset. To better understand how it works we will use an example. We will draw a diagonal line first, then we will offset the line with 10 pixels horizontally and 15 pixels vertically.

```
//Renders a red diagonal line not offset.
e.Graphics.DrawLine(Pens.Red, 0, 0, 30, 30);
```

The result is as follows:

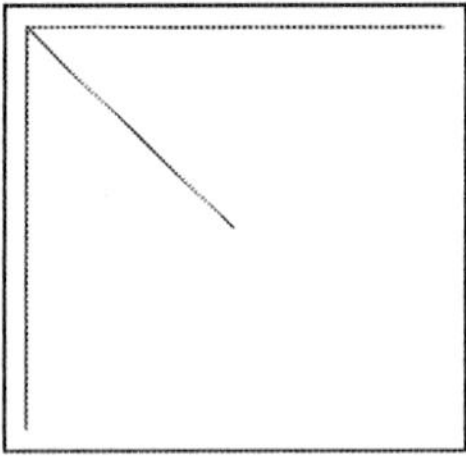

Now let's translate the line:

```
//Translates the following drawing by 10 pixels to the right
// and 15 pixels down
e.Graphics.TranslateTransform(10, 15);
//Renders a red diagonal line not offset.
e.Graphics.DrawLine(Pens.Red, 0, 0, 30, 30);
//Resets the transformation
e.Graphics.ResetTransform();
```

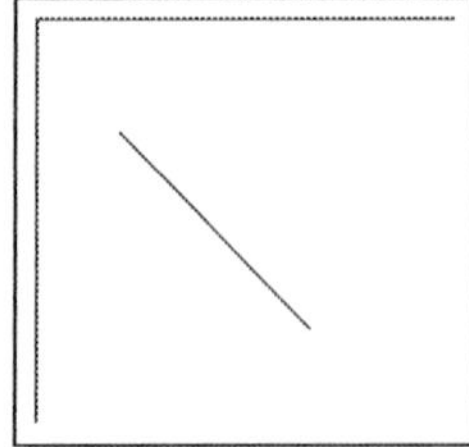

Notice that even if the starting point of the line is specified to be X=0 and Y=0 the line is offset as specified in the transformation.

Transformations are useful when you need all figures to be offset by a specified amount or if a figure has variable positions. If it's composed of 15 points, it is unprofessional to have formulas to calculate each point's coordinates. It is easier to render the figure using any origin and use the translation transformation to move it around.

Rotation

The rotation transformation rotates the axes of the coordinate system by a specified angle. The effect of this is that every figure drawn after this will be rotated by that angle. In the following illustration you can see how it's done:

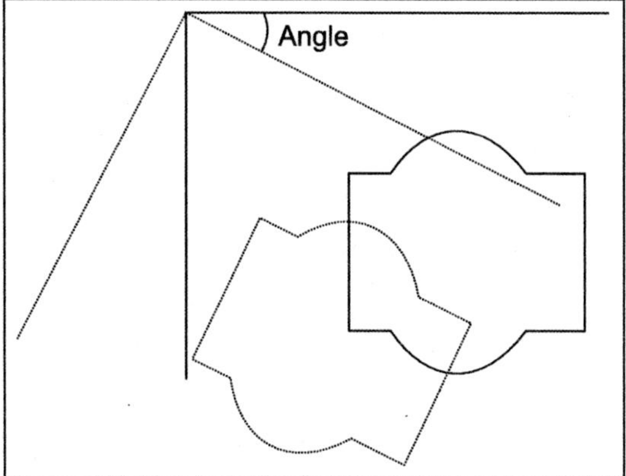

Now let's see how this is done in practice by rotating a line by 30 degrees:

```
//Draws a horizontal red line
e.Graphics.DrawLine(Pens.Red, 10, 10, 60, 10);
```

The result is as follows:

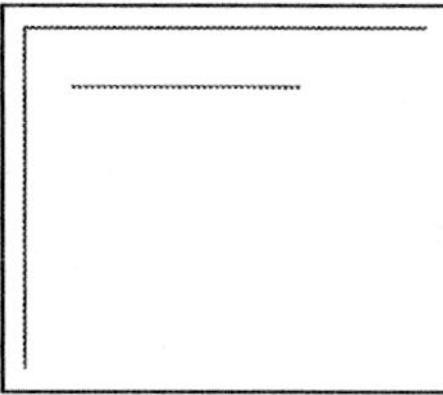

Now let's see what happens if we use the rotation transformation to rotate the line by 30 degrees.

```
//Rotates the following drawing by 30 degrees
e.Graphics.RotateTransform(30);
//Draws a horizontal red line
e.Graphics.DrawLine(Pens.Red, 10, 10, 60, 10);
//Resets the transformation
e.Graphics.ResetTransform();
```

The result is as follows:

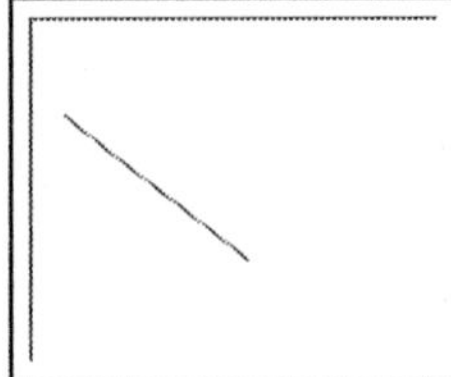

Notice that the first point of the line was also changed. This is because the line was rotated around the origin of the coordinate system, not around the first point of the line as seen in the illustration above. To only rotate the line, you must set the origin of the coordinate system to the first point of the line by using the translation transformation presented earlier.

```
//Translates the origin to the first point of the line
e.Graphics.TranslateTransform(10, 10);
//Rotates the following drawing by 30 degrees
e.Graphics.RotateTransform(30);
//Draws a horizontal red line. Notice that the coordinates have changed
//because the origin has been translated
e.Graphics.DrawLine(Pens.Red, 0, 0, 50, 00);
//Resets the transformation
e.Graphics.ResetTransform();
```

The result is as follows:

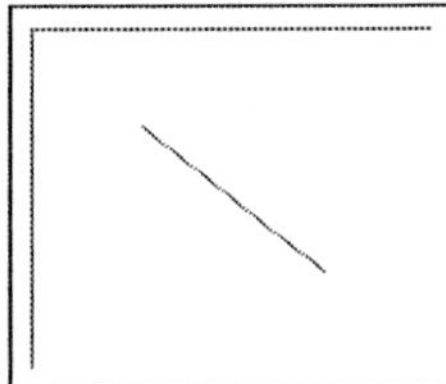

Notice that the first point of the line now matches the first point of the original horizontal line and the line is rotated by 30 degrees. This practice will be used in drawing the `Clock` control's lines.

Scaling

The scaling transformation changes the axis vectors of the coordinate system. Their modulus is set as parameters of the transformation. In other words, scaling multiplies everything with the specified factors. It is useful if you want to enlarge something without the need to calculate anything. After the transformation has been specified, every coordinate and size will be multiplied by the scaling factors.

We will next see how scaling works, and how to implement it, by scaling an ellipse. First let's draw the ellipse without setting the scaling transformation, to see the difference after the transformation has been applied:

```
//Draws a small ellipse
e.Graphics.DrawEllipse(Pens.Red, 5, 5, 20, 20);
```

We get the following result:

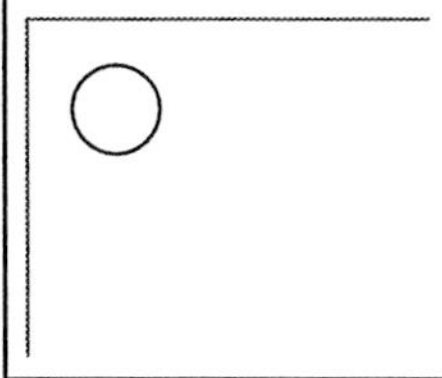

Now let's scale this ellipse. We'll make it 5 times wider and 2 times higher.

```
//Scales the following drawing
e.Graphics.ScaleTransform(5, 2.5f);
//Draws a small ellipse
e.Graphics.DrawEllipse(Pens.Red, 5, 5, 20, 20);
//Resets the transformation
e.Graphics.ResetTransform();
```

We get the following result:

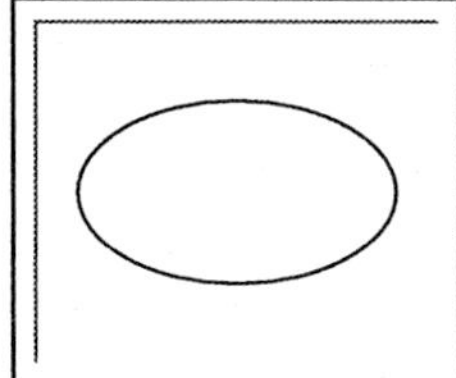

Notice how the location coordinates of the ellipse and the line width are also scaled. To keep the location the same, use the translation as in the rotation example.

Now that you have seen how to render complex shapes and used transformations to obtain different effects, we will put everything into practice by creating a functional control, using what we learned.

Creating the Clock Control

It's time to put everything into practice to create the `Clock` control. This control displays the current system time, drawing a clock-like figure. We will use the Timer component to refresh the clock's appearance every second.

Time for Action—Creating the Clock Control

1. Start Visual C# 2005 Express and create a new Windows Application project named `ClockTest`.
2. Add a custom control named Clock to the project and add it to the form's surface. You might want to change its background color to make it visible on the form.

Now let's add the Timer component that refreshes the clock every second, and handle its `Tick` event.

3. In `ClockControl`'s designer view drag a Timer component from the Toolbar on to the control's surface. Change its name to timer and set its `Interval` property to 1000 (the interval in milliseconds at which to refresh the clock).
4. Add an event handler to the timer's `Tick` property in the clock control and add functionality to refresh the control when it is fired.

```
private void timer_Tick(object sender, EventArgs e)
{
  Invalidate();
}
```

Now the control refreshes its appearance every second.

5. Modify the constructor of the control to optimize the rendering and to enable the timer.

```
public Clock()
{
  //Sets the rendering mode of the control to double buffer to stop
  // flickering
  this.SetStyle(ControlStyles.OptimizedDoubleBuffer, true);
  InitializeComponent();
  //Enables the timer so the clock refreshes every second
  timer.Enabled = true;
}
```

6. Now let's build the control's structure. We'll implement the control's members and properties. The properties will allow the clock line colors to be configured.

```
private Color hourColor = Color.Black;
private Color minuteColor = Color.Black;
private Color secondColor = Color.Black;
public Color HourColor
{
  get
  {
    return hourColor;
  }
  set
  {
    if (hourColor != value)
    {
      hourColor = value;
      Invalidate();
    }
  }
}
public Color MinuteColor
{
  get
  {
    return minuteColor;
  }
  set
  {
    if (minuteColor != value)
    {
      minuteColor = value;
      Invalidate();
    }
  }
}
public Color SecondColor
{
  get
  {
```

```
            return secondColor;
        }
        set
        {
            if (secondColor != value)
            {
                secondColor = value;
                Invalidate();
            }
        }
    }
```

The control's user interface is complete. We will now focus on rendering the control.

7. Make sure you add the `using System.Drawing.Drawing2D` directive.
8. We'll override the `OnPaint()` method of the control and implement rendering code. We will render the control from the center by using calculated radii to draw the points representing the hours, the text, and the lines.
9. First, we will calculate these radii based on the control's size so when the control's size is changed, everything will change according to its new size.

```
protected override void OnPaint(PaintEventArgs e)
{
    //Calls the base class's OnPaint method
    base.OnPaint(e);
    //Smoothes out the appearance of the control
    e.Graphics.SmoothingMode = SmoothingMode.AntiAlias;
    //The center of the control, which is used as center for the clock
    PointF center = new PointF(this.Width / 2, this.Height / 2);
    //The distance of the text from the center
    float textRadius = (Math.Min(Width, Height) - Font.Height) / 2;
    //The distance of the margin points from the center
    float outerRadius = Math.Min(Width, Height) / 2 - Font.Height;
    //The length of the hour line
    float hourRadius = outerRadius * 6 / 9;
    //The length of the minute line
    float minuteRadius = outerRadius * 7 / 9;
    //The length of the second line
    float secondRadius = outerRadius * 8 / 9;
}
```

10. We will now add a method that calculates the angle of a value on the clock, given as parameters the total number of divisions, and the current value. For example, this method will find out the angle of the hour line when the hour is 2 o'clock, knowing that we have a total of 12 hours represented.

```
private float GetAngle(float clockValue, float divisions)
{
    //Calculates the angle
    return 360 - (360 * (clockValue) / divisions) + 90;
}
```

11. Also we need to find a way to get the point from the center at a given angle and a given radius. This functionality is implemented in the `GetPoint()` method.

```
private PointF GetPoint(PointF center, float radius, float angle)
{
    //Calculates the X coordinate of the point
    float x = (float)Math.Cos(2 * Math.PI * angle / 360) * radius +
              center.X;
    //Calculates the Y coordinate of the point
    float y = -(float)Math.Sin(2 * Math.PI * angle / 360) * radius +
              center.Y;
    return new PointF(x, y);
}
```

The implementation of these two methods is math based, and it is used to calculate things, and is not fundamental in creating controls. This is the reason they are not thoroughly explained. We will focus on their use rather than on their implementation.

12. We will now render the outer dots and text of the clock. Implement the following code in the `OnPaint()` method after the last line of code:

```
for (int i = 1; i <= 60; i++)
  {
    //Gets the angle of the outer dot
    float angle = GetAngle(i / 5f, 12);
    //Gets the location of the outer dot
    PointF dotPoint = GetPoint(center, outerRadius, angle);
    //Indicates the size of the point
    int pointSize = 2;
    //Is true when a large dot needs to be rendered
    if (i % 5 == 0)
    {
      //Sets the size of the point to make it bigger
      pointSize = 4;
      //The hour number
      string text = (i / 5).ToString();
      SizeF sz = e.Graphics.MeasureString(text, Font);
      //The point where the text should be rendered
      PointF textPoint =
                           GetPoint(center, textRadius, angle);
      //Offsets the text location so it is centered in that point.
      textPoint.X -= sz.Width / 2;
      textPoint.Y -= sz.Height / 2;
      //Draws the hour number
      e.Graphics.DrawString(text, Font,
          new SolidBrush(this.ForeColor), textPoint);
    }
    Pen pen = new Pen(new SolidBrush(this.ForeColor), 1);
    //Draws the outer dot of the clock
    e.Graphics.DrawEllipse(pen, dotPoint.X - pointSize / 2,
          dotPoint.Y - pointSize / 2, pointSize, pointSize);
    pen.Dispose();
  }
```

The clock looks like this:

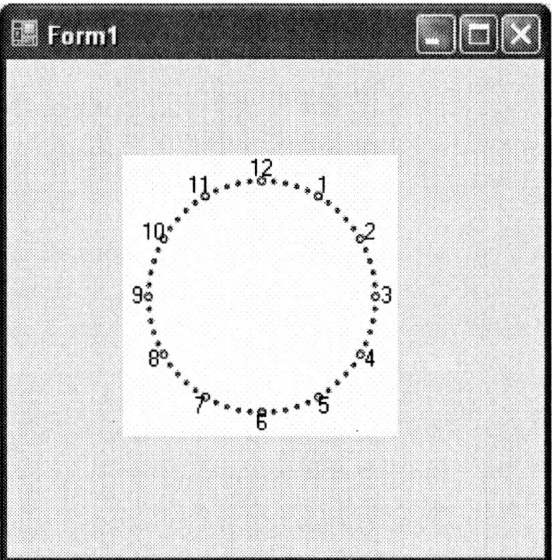

13. Now we will render the clock hand lines. To keep the rendering code clean, it's a good practice to use helper methods. We will first implement a method called `DrawLine()` that renders a clock hand line given a color, a line width, a radius, and an angle.

```
private void DrawLine(Graphics g, Color color, int penWidth, PointF
                  center, float radius, float angle)
{
  //Calculates the end point of the line
  PointF endPoint = GetPoint(center, radius, angle);
  //Creates the pen used to render the line
  Pen pen = new Pen(new SolidBrush(color), penWidth);
  //Renders the line
  g.DrawLine(pen, center, endPoint);
  pen.Dispose();
}
```

14. Render the lines using the helper methods. Add the following code in the `OnPaint()` method in `clock.cs`:

```
//Gets the system time
DateTime dt = DateTime.Now;
//Calculates the hour offset from the large outer dot
float min = ((float)dt.Minute) / 60;
//Calculates the angle of the hour line
float hourAngle = GetAngle(dt.Hour + min, 12);
//Calculates the angle of the minute line
float minuteAngle = GetAngle(dt.Minute, 60);
//Calculates the angle of the second line
float secondAngle = GetAngle(dt.Second, 60);
//Draws the clock lines
DrawLine(e.Graphics, this.secondColor, 1, center, secondRadius,
                  secondAngle);
DrawLine(e.Graphics, this.minuteColor, 2, center, minuteRadius,
                  minuteAngle);
 DrawLine(e.Graphics, this.hourColor, 3, center, hourRadius,
         hourAngle);
```

Now the clock lines are visible:

15. Now we'll see how to shape a control. Shaping a control means giving it a shape different from its default rectangular shape. This is done by creating a `Region` object and setting it to the control. We will shape the clock into a circle.

16. We will implement a method that makes the control's region a circle based on its size.

```
private void MakeRound()
{
  GraphicsPath gp = new GraphicsPath();
  float min = Math.Min(Width, Height);
  //Creates the ellipse shape
  gp.AddEllipse((Width - min) / 2, (Height - min) / 2, min, min);
  //Creates the ellipse region
  Region rgn = new Region(gp);
  //Sets the ellipse region to the control
  this.Region = rgn;
}
```

17. This method needs to be called in the constructor and every time the control's size changes.

```
protected override void OnSizeChanged(EventArgs e)
{
  MakeRound();
  Invalidate();
}
public Clock()
{
Makeround();
}
```

Compile and execute the project. You will get output as shown in the earlier figure.

Time for Action—Updating the Clock to Use Transformations

We will now see how transformations make everything easier. We will render the lines using transformations. First, we will translate the origin to the center of the clock and then we will rotate the coordinate system with the angle of each line, and render horizontal lines whose length is the radius of the line.

1. First, you will modify the `GetAngle()` method to calculate the angle of the line because `Graphics` rotations' sense is inversed from the trignometrical sense.

```
 private float GetAngle(float clockValue, float divisions)
{
  return (360 * (clockValue) / divisions) - 90;
}
```

2. You will have to modify the next line in the `OnPaint()` method so as to get a correct view of the clock numbers:

```
PointF textPoint = GetPoint(center, textRadius, angle);
PointF textPoint = GetPoint(center, textRadius, -angle);
```

3. We will modify the rendering method to use the new method and translate the origin to the center of the clock:

```
  float hourAngle = GetAngle(dt.Hour + min, 12);
  float minuteAngle = GetAngle(dt.Minute, 60);
  float secondAngle = GetAngle(dt.Second, 60);
  e.Graphics.TranslateTransform(center.X, center.Y);
DrawLine(e.Graphics,this.secondColor,1,center,secondRadius,secondAngle);
DrawLine(e.Graphics,this.minuteColor,2,center,minuteRadius,minuteAngle);
DrawLine(e.Graphics,this.hourColor,3,center,hourRadius,hourAngle);
  e.Graphics.ResetTransform();
```

4. Now that we have changed the way the lines will be rendered, it's time to change the `DrawLine()` method.

```
private void DrawLine(Graphics g,Color color,int penWidth,
                      PointF center,float radius, float angle)
{
  g.RotateTransform(angle);
  Pen pen = new Pen(new SolidBrush(color),penWidth);
  g.DrawLine(pen,0,0,radius,0);
  pen.Dispose();
  g.RotateTransform(-angle);
}
```

Notice how no extra calculations are needed to render the line (the `GetPoint()` method isn't used any more). First the coordinate system was rotated by the line's angle, then the horizontal line was drawn (because with the system rotated it will appear at the right angle), and then the system is rotated back.

What Just Happened?

In this exercise you have learned how to put into practice the drawing techniques learned so far. You have created a functional `Clock` control and then improved its rendering to use transformations.

Now that you have created a fully functional custom control that represents a clock and you have learned more GDI+ drawing techniques, it is time for you to use your knowledge. Try to draw the clock hands as arrows. This is good exercise to see that you can actually improve the quality of a custom control just by putting into practice what you have learned.

Summary

Having gone through the previous chapter and this chapter, you now have the knowledge to render many paths with any line type and any shape with any filling brush. Then you learned how to apply graphic transformations to improve rendering, and to minimize the use of complex mathematical formulas. In this chapter you have learned the most important three operations in GDI+: translation, rotation, and scaling.

5

Drawing Control Parts, Borders, and Adornments

If you've read the book so far and you are wondering "What if I want to implement a control that contains a different kind of checkbox?" or "What if I want my control's border to be configurable with the theme of the application?" and your question is "Do I have to render them myself?" The answer is "No". The .NET Framework has a set of tools, which you can use to render control parts, borders, and adornments. These features are implemented in the `ControlPaint` helper class with static methods that draw the specified control parts and borders. More specifically in this chapter you will:

- Explore .NET's `ControlPaint` class and use it to render controls
- Learn how to reuse code by creating base controls and deriving from them

Along the way you'll build a few custom controls, to have a little fun with the help of this new theory.

Rendering Common Control Parts

The star of this chapter will be the `ControlPaint` class. The `ControlPaint` class is a .NET helper class that facilitates rendering common control parts, borders, adornments, and obtaining different shades of a specified color. In other words, it contains built-in functionality for rendering standard control parts that the user is familiar with.

To better understand what control parts are, let's consider some examples. A checkbox is composed of a check button and a label. These are called control parts. The same principle applies to radio buttons, scroll buttons, and sizing grips. These parts can't be found as standalone controls, which you could use when creating a form or custom control. However, the `ControlPaint` helper class wraps the required functionality of rendering these parts, in any of their states (for example, it knows how to draw a checked or unchecked check button).

We will now explore the methods of `ControlPaint`, and we'll see how they facilitate control rendering. These methods take as parameters the `Graphics` object, a rectangle, button styles, and states. For the demonstrations, we'll create simple helper methods that use `ControlPaint` methods in order to draw control parts, such as:

- Buttons
- Caption buttons
- Checkboxes
- Drop-down buttons
- Radio buttons
- Scroll buttons

Let's take them one by one.

Drawing Buttons

Drawing buttons is done using the `DrawButton()` method of the `ControlPaint` class. The method draws a button that fits inside a specified rectangle with a specified state. The best way to understand this is by using an example. Consider this method:

```
private void DrawButton(Graphics g, ref Rectangle rc, ButtonState state)
{
  ControlPaint.DrawButton(g, rc, state);
  // write the state just rendered 5 pixels to the right of the button
  g.DrawString(state.ToString(), Font, Brushes.Black,
               rc.Width + 5, rc.Y + (rc.Height-Font.Height)/2);
  // offset the bounding rectangle, and leave a 5 pixel gap
  rc.Offset(0, rc.Height + 5);
}
```

This helper method called `DrawButton()` simply uses the `ControlPaint.DrawButton()` method to draw a button, and also draw a text specifying the button's state to the right of the button.

Now, you could use this method in your form or control to easily render the button states:

```
//The size of the button.
Rectangle rc = new Rectangle(0, 0, 50, 25);
DrawButton(e.Graphics, ref rc, ButtonState.All);
DrawButton(e.Graphics, ref rc, ButtonState.Checked);
DrawButton(e.Graphics, ref rc, ButtonState.Flat);
DrawButton(e.Graphics, ref rc, ButtonState.Inactive);
DrawButton(e.Graphics, ref rc, ButtonState.Normal);
DrawButton(e.Graphics, ref rc, ButtonState.Pushed);
```

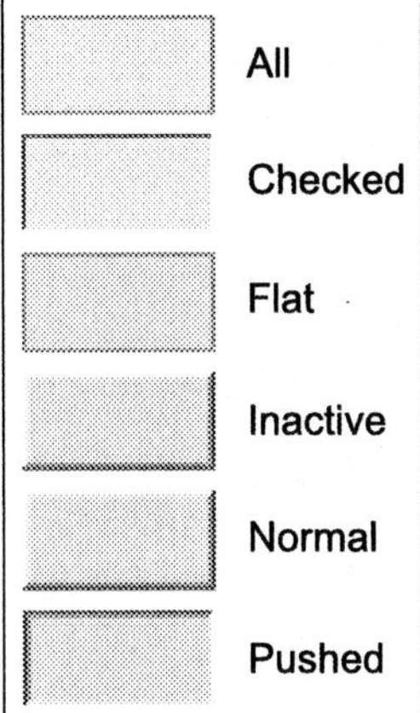

As you can see, there's no rocket science around. You could simply use code like this to create a new control, and this very simple implementation was possible by using `ControlPaint.DrawButton()` and `Graphics.DrawString()`. Quite amazing, huh? Let's see some more!

Drawing Caption Buttons

Caption buttons are the buttons that appear in the top right of the title bar of any application. They are the Minimize, Restore, Maximize, Help, and Close buttons. These buttons can be drawn using the `ControlPaint.DrawCaptionButton()` method. This method takes the same parameters as `DrawButton()`, adding a `CaptionButton` enum parameter that specifies the type of caption button. To verify the functionality, you can modify the `DrawButton()` helper method to draw caption buttons:

```
private void DrawCaptionButton(Graphics g, ref Rectangle rc,
                                    CaptionButton button, ButtonState state)
{
  ControlPaint.DrawCaptionButton(g, rc, button, state);
  // Write the state just rendered 5 pixels to the right of the button
  g.DrawString(state.ToString() + ", " + button.ToString(), Font,
               Brushes.Black, rc.Width + 5, rc.Y + (rc.Height -
                                                    Font.Height) / 2);
  // Offset the bounding rectangle, and leave a 5 pixel gap
  rc.Offset(0, rc.Height + 5);
}
```

You could make use of this method by using it in the `OnPaint()` method of your control or form. The size of the buttons has changed to make them square.

```
// The size of the button.
Rectangle rc = new Rectangle(0, 0, 25, 25);
DrawCaptionButton(e.Graphics, ref rc, CaptionButton.Close,
                                      ButtonState.All);
DrawCaptionButton(e.Graphics, ref rc, CaptionButton.Help,
                                      ButtonState.Checked);
DrawCaptionButton(e.Graphics, ref rc, CaptionButton.Maximize,
                                      ButtonState.Flat);
DrawCaptionButton(e.Graphics, ref rc, CaptionButton.Minimize,
                                      ButtonState.Inactive);
DrawCaptionButton(e.Graphics, ref rc, CaptionButton.Restore,
                                      ButtonState.Normal);
DrawCaptionButton(e.Graphics, ref rc, CaptionButton.Close,
                                      ButtonState.Pushed);
```

Drawing Checkboxes

To draw checkbox buttons, the `ControlPaint.DrawCheckbox()` method is used. The `DrawCheckBox()` method is similar to the `DrawButton()` method, so the helper method will look the same:

```
private void DrawCheckBox(Graphics g, ref Rectangle rc, ButtonState state)
{
  ControlPaint.DrawCheckBox(g, rc,  state);
  // Write the state just rendered 5 pixels to the right of the button
  g.DrawString(state.ToString() , Font, Brushes.Black,
             rc.Width + 5, rc.Y + (rc.Height - Font.Height) / 2);
  // Offset the bounding rectangle, and leave a 5 pixel gap
  rc.Offset(0, rc.Height + 5);
}
```

The code that uses this method can look like this:

```
// The size of the button.
Rectangle rc = new Rectangle(0, 0, 25, 25);
DrawCheckBox(e.Graphics, ref rc,  ButtonState.All);
DrawCheckBox(e.Graphics, ref rc,  ButtonState.Checked);
DrawCheckBox(e.Graphics, ref rc,  ButtonState.Flat);
DrawCheckBox(e.Graphics, ref rc,  ButtonState.Inactive);
DrawCheckBox(e.Graphics, ref rc,  ButtonState.Normal);
DrawCheckBox(e.Graphics, ref rc,  ButtonState.Pushed);
```

The result is shown in the following figure:

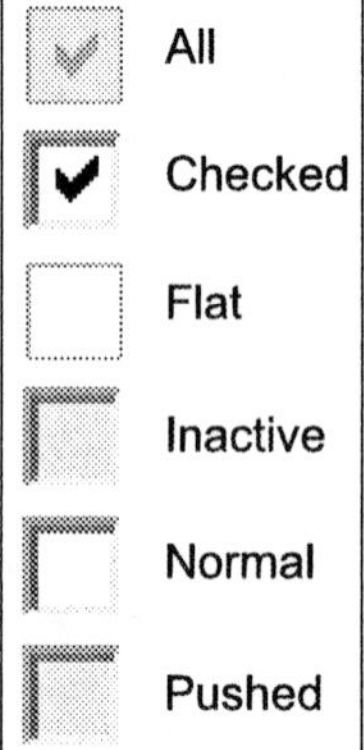

Drawing Drop-Down Buttons

Use the `ControlPaint.DrawComboButton()` method to draw drop-down buttons. Its signature is the same as the `DrawButton()` and `DrawCheckBox()` methods.

```
private void DrawComboButton(Graphics g, ref Rectangle rc, ButtonState state)
{
  ControlPaint.DrawComboButton(g, rc,  state);
  // Write the state just rendered 5 pixels to the right of the button
  g.DrawString(state.ToString() , Font, Brushes.Black, rc.Width + 5, rc.Y
                                        + (rc.Height - Font.Height) / 2);
  // Offset the bounding rectangle, and leave a 5 pixel gap
  rc.Offset(0, rc.Height + 5);
}
```

You can use this method as follows:

```
  // The size of the button.
  Rectangle rc = new Rectangle(0, 0, 25, 25);
  DrawComboButton(e.Graphics, ref rc, ButtonState.All);
  DrawComboButton(e.Graphics, ref rc, ButtonState.Checked);
  DrawComboButton(e.Graphics, ref rc, ButtonState.Flat);
  DrawComboButton(e.Graphics, ref rc, ButtonState.Inactive);
  DrawComboButton(e.Graphics, ref rc, ButtonState.Normal);
  DrawComboButton(e.Graphics, ref rc, ButtonState.Pushed);
```

The result would look like the following figure:

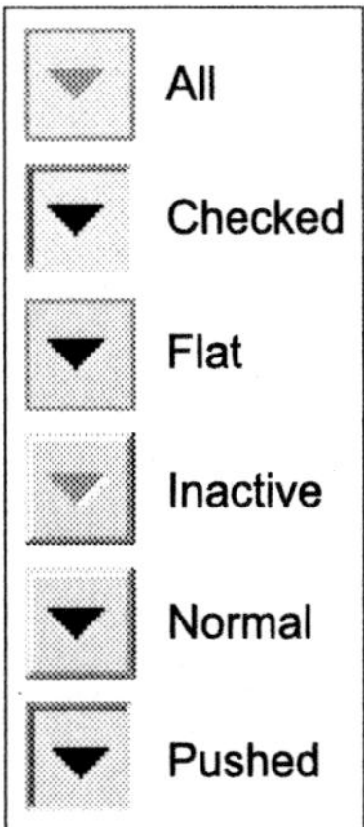

Drawing Radio Buttons

Drawing radio buttons is made easy using the `ControlPaint.DrawRadioButton()` method. With the usual signature, it is easy to render them:

```
private void DrawRadioButton(Graphics g, ref Rectangle rc, ButtonState state)
{
  ControlPaint.DrawRadioButton(g, rc,  state);
  // Write the state just rendered 5 pixels to the right of the button
  g.DrawString(state.ToString() , Font, Brushes.Black, rc.Width + 5,
               rc.Y + (rc.Height - Font.Height) / 2);
  // Offset the bounding rectangle, and leave a 5 pixel gap
  rc.Offset(0, rc.Height + 5);
}
```

Use the code as shown below:

```
// The size of the button.
Rectangle rc = new Rectangle(0, 0, 16, 16);
DrawRadioButton(e.Graphics, ref rc, ButtonState.All);
DrawRadioButton(e.Graphics, ref rc, ButtonState.Checked);
DrawRadioButton(e.Graphics, ref rc, ButtonState.Flat);
DrawRadioButton(e.Graphics, ref rc, ButtonState.Inactive);
DrawRadioButton(e.Graphics, ref rc, ButtonState.Normal);
DrawRadioButton(e.Graphics, ref rc, ButtonState.Pushed);
```

The results should look like the figure shown below:

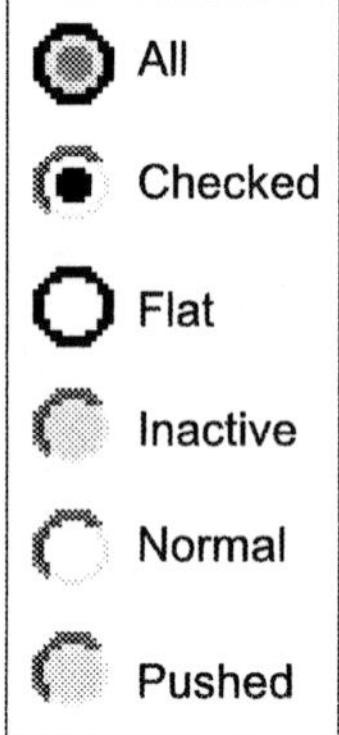

Drawing Scroll Buttons

Scroll buttons are the arrow buttons seen in scrollbars, up-down controls, and other controls with arrow buttons. Rendering them is easy as before. The helper method will now take as parameter a `ScrollButton` enum that specifies which button to render as seen in the example.

```
private void DrawScrollButton(Graphics g, ref Rectangle rc,
                              ScrollButton button, ButtonState state)
{
  ControlPaint.DrawScrollButton(g, rc, button, state);
  // Write the state just rendered 5 pixels to the right of the button
  g.DrawString(button.ToString() +", "+state.ToString() , Font,
      Brushes.Black, rc.Width + 5, rc.Y + (rc.Height - Font.Height) / 2);
  // Offset the bounding rectangle, and leave a 5 pixel gap
  rc.Offset(0, rc.Height + 5);
}
```

Use the code like this:

```
// The size of the button.
Rectangle rc = new Rectangle(0, 0, 25, 25);
DrawScrollButton(e.Graphics, ref rc, ScrollButton.Down,
                 ButtonState.All);
DrawScrollButton(e.Graphics, ref rc, ScrollButton.Left,
                 ButtonState.Checked);
DrawScrollButton(e.Graphics, ref rc, ScrollButton.Max,
                 ButtonState.Flat);
DrawScrollButton(e.Graphics, ref rc, ScrollButton.Min,
                 ButtonState.Inactive);
DrawScrollButton(e.Graphics, ref rc, ScrollButton.Right,
                 ButtonState.Normal);
DrawScrollButton(e.Graphics, ref rc, ScrollButton.Up,
                 ButtonState.Pushed);
```

The result should resemble the figure shown below:

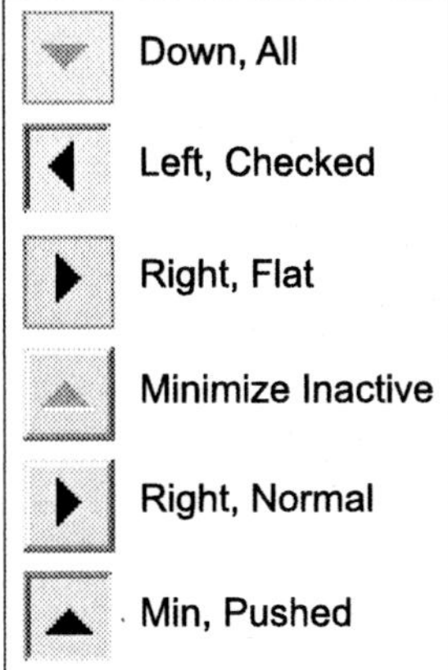

These are the common control parts that can be rendered using the `ControlPaint` class. We will now focus our attention on drawing control adornments.

Rendering Borders and Frames

Borders are important for both the appearance and the functionality of a control. The border style can reflect some states of the control. For example, the border of a button control reflects whether it is pushed or not. In this section you will learn how to make controls' appearance look good and be more configurable using borders.

Rendering Button Borders

Rendering button borders is done using the `ControlPaint.DrawBorder()` method. We will be using the same helper method to render all the button border styles.

```
private void DrawBorder(Graphics g, ref Rectangle rc,Color color,
                        ButtonBorderStyle borderStyle)
{
  ControlPaint.DrawBorder(g, rc, color, borderStyle);
  // Write the state just rendered 5 pixels to the right of the glyph
  g.DrawString(borderStyle.ToString(), Font, Brushes.Black, rc.Width + 5,
                        rc.Y + (rc.Height - Font.Height) / 2);
  // Offset the bounding rectangle, and leave a 5 pixel gap
  rc.Offset(0, rc.Height + 5);
}
```

You would use this method as follows:

```
Rectangle rc = new Rectangle(0, 0, 50, 25);
DrawBorder(e.Graphics, ref rc, Color.Black, ButtonBorderStyle.Dashed);
DrawBorder(e.Graphics, ref rc, Color.Black, ButtonBorderStyle.Dotted);
DrawBorder(e.Graphics, ref rc, Color.Black, ButtonBorderStyle.Inset);
DrawBorder(e.Graphics, ref rc, Color.Black, ButtonBorderStyle.None);
DrawBorder(e.Graphics, ref rc, Color.Black, ButtonBorderStyle.Outset);
DrawBorder(e.Graphics, ref rc, Color.Black, ButtonBorderStyle.Solid);
```

The result:

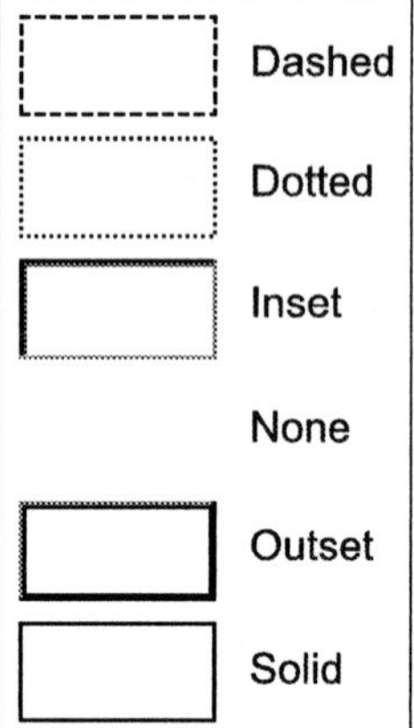

Rendering 3D Borders

Rendering 3D borders is done in the same way as rendering other control parts.

```
private void DrawBorder3D(Graphics g, ref Rectangle rc,
                          Border3DStyle borderStyle)
{
  ControlPaint.DrawBorder3D(g, rc,  borderStyle);
  // Write the state just rendered 5 pixels to the right of the glyph
  g.DrawString(borderStyle.ToString(), Font, Brushes.Black,
              rc.Width + 5, rc.Y + (rc.Height - Font.Height) / 2);
  // Offset the bounding rectangle, and leave a 5 pixel gap
  rc.Offset(0, rc.Height + 5);
}
```

You would use this method as follows:

```
Rectangle rc = new Rectangle(0, 0, 50, 25);
DrawBorder3D(e.Graphics, ref rc,Border3DStyle.Adjust);
DrawBorder3D(e.Graphics, ref rc, Border3DStyle.Bump);
DrawBorder3D(e.Graphics, ref rc, Border3DStyle.Etched);
DrawBorder3D(e.Graphics, ref rc, Border3DStyle.Flat);
DrawBorder3D(e.Graphics, ref rc, Border3DStyle.Raised);
DrawBorder3D(e.Graphics, ref rc, Border3DStyle.RaisedInner);
DrawBorder3D(e.Graphics, ref rc, Border3DStyle.RaisedOuter);
DrawBorder3D(e.Graphics, ref rc, Border3DStyle.Sunken);
DrawBorder3D(e.Graphics, ref rc, Border3DStyle.SunkenInner);
DrawBorder3D(e.Graphics, ref rc, Border3DStyle.SunkenOuter);
```

The result is shown in the following figure:

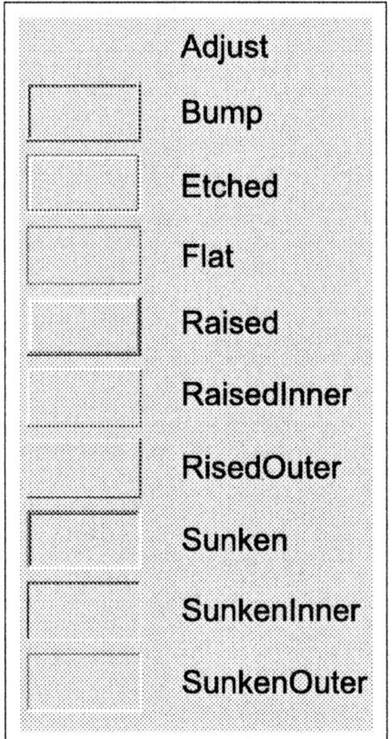

Rendering Control Adornments

Control adornments are shapes rendered on the surface of a control to indicate that a specific action can be performed on the control by clicking on them. For example, the little squares that appear in the corners of controls to indicate that they are sizable, are adornments. The rectangle that appears inside a button to indicate that it has focus is an adornment. Most of the adornments are defined by the Windows user interface and are familiar to most users because of it. Adornments help you create an intuitive interface for the control. The `ControlPaint` class contains functionality for drawing adornments. The adornments that can be rendered will be presented in the next table along with the code that renders them.

Description	Method	Appearance
Container grab handle: Used for changing the location of controls.	`ControlPaint.DrawContainerGrabHandle (e.Graphics, new Rectangle(0, 0, 25, 25));`	
Size grip: Used to resize windows.	`ControlPaint.DrawSizeGrip(e.Graphics,Color.Gray,new Rectangle(0,0,25,25));`	
Grab handle: Used in the corners of controls for resizing.	`ControlPaint.DrawGrabHandle(e.Graphics, new Rectangle(0, 0, 25, 25), true, false);`	
Grid: Used in forms to align controls.	`ControlPaint.DrawGrid(e.Graphics, new Rectangle(0, 0, 100, 100), new Size(5, 5), Color.Red);`	

<table>
<tr><th>Description</th><th>Method</th><th>Appearance</th></tr>
<tr><td>Menu glyph: Symbols used in rendering common control interfaces.</td><td><pre>private void DrawMenuGlyph(Graphics g,
     ref Rectangle rc, MenuGlyph glyph)
{
  ControlPaint.DrawMenuGlyph(g, rc,
                              glyph);
  // Write the state just rendered 5
  // pixels to the right of the glyph
  g.DrawString(glyph.ToString() , Font,
    Brushes.Black, rc.Width + 5, rc.Y +
    (rc.Height - Font.Height) / 2);
  // Offset the bounding rectangle, and
  // leave a 5 pixel gap
  rc.Offset(0, rc.Height + 5);
}
Rectangle rc = new Rectangle(0, 0, 16,
                              16);
DrawMenuGlyph(e.Graphics, ref rc,
              MenuGlyph.Arrow);
DrawMenuGlyph(e.Graphics, ref rc,
              MenuGlyph.Bullet);
DrawMenuGlyph(e.Graphics, ref rc,
              MenuGlyph.Checkmark);</pre></td><td>▶ Arrow
● Bullet
✓ Checkmark</td></tr>
<tr><td>Focus rectangle: Use to indicate that a control has focus.</td><td><pre>ControlPaint.DrawFocusRectangle(e.Graphics,
new Rectangle(5, 5, 50, 25));</pre></td><td></td></tr>
</table>

With adornments we conclude the presentation of how to render control parts, borders, and adornments. We will now use them in a few examples to demonstrate their functionality.

Creating Multiple Controls that Reuse the Same Functionality

When planning an application, you sometimes notice that two or more of the controls you want to implement either have a similar part of their interface or similar parts of their behaviors. To build the application in a professional way, and to save time and money implementing and debugging controls, the best way to tackle this issue is by creating a base control that implements the common features of the controls, and then deriving from it to create the specific features of each of them. To best understand this practice we will look at an example.

Let's say that in our application we need to build controls that include control parts. For example, a checkbox when clicked changes its check state and a radio button does the same thing, but their appearance is clearly not the same. You can create a base class that is a common button that has the functionality embedded. For each button type, you will derive from the base class, creating a new class. This derived class will inherit all the base functionality, and add some specific properties. When checked and clicked, the radio button will remain checked while the checkbox will uncheck. Here, in the derived classes you will also change the look and feel of the button by overriding the `OnPaint()` method. We will implement a `ControlPart` base class that contains the common behavior of all parts that can be rendered using the `ControlPaint` class.

Creating a Base Class for Two or More Controls

Creating base classes for controls to encourage code reusability, and to minimize the amount of time to create similar controls, is used as a best practice when implementing controls. Using this technique has many advantages with virtually no disadvantage, so learning to use it is a good way to implement an application faster and better.

In our example, we will create a `ControlPart` base class that implements common mouse functionality of all controls we will derive from it. The control will have a field that indicates whether it is checked or unchecked, and another that indicates the mouse action performed over its surface (clicked, mouse hover, etc.).

The `ControlPart` base class will practically be a class that holds information about mouse events that have happened and are happening on the surface of the control. However, it is not intended to be a functional and independent control, but to ease implementing of other controls that derive from it. There will be two main fields that hold the mouse information. One of them (`buttonState`) will hold information on what is happening with the mouse at present on the surface of the control (`MouseHover`, `MouseClick`, etc.) and the other (`checkState`) will hold information on the number of clicks that have been performed on the surface of the control. The `buttonState` field can have multiple values defining the state of a button such as `Flat`, `Normal`, `Pushed`, etc., and the `checkState` can have one of three values: `Checked`, `Unchecked`, and `Indeterminate`. The information held in these fields is then used by the derived controls to render their states accordingly. This is done by creating virtual methods in the base class, which are then overridden by the derived controls to render their specific appearances.

Time for Action—Creating the ControlPart Base Class

1. Create a new Windows Application project in Visual C# Express called `CreatingControlParts`.
2. Add a new class to the project called `ControlPart`, and derive it from the `Control` class.

```
public class ControlPart: Control
{
  private ButtonState buttonState = ButtonState.Flat;
  private CheckState checkState = CheckState.Unchecked;
  // indicates whether the mouse is hovering over the control
  protected bool mouseOver = false;
  public ControlPart()
  {
    SetStyle(ControlStyles.OptimizedDoubleBuffer |
             ControlStyles.ResizeRedraw, true);
  }
}
```

3. It's time to add the mouse event handlers that manipulate the two fields. You will have to override the `OnMouseEnter()`, `OnMouseLeave()`, `OnMouseDown()`, and `OnMouseUp()` methods.

   Handling mouse events is very easy. The base `Control` class fires events when any relevant mouse action happens on the surface of the control, so handling mouse events only requires you to override the methods that fire the events. These events start with "Mouse" and end with the action that is occurring or has just happened. To better understand this theory we will put it into practice in our example. We need to know when mouse actions occur in our control so we can change the two fields that indicate to the derived controls what to render. The default `buttonState` is chosen to be `Flat`.

> You will learn more about handling mouse events in Chapter 10.

4. When the mouse cursor enters the control we set our `buttonState` to `Normal`, to highlight the control and then invalidate the control.

```
protected override void OnMouseEnter(EventArgs e)
{
  base.OnMouseEnter(e);
  buttonState = ButtonState.Normal;
  mouseOver = true;
  Invalidate(true);
}
```

5. Now when the mouse cursor enters the surface of the control, this method will be called. We will implement similar behavior for other mouse events.

```
protected override void OnMouseLeave(EventArgs e)
{
  base.OnMouseLeave(e);
  buttonState = ButtonState.Flat;
  mouseOver = false;
  Invalidate(true);
}
```

6. When the mouse cursor leaves the surface of the control, its appearance will turn back to its default state, which is `Flat`.

```
protected override void OnMouseDown(MouseEventArgs e)
{
  base.OnMouseDown(e);
  this.Focus();
  if(!(e.Button==MouseButtons.Left)) return;
  buttonState = ButtonState.Pushed;
  switch(checkState)
  {
    case CheckState.Checked: checkState = CheckState.Unchecked; break;
    case CheckState.Unchecked: checkState = CheckState.Checked; break;
    case CheckState.Indeterminate: checkState = CheckState.Unchecked;
         break;
  }
  Invalidate(true);
}
```

7. When the user clicks the control, the `buttonState` is set to `Pushed` to indicate this, and the `checkState` is changed.

```
protected override void OnMouseUp(MouseEventArgs e)
{
  base.OnMouseUp(e);
  if(!((e.Button & MouseButtons.Left)==MouseButtons.Left)) return;
  buttonState = ButtonState.Normal;
  Invalidate(true);
}
```

After the click has been performed, the `buttonState` is returned to `Normal`.

8. Now let's add the virtual method that will be overridden in the derived controls to render them. This method passes the `buttonState` and `checkState` as parameters to the derived control and will be called from the `OnPaint()` event handler.

```
protected virtual void RenderControl(Graphics g,
                                     ButtonState buttonState,
                                     CheckState checkState)
{
}
protected override void OnPaint(PaintEventArgs e)
{
  base.OnPaint(e);
  RenderControl(e.Graphics,buttonState,checkState);
}
```

Now the base class is created and all we need to do to start building control parts is to derive from it and override the `RenderControl()` method.

What Just Happened?

You have successfully created a `ControlPart` base class that implements the default behavior of the buttons. You have developed mouse action functionality. It also contains a `RenderControl()` method that will be called from the derived class code for drawing the buttons.

Creating Derived Controls

Now we will see how easy it is to create controls using the base class we just created. Because the behavior is packed in the base class, the derived class only implements the differences, which in this case is what is rendered. We will override the `RenderControl()` method, and with the help of the `ControlPaint` class presented earlier we will build controls very quickly.

We will now create a `ScrollArrowButton` control that can be rendered using the `ControlPaint.DrawScrollButton()` method, and a `CheckButton` control that represents only the square check area of a checkbox. Both controls derive from the `ControlPart` base control.

Time for Action—Creating the ScrollArrowButton Control

1. Add a `ScrollArrowButton` class to the project `CreatingControlParts` and derive it from `ControlPart`.

```
public class ScrollArrowButton: ControlPart
{
}
```

2. Override the `RenderControl()` method to render the scroll button according to the `buttonState` and `checkState` manipulated in the base class and given as parameters.

```
public class ScrollArrowButton : ControlPart
{
  protected override void RenderControl(Graphics g,
                                        ButtonState buttonState,
                                        CheckState checkState)
  {
    ControlPaint.DrawScrollButton(g, ClientRectangle,
                                  ScrollButton.Up, buttonState);
  }
}
```

This is everything that needs to be done to have a functional `ScrollButton` control because the rest of the functionality is implemented in the base class. Notice that the `checkState` parameter is never used in this example because it isn't required to know how many times the button has been clicked, but it will be used in the next control part we build.

3. The `ControlPaint.DrawScrollButton()` takes as third parameter a `ScrollButton` enum that indicates the type of button to render (up, down, left, or right), so to make the control more complete, we can make this option `public` to the user through a field-property pair.

```
private ScrollButton sButton = ScrollButton.Up;
    public ScrollButton ButtonType
    {
      get
      {
        return sButton;
      }
      set
      {
        if (sButton != value)
        {
          sButton = value;
          Invalidate();
        }
      }
    }
```

4. And in the rendering code, modify the parameter of the method:

```
protected override void RenderControl(Graphics g,
                  ButtonState buttonState,CheckState checkState)
{
  ControlPaint.DrawScrollButton(g, ClientRectangle, sButton,
                              buttonState);
}
```

Now the type of button can be chosen by the user.

To test the `ScrollArrowButton` control, add 4 controls to the application's form, and set their `ButtonType` property differently to the four buttons, then run the application and see how they work.

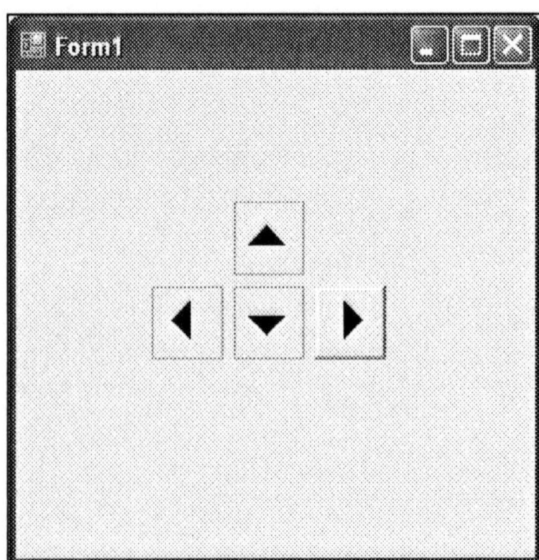

What Just Happened?

In this example you have learned to create a derived control. You have inherited functionality from the base class `ControlPart`, and you have successfully created a `ScrollArrowButton` control.

We'll continue by creating yet another derived control: the `CheckButton`!

Time for Action—Creating the CheckButton Control

1. Add a new class to the project, name it `CheckButton`, and derive it from the `ControlPart` base class.
2. Override the `RenderControl()` method to render the check button.

```
public class CheckButton : ControlPart
{
  protected override void RenderControl(Graphics g,ButtonState
                                        buttonState,CheckState
                                        checkState)
  {
   ButtonState bstate = buttonState;
   switch(checkState)
   {
     case CheckState.Checked: bstate = ButtonState.Checked; break;
     case CheckState.Indeterminate: bstate = ButtonState.All; break;
   }
   ControlPaint.DrawCheckBox(g,ClientRectangle,bstate);
  }
}
```

   Note that the `ControlPaint.DrawCheckBox()` method takes as parameter a `ButtonState` object so we have to set it according to our `checkState`.

3. Again, this is everything required to build a functional `CheckButton`.Test the `CheckButton` control on the application's form.

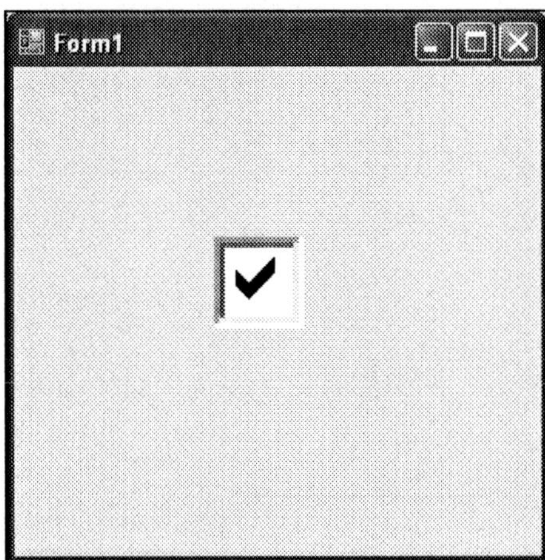

The advantages of implementing common behaviors in base classes are clearly visible: the amount of code required for building a new control is minimal. Using the same technique you can create combobox buttons, caption buttons, and many more. You could even render your own controls in the `RenderControl()` method based on the `buttonState` and `checkState` parameters.

What Just Happened?

In this example, you have implemented a `CheckButton` control. So you have seen how easily you can create controls by deriving from a base `Control` class. Even though implementing the derived controls is a piece of cake, the development of a base control from which you can derive is somewhat harder. You saved a lot of time creating this control by deriving it from an existing one instead of writing it from scratch.

Extending Existing Controls

In this section we will see how we can adapt existing controls to better fit our needs, with minimum effort. Sometimes when creating a new control, you can notice that some of the features you want are already implemented in another control. You can use some features implemented in other basic controls by deriving from them and building functionality on top of them.

We will demonstrate this concept by creating a `BorderGradientPanel` control that is nothing more than a panel with a choice of borders and a gradient background. The control can be used individually to create a nice looking background for other controls and is not specifically created for extending it. We will then derive from it to create a `GradientButton` control based on the functionality of the `BorderGradientPanel`.

Time for Action—Creating the BorderGradientPanel Control

This control will have three field-property pairs that specify the border type, the start color of the gradient, and the end color of the gradient.

1. Add a new control to the application and name it `BorderGradientPanel`, and add the three field-property pairs that specify the appearance settings of the control.

```
public class BorderGradientPanel : Control
{
  private Border3DStyle borderStyle = Border3DStyle.Sunken;
  private Color startColor = SystemColors.Control;
  private Color endColor = SystemColors.Control;
  public Color EndColor
  {
    get
    {
      return endColor;
    }
    set
    {
      if (endColor != value)
      {
        endColor = value;
        Invalidate();
      }
  }
  public Color StartColor
  {
    get
    {
      return startColor;
    }
```

```
            set
            {
              if (startColor != value)
              {
                startColor = value;
                Invalidate();
              }
            }
          }
        }
        public Border3DStyle BorderStyle
        {
          get
          {
            return borderStyle;
          }
          set
          {
            if (borderStyle != value)
            {
              borderStyle = value;
              Invalidate();
            }
          }
        }
        public BorderGradientPanel()
        {
          SetStyle(ControlStyles.OptimizedDoubleBuffer |
                   ControlStyles.ResizeRedraw, true);
        }
      }
```

2. Now override the OnPaint() method to render the panel's background.

```
      protected override void OnPaint(PaintEventArgs e)
      {
        base.OnPaint(e);
        LinearGradientBrush brush = new LinearGradientBrush(new Point(0, 0),
                                    new Point(0, Height), startColor,
                                    endColor);
        e.Graphics.FillRectangle(brush, ClientRectangle);
        ControlPaint.DrawBorder3D(e.Graphics, ClientRectangle, borderStyle);
        brush.Dispose();
      }
```

The simple control is now ready for testing.

3. Add the control to the form, compile the project, and then execute.

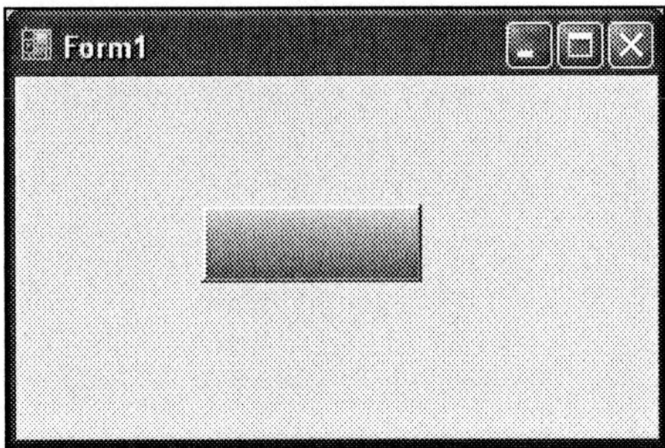

What Just Happened?

In this example you have created a `GradientPanel` control. Although simple, the `BorderGradientPanel` is a functional control. We can use its features to create a `GradientButton` control by deriving from it without having to implement the features already there.

Time for Action—Implementing the GradientButton Control

We will now implement a `GradientButton` control based on the functionality of the `BorderGradientPanel` control. We will have a private field that will indicate whether the button has been clicked to update its appearance.

Let's start building the control.

1. Create a new control class derived from `BorderGradientPanel`.

```
public class GradientButton : BorderGradientPanel
{

}
```

2. We will now add the property that indicates whether the button has been clicked, and a method that updates the appearance properties so that the button appears to be clicked. To achieve this effect, the gradient colors will be interchanged. Also we will call the method in the control's constructor to initialize the properties.

```
private bool clicked = false;
   public GradientButton()
   {
     UpdateAppearance();
   }
   private void UpdateAppearance()
   {
     if (clicked)
     {
       StartColor = SystemColors.Control;
       EndColor = SystemColors.ControlLight;
       BorderStyle = Border3DStyle.Sunken;
     }
     else
     {
       StartColor = SystemColors.ControlLight;
       EndColor = SystemColors.Control;
       BorderStyle = Border3DStyle.Raised;
     }

   }
```

3. Let's now add the mouse behavior specific to a button. When the mouse is clicked on the surface of the control, the `clicked` property is set to true and the appearance properties are changed as needed by calling the `UpdateAppearance()` method. After the mouse button has been released, the button appearance will return to `Normal`.

```
protected override void OnMouseDown(MouseEventArgs e)
{
  if (e.Button == MouseButtons.Left)
  {
    clicked = true;
    UpdateAppearance();
  }
}
```

```
protected override void OnMouseUp(MouseEventArgs e)
{
  if (e.Button == MouseButtons.Left)
  {
    clicked = false;
    UpdateAppearance();
  }
}
```

4. Finally, we will render the control. The `base.OnPaint(pe)` call will render the border and the gradient, according to the base class, and after that, we will add what is new to the button, which is the text. The button text will be offset by 2x2 pixels when it is clicked to give the impression that it is pressed.

```
  protected override void OnPaint(PaintEventArgs pe)
  {
    base.OnPaint(pe);
    Brush foreBrush = new SolidBrush(ForeColor);
    SizeF size = pe.Graphics.MeasureString(Text, Font);
    PointF pt = new PointF((Width - size.Width) / 2, (Height -
                size.Height) / 2);
    if (clicked)
    {
      pt.X += 2;
      pt.Y += 2;
    }
    pe.Graphics.DrawString(Text, Font, foreBrush, pt);
    foreBrush.Dispose();
  }
}
```

Now the button control is complete:

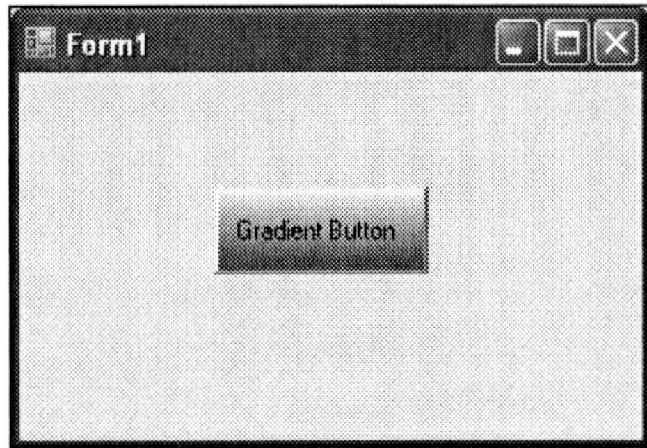

What Just Happened?

You have simply created a `GradientButton` control by deriving the `GradientButton` class from the `BorderGradientPanel`. From the base class you have inherited the appearance and you have overridden the mouse functionality. Also you have overridden the `OnPaint()` method for displaying the button text. Notice that in the beginning of the `OnPaint()` method you have called the `base.OnPaint()` method, which is the `BorderGradientPanel` rendering method.

Summary

In this chapter, you have learned how to render standard parts of controls using the .NET Framework and the `ControlPaint` class. This is useful when trying to replicate user interfaces that the end users are familiar with but at the same time have the functionality needed in the application.

You also saw how reusing functionality can easily be implemented using OOP's principles. Designing a fully structured set of classes can prove to be challenging, but it has benefits in the long term. Most of the work consists of finding common behaviors of the derived classes and implementing these behaviors in the base class. The greater the set of classes will be, the more generic the base class will need to be.

You have also seen how to build controls that combine similar appearance or functionality much more easily by building a base class that encapsulates the common features and then deriving from it to create the specifics of each control.

6
Working with Images

Ever since **Graphical User Interfaces** (**GUIs**) were invented, developers have been keen to use images to make their programs easier to use, and more attractive and intuitive to their users. Images brighten up an otherwise boring and clinical computer screen, and make the general computing experience more enjoyable.

Visual support facilitates the information absorption and presentation of up-to-date information. Any user can more easily understand information just by looking at a picture. Images are the most intuitive memories because the human mind in most cases has a visual memory. This means that when you recall a memory it is frequently a visual one. Think briefly of a tree. What comes to your mind first? Is it the roughness of bark, the taste of fruit or nuts, the smell of tree, the rustle of leaves—or is it a picture of a tree?

Have you ever wondered what it was like before the GUI? There were just text-mode applications. The GUI tried and succeeded in emulating different features of reality. Today, computers can easily reproduce the image and the sound of a tree and in the years to come they will become increasingly better at it.

As regards to the custom controls, these can be user-friendly, if you do the job the right way. It is up to you to develop a custom control that has a good-looking interface. The rendering can be done using drawing lines and curves, using brushes and text; but sometimes it can be improved using images. For example, the Save button in a common application has a floppy disk picture associated, loaded from an image file.

In this chapter, we will discuss how .NET deals with images, and how it can be used to improve your software. We'll visit the `Image`, `Bitmap`, and `Graphics` objects and create a powerful component that you can include in your own programs. You'll learn how to create a picture from scratch without any user intervention, and you'll see some of the cool capabilities of GDI+ in action. Most of the examples take the form of short code snippets, although we will look at creating a small but powerful component that will fast-track you towards some of the more detailed image effects that .NET has to offer.

For the rest of this chapter, you will:

- Learn about the basic .NET classes that deal with images: `Image` and `Bitmap`
- Display images
- Apply various effects on images
- Use images to build better-looking custom controls

As usual, at the end of the chapter you'll build a full custom control where you'll apply the new theory. Let's get started.

Drawing Images

All of the examples in this chapter will require the use of a few namespaces. Make sure each C# file has the following `using` clauses:

```
using System;
using System.Drawing;
using System.Drawing.Imaging;
using System.Drawing.Drawing2D;
```

This will make sure that C# knows where to find each of the classes we will be using.

Using the Image Class

The `Image` class is usually your first port of call when using images in .NET programming. It enables you to store a picture in memory so that it can be manipulated, and it exposes many pieces of information about that picture, including its size and how many colors are used. `Image` is the base class from which another class, `Bitmap`, is derived. We'll be looking at `Bitmap` in a while, but we should look at `Image`'s capabilities first.

The `Image` class comes packed with lots of useful functionality, such as:

- Loading an image from a file and exposing information about it.
- Saving a picture to a file in a specified format such as JPEG or GIF.
- Rotating or flipping a picture.
- Enabling detailed manipulation of the picture by using other classes in conjunction with the `Image` object. For example, you can draw lines on the picture by using an associated `Graphics` object.

There are of course many other properties and methods of the `Image` class but the ones outlined above are by far the most commonly used. To introduce the `Image` class we'll use three of the above features in one go!

Besides being a programmer, I am also an amateur photographer, and I like to take personal portraits. I often take several dozen photographs on my digital camera over the course of a day. One problem I face is that I hold my camera at 90 degrees to the horizontal; so that I can fit the chosen subject in the viewfinder properly.

This is annoying because all the saved pictures on my camera are stored sideways and my camera doesn't have an auto-rotate feature. So every day I have to open all the new photographs on my computer, rotate them by 90 degrees to make them appear the right way up and then save them again. I like to save them as JPEG files to save space.

How could I use C# to make my life easier? Simple, just by creating a method that will rotate the image 90 degrees.

```
private void RotateAndSaveImage(String input, String output)
{
  //create an object that we can use to examine an image file
  Image img = Image.FromFile(input);
  //rotate the picture by 90 degrees
  img.RotateFlip(RotateFlipType.Rotate90FlipNone);
  //re-save the picture as a Jpeg
  img.Save(output, System.Drawing.Imaging.ImageFormat.Jpeg);
  //tidy up after we've finished
  img.Dispose();
}
```

That's an outline of the whole process of loading, rotating, and saving a picture, all wrapped in a short method; exception handling and parameter validation were omitted for clarity. Let us look at it in detail.

Firstly, the `RotateAndSaveImage()` method takes two string parameters: `input` and `output`. The `input` parameter is the path of the picture file we want to use. The `output` parameter is the name of the new file that will be created when the `Image.Save()` method is called.

Further I could use a `for` loop to iterate through all the files within a folder on my computer. I can even try this on my camera's memory card directly and pass each filename to this `RotateAndSaveImage()` method. So in doing this, I can save valuable time, being free to travel further from home in pursuit of my hobby.

Using the Bitmap Class

We used the `Image` class to load an existing picture, and in earlier chapters we saw how graphical effects could be drawn onto controls. These two processes can be combined to enable the creation of brand new images purely by writing code.

So let's do exactly that, create a usable picture from scratch. Since the `Image` class is abstract, it does not have a constructor that would allow creating an image that doesn't already exist; but we still need a blank `canvas` to paint onto. This is where the `Bitmap` class comes in. `Bitmap` does have a constructor that lets us immediately create a blank picture in memory. The following code helps us understand the concept better:

```
private Image CreatePicture()
{
  // Create a new Bitmap object, 50 x 50 pixels in size
  Image canvas = new Bitmap(50, 50);
  // create an object that will do the drawing operations
  Graphics artist = Graphics.FromImage(canvas);
  // draw a few shapes on the canvas picture
  artist.Clear(Color.Lime);
  artist.FillEllipse(Brushes.Red, 3, 30, 30, 30);
  artist.DrawBezier(new Pen(Color.Blue, 3), 0, 0, 40, 15, 10, 35, 50, 50);
```

```
        // now the drawing is done, we can discard the artist object
        artist.Dispose();
        // return the picture
        return canvas;
    }
```

`CreatePicture()` is a function that returns an `Image` object. As you can see, it takes no parameters. The first thing that happens is the declaration of an `Image` object called `canvas`. The `canvas` variable is initialized by a call to one of `Bitmap`'s several constructors, the one that enables us to define the dimensions of the new picture. This line of code also demonstrates the "is a" OOP concept, because "`Bitmap` is an `Image`". `Image` is the base class of the `Bitmap` class and so we can happily assign a `Bitmap` object to an `Image` variable.

So, now that we literally have a blank canvas to paint on, we need to have a way to get the paint onto it; to achieve this we create a `Graphics` object called `artist`. For anything to appear on our `canvas`, the `Graphics` object must be associated with the image. So we use one of the `Graphics` class's static methods, `FromImage()`, to create a new `Graphics` object that is bound to our `canvas`. So from this point onwards, anything that we ask `artist` to draw will appear on our `canvas`.

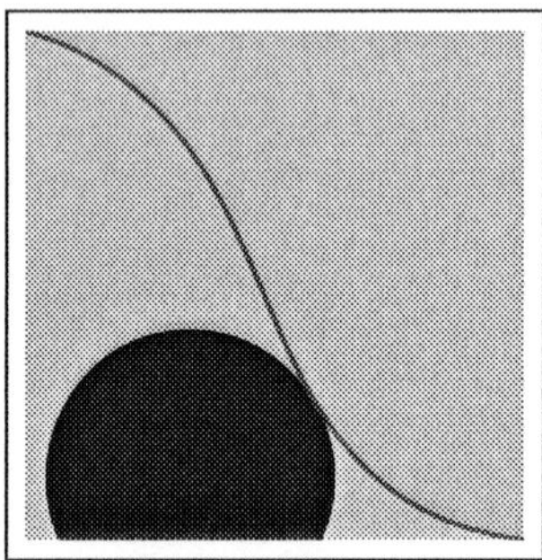

The next three lines of code are dedicated to drawing the picture itself. The image you see above is drawn (in memory) by this code.

We discussed simple drawing operations in the first chapters so these lines of code should be recognizable. The `background`, the `ellipse`, and the `Bezier` curve are all drawn by calls on the `artist` object, and they are all drawn onto our `canvas` object.

The last two lines finish the job. First we `dispose` of the `artist` object because it is no longer of any use to us. Note that even though we have destroyed the `Graphics` object, the drawing that it created remains unharmed inside the `Bitmap` object. The last line returns our freshly created picture back to the calling method.

We'll use the `CreatePicture()` method throughout the examples in this chapter to demonstrate some interesting graphical techniques, saving us the time to select and load images each time.

Displaying Images

So now we have designed a function to draw a nice image for us, how are we going to appreciate its magnificence if we can't even see it?

It's a fair point and one we can easily address. Fire up a new Windows Application project in C# and add a `PictureBox` control to your form. Add the `CreatePicture()` function code (above) to the form's code. Finally, go to the form's `load` event handler and insert the following code:

```
pictureBox1.Image = CreatePicture();
```

Now run the program. In the top left of your `PictureBox` you can see the image that was created by the `CreatePicture()` function. Setting a `Picturebox`'s `Image` property is the simplest way to use a `PictureBox` to display an image but it doesn't allow you to control exactly where the image is drawn on the `PictureBox`'s visible area. You can use the `SizeMode` property to do things like force the image to expand or shrink to fill the control. Still, this isn't very useful if we want to draw an image at specific coordinates.

Luckily, the `Graphics` object has the tool for the job. We'll add a private member variable to hold our picture so we don't have to keep calling the `CreatePicture()` method all the time. We'll assign the image to this variable in the form's `Load` event.

Time for Action—Displaying Images

1. Create a Windows Application and name it `DisplayImage`.
2. Add the following member variable to the code in the `Form1.cs` file:
   ```
   private Image myPicture = null;
   ```
3. While in the designer, double-click the Form; this will bring you to the following method:
   ```
   private void Form1_Load(object sender, EventArgs e)
   {
   ...
   }
   ```
4. Add the following code in the `Form1_Load()` method:
   ```
   private void Form1_Load(object sender, EventArgs e)
   {
     myPicture = CreatePicture(); //create and store
   }
   ```
5. Switch the Form to Design View mode, and drag a `PictureBox` control from the Toolbox to the form.
6. Right-click your newly added `PictureBox`, and open its Properties window. In the Properties window select the Events tab, and double-click the `Paint` event to have Visual C# Express generate the event handler for you.
7. Add the following code to the `pictureBox1_Paint()` method:
   ```
   private void pictureBox1_Paint(object sender, PaintEventArgs e)
   {
     // draw the image onto the picturebox using the supplied
                         graphics object
     e.Graphics.DrawImage(myPicture, 30, 50); //draw the image
   }
   ```

8. Add the `CreatePicture()` method as shown below to the `Form1.cs` file.

```
private Image CreatePicture()
{
  // Create a new Bitmap object, 50 x 50 pixels in size
  Image canvas = new Bitmap(50, 50);
  // create an object that will do the drawing operations
  Graphics artist = Graphics.FromImage(canvas);
  // draw a few shapes on the canvas picture
  artist.Clear(Color.Lime);
  artist.FillEllipse(Brushes.Red, 3, 30, 30, 30);
  artist.DrawBezier(new Pen(Color.Blue, 3), 0, 0, 40, 15, 10,
                                          35, 50, 50);
  // now the drawing is done, we can discard the artist object
  artist.Dispose();
  // return the picture
  return canvas;
}
```

9. Change the BackColor of the `picturebox` to ControlLightLight (Window color) and the BorderStyle to Fixed3D border.
10. Build and then execute the project.

What Just Happened?

In the sequence that the program runs, the member variable `myPicture` is declared and initialized to `null`. Then the form's `Load` event handler calls `CreatePicture()` and passes the resultant image to the `myPicture` variable. From this point onwards, every time the `Paint` event of the `PictureBox` fires, it uses the `Graphics` object supplied by the `PaintEventArgs` parameter to draw the image onto the `PictureBox`. Its position is 30 pixels to the right and 50 pixels below the top left corner of the `PictureBox`. We should end up with a form that looks something like the one that follows:

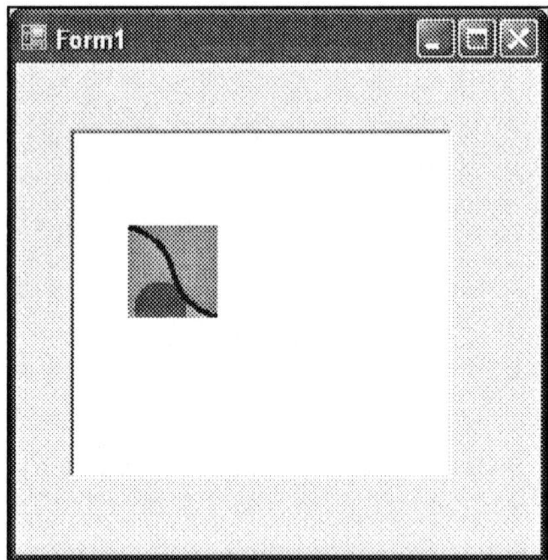

Image Effects

GDI+ provides a host of exciting tools to let you draw your images in complex ways. Skewing, rotating, and even tiling are all possible. We'll have a go at tiling first because it's quick and easy to set up.

You'll need to have the `CreatePicture()` function ready again, and also have a `PictureBox` set up on your form. We'll use the `Paint` event of the `PictureBox` to demonstrate this effect.

```
// declare a member variable to cache the image
private Image myPicture = null;
// use form load to create and store our image
private void Form1_Load(object sender, EventArgs e)
{
  myPicture = CreatePicture(); //create and store
}
private void pictureBox1_Paint(object sender, PaintEventArgs e)
{
  // create a texturebrush that will do the tiling for us
  TextureBrush tex = new TextureBrush(myPicture, WrapMode.Tile);
  // draw the effect onto the picturebox using the supplied graphics object
  e.Graphics.FillRectangle(tex, e.ClipRectangle);
  tex.Dispose();
}
```

You will no doubt have noticed a new class, `TextureBrush`. As you can imagine, given its name, it is derived from the `Brush` class that we looked at earlier in the book. Brushes are used to fill areas rather than to draw outlines of shapes. This means we can use `TextureBrush` to fill rectangles, ellipses, `GraphicsPath` objects, or anything else. We supply an `Image` object to initialize the `TextureBrush` instead of initializing it with a color as we do with other normal brushes. This image will become the 'paint' that this brush applies to our drawing surfaces.

The second parameter of the `TextureBrush's` constructor lets us specify what kind of behavior the brush will exhibit. There are a few different **WrapMode** styles to play with; so feel free to experiment with different ones and look at their effects. For the time being, we just want to `Tile` the background of our `PictureBox` with our now familiar picture. Enter the previous code into your program and run it.

You will get a result that looks similar to the following screenshot:

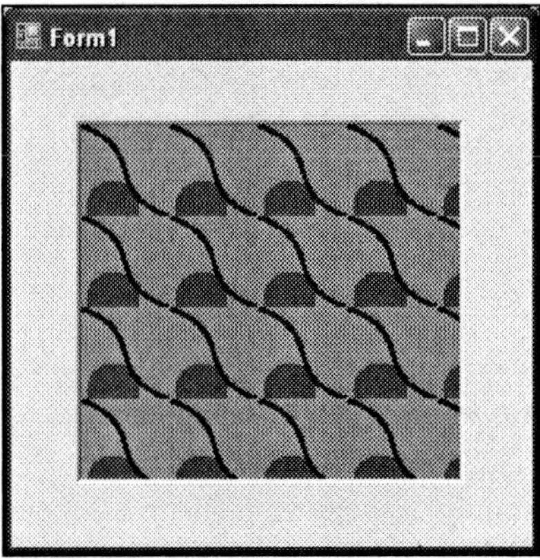

You may also have noticed that this is identical to the effect that the `PictureBox` uses when its `BackgroundImageLayout` property is set to `Tile`. So why bother using all those lines of code when we can just set a property? Good question, and if you only wanted to tile the image horizontally and vertically then you probably would just pass an image to the `pictureBox1.BackgroundImage` and set its `BackgroundImageLayout` to `Tile` and forget about it. But that's just not good enough for us, is it? No, it's not.

What if we want to choose the angle at which the tiles are displayed? We stay with our `TextureBrush` and modify our `Paint` event handler a little. By adding a transformation to the `TextureBrush` we can alter the way it paints our tiles.

Take this example:

```
private void pictureBox1_Paint(object sender, PaintEventArgs e)
{
  //create a texturebrush that will do the tiling for us
  TextureBrush tex = new TextureBrush(myPicture, WrapMode.Tile);
  //Rotate the brush by 45 degrees clockwise
  tex.RotateTransform(45);
  //draw the effect onto the picturebox using the supplied graphics object
  e.Graphics.FillRectangle(tex, e.ClipRectangle);
  tex.Dispose();
}
```

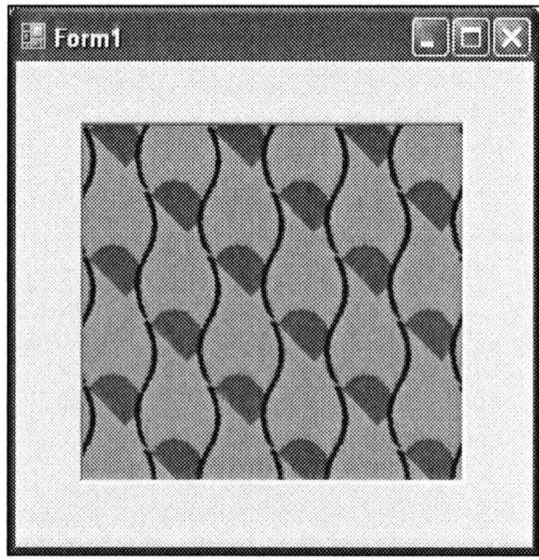

Run the program again. By adding a single line we have radically altered the tile effect; basically instead of tiling horizontally from left to right, it is now striping the image from top left to bottom right. This is due to our specified angle of 45 degrees, that we have passed to the `RotateTransform()` method of the `TextureBrush`.

Other kinds of transformation are also available to the `TextureBrush`, such as `TranslateTransform`, which slides the tiles left, right, up, or down. Finally, `ScaleTransform` enables us to change the size of the image before it is tiled onto the screen. Experiment with them and you will be able to see the effects of each.

Skewing, Rotation, and Scaling

We are going to build a class to help us apply these effects on images. Skewing, rotating, and scaling images (if handled separately) can seem daunting, but if you take the right approach, they are closely related to each other. It is convenient to design a control (or a helper class) for this task because it's quite possible that you may want to include these features in several of your programs. This kind of code re-use is a central tenet of Object Orientated Programming and we shall once again see its benefits here.

First we should understand what each of these three terms means.

Skewing is the act of making a rectangular image slanted. That is to make it fit into a parallelogram instead of a rectangle.

This figure shows an image before (left) and after skewing:

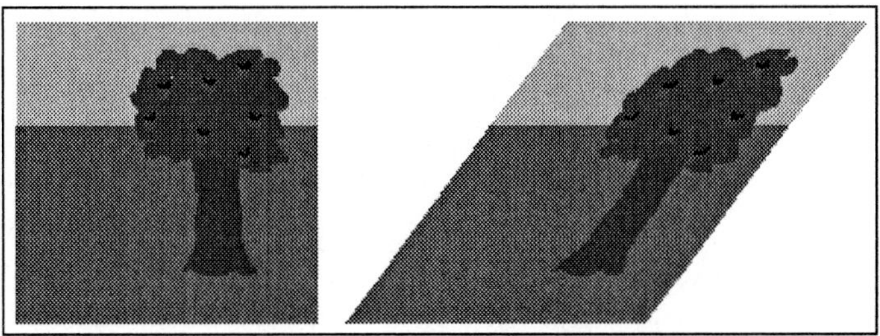

The image shown here has been skewed along the X-axis by approximately two thirds of its width. Skewing can also be done along the Y-axis in the same fashion, or even both X and Y axes at once. This effect is often used in animation and 2D computer games: imagine a character running quickly from left to right; the sprites can be skewed slightly to the right to give the impression of acceleration. It can be quite an effective way to enhance graphics without sacrificing speed or writing lots of additional code.

Rotation is pretty much what you'd imagine. An image turns through a known angle but remains rectangular and maintains its dimensions throughout. It should be made clear at this point that when we rotated the pictures earlier in the chapter we were only able to rotate in multiples of 90 degrees, which is fine for photographic work but a little too restrictive for anything more elaborate such as animation or computer games. It would be cool if we could say exactly how much we wanted to rotate our picture, 30, 45, 90 or even 132.677 degrees!

Scaling is simply making an image larger or smaller. To scale an image, the user is normally asked to supply a single value. The width and height values are then both multiplied by this number to alter the size of the image. Scaling preserves the height:width ratio of the picture. For example, if we have an image that we want to double in both width and height then we would specify a scaling factor of 2.0. If we wanted to reduce the image down to one third of its width and height then our scaling factor would be 0.33333. The scaling factor must be greater than zero.

Building the ImageWarper Class

So you've learned how to create, draw, and apply different effects on image objects. These skills are important for custom control builders, since the appearance of a control is very important for its success with end users.

We'll build a simple but powerful control to help us with drawing images and adding graphical effects to your custom controls. This control will take advantage of the `Graphics.DrawImage()` method to unify skewing, rotation, and scaling into a single operation. You may have noticed that this method has about thirty different overload implementations! Do not fear, we will be using only one of them.

In order to unify skewing, rotation, and scaling into a single operation we need to identify some common ground that all three things share. What these operations have in common is that they all work with the coordinates system. A normal image can be drawn anywhere if you supply the right coordinates, but we will do something a little more complicated than that. The particular overload of `DrawImage()` that we will use is given below:

```
Graphics.DrawImage(Image, PointF[])
```

This method accepts an image object (the one that we want to draw) and also an array of three `PointF` objects. This array defines the parallelogram that the image is to be drawn inside. We only need to define three of these points because the GDI+ is able to extrapolate the fourth corner from the first three; this saves us having to work it out ourselves. The array should contain the top-left, top-right, and bottom-left points in that order. This may sound like advanced mathematics but it really looks quite simple when illustrated:

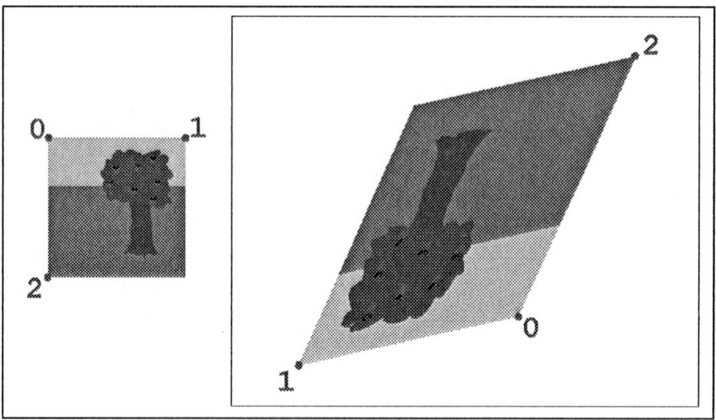

In the above illustration, you can see the original image on the left, where the points of the array are shown numbered at the three corners of the image. Now look at the image on the right. The rectangle box represents the control onto which we are drawing, be it a control, or a form, or whatever. You can see the same numbered points but in a different formation.

The picture on the right has had all three effects applied to it. We can see that it is skewed because it is no longer square. We know it has been rotated because it is upside down. And because it is much larger than the image on the left, we can deduce that it has been scaled. We can do all of this simply by manipulating three points on a two dimensional plane. That is pretty amazing isn't it?

Let's just write this control and examine how it works.

Time for Action—Creating the ImageWarper Class

1. In Visual C# Express, go to File | New Project, select Visual C# project types, and the Windows Application project type.
2. Write WarpControlApp as the project's name, as shown in the following screenshot, and click OK:

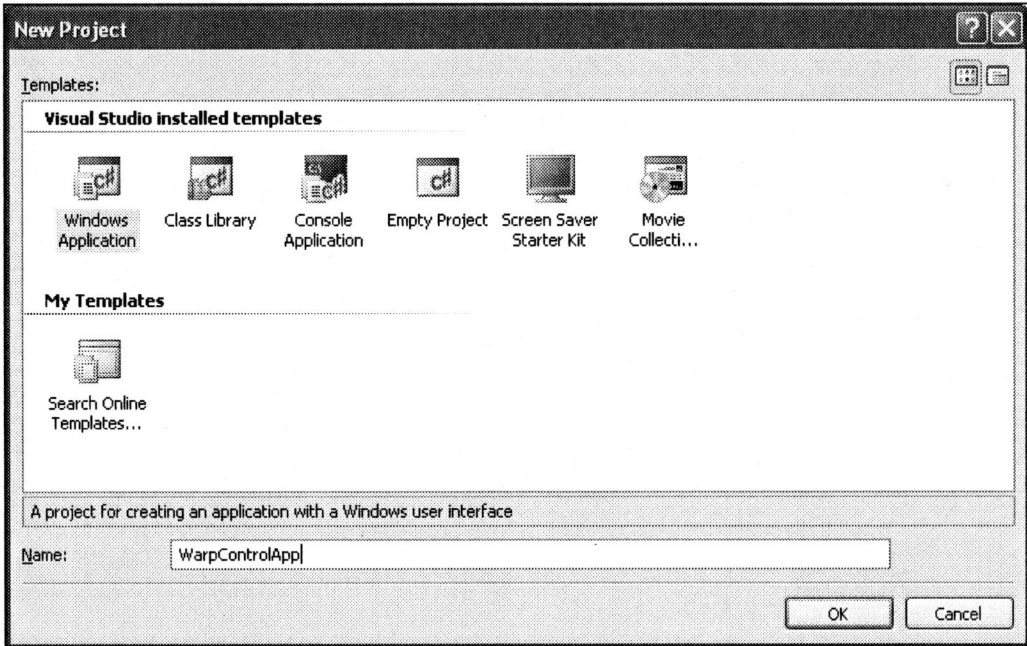

3. Add the `CreatePicture()` method to your form's code:

```
namespace ImageWarperTest
{
  public partial class Form1 : Form
  {
    public Form1()
    {
      InitializeComponent();
    }
    private Image CreatePicture()
    {
      // Create a new Bitmap object, 50 x 50 pixels in size
      Image canvas = new Bitmap(50, 50);
      // create an object that will do the drawing operations
      Graphics artist = Graphics.FromImage(canvas);
      // draw a few shapes on the canvas picture
      artist.Clear(Color.Lime);
```

```
            artist.FillEllipse(Brushes.Red, 3, 30, 30, 30);
            artist.DrawBezier(new Pen(Color.Blue, 3), 0, 0, 40, 15, 10,
                                                       35, 50, 50);
            // now the drawing is done, we can discard the artist object
            artist.Dispose();
            //return the picture
            return canvas;
        }
    }
}
```

4. Right-click the project name in Solution Explorer, and select Add | New Item. Choose the Class template, change its name to `ImageWarper.cs`, and press Add.
5. Change the default generated code to:

```
using System;
using System.Drawing;
using System.Drawing.Drawing2D;
using System.ComponentModel;
public class ImageWarper : Component
{
  public void DrawWarpedPicture(
  Graphics surface,  // the surface to draw on
  Image img,         // the image to draw
  PointF sourceAxle, // pivot point passing through image.
  PointF destAxle,   // pivot point's position on destination surface
  double degrees,    // degrees through which the image is rotated
                        clockwise
  double scale,      // size multiplier
  SizeF skew         // the slanting effect size, applies BEFORE
                        scaling or rotation
)
{
 // give this array temporary coords that will be overwritten in the
    loop below
 // the skewing is done here orthogonally, before any trigonometry is
    applied
 PointF[] temp = new PointF[3] {  new
                 PointF(skew.Width, -skew.Height),
 new PointF((img.Width - 1) + skew.Width, skew.Height),
 new PointF(-skew.Width,(img.Height - 1) - skew.Height) };
 double ang, dist;
 double radians = degrees * (Math.PI / 180);
 // convert the images corner points into scaled, rotated, skewed and
    translated points
 for (int i = 0; i < 3; i++)
 {
   // measure the angle to the image's corner and then add the
      rotation value to it
   ang = GetBearingRadians(sourceAxle, temp[i], out dist) + radians;
   dist *= scale; // scale
   temp[i] = new PointF((Single)((Math.Cos(ang) * dist) + destAxle.X),
   (Single)((Math.Sin(ang) * dist) + destAxle.Y));
 }
 surface.DrawImage(img, temp);
}

private double GetBearingRadians(PointF reference, PointF target, out
                                  double distance)
{
  double dx = target.X - reference.X;
  double dy = target.Y - reference.Y;
  double result = Math.Atan2(dy, dx);
  distance = Math.Sqrt((dx * dx) + (dy * dy));
  if (result < 0)
```

```
        result += (Math.PI * 2); // add the negative number to 360 degrees
                                 // to correct the atan2 value
      return result;
    }
  }
```

6. To demonstrate the usefulness of the `ImageWarper` class, we will use a random object to randomly select rotation, skewing, and scaling values, so that we can see a wide range of different combinations without having to keep recompiling or manually choosing values—plus it's a quick bit of code to write anyway. First, while in the designer, double-click the form to have the `Form1_Load` event handler generated for you, and then complete it with the code given below:

```
public partial class Form1 : Form
{
  Image img = null;
  private void Form1_Load(object sender, EventArgs e)
  {
    img = CreatePicture();
  }
```

7. Use the **Properties** window in the **Visual C# Express** designer to have the `Form1_MouseUp()` event handler generated for you, then complete its code like this:

```
private void Form1_MouseUp(object sender, MouseEventArgs e)
{
  Random rand = new Random(); // randomizes our drawing parameters
  // set up all our parameters first before calling DrawWarpedPicture.
  Graphics target = this.CreateGraphics(); // draw onto the form's
                                            // surface
  PointF pivotOnImage = new PointF(img.Width / 2, img.Height / 2);
  PointF pivotOnTarget = new PointF((Single)e.X, (Single)e.Y);
  double rotate = rand.NextDouble() * 360;
  double scaleFactor = 0.2 + (rand.NextDouble() * 2);
  SizeF skewing = new SizeF(rand.Next(-20, 21), rand.Next(-20, 21));
// draw it!
  ImageWarper warper = new ImageWarper();
   warper.DrawWarpedPicture(target, img, pivotOnImage, pivotOnTarget,
                            rotate, scaleFactor, skewing);
}
```

8. Fire up the program and click on the centre of the form. Every time you click, a randomly warped version of the picture appears at your mouse coordinates. Notice that each one's centre is aligned to the mouse pointer.

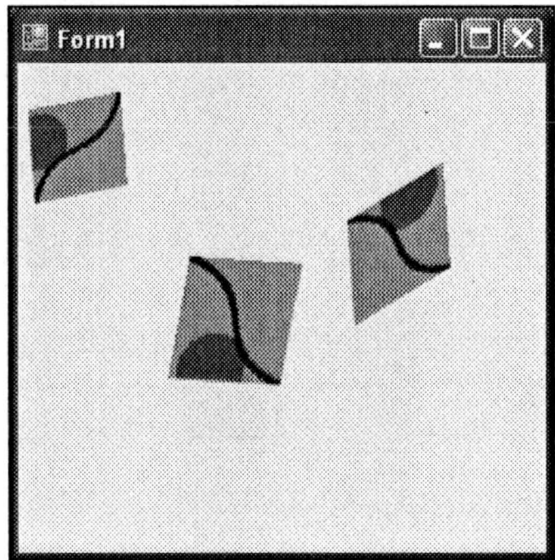

What Just Happened?

The main focus of this exercise is the `ImageWarper` class, so we'll discuss it first. The `ImageWarper` class serves to skew, rotate, scale, and draw an image using a `Graphics` object. It has only two methods, of which only one is public (and consequently, available to our program). Before demonstrating its use, we should briefly discuss its working.

Let's look at the parameters of the `DrawWarpedPicture()` method:

Parameters	Description
`Graphics surface`	This can be any `Graphics` object that you want to draw to.
`Image img`	This is the image object that you want to warp and draw. The actual image is unaffected but it is drawn warped; this allows for repeated draw operations to be done without damaging the original.
`PointF sourceAxle`	The point around which the image is rotated. Coordinates are relative to the top left corner of the image. This enables us to pick a feature on the image and make that point stationary while the image rotates around it.
`PointF destAxle`	This is the point on the target surface where the `sourceAxle` is snapped to. Imagine you pin the image to the screen with a needle; the image can only spin around the needle. The needle passes through both `sourceAxle` and `destAxle`.
`double degrees`	The angle that you want to rotate the image by. The method could be easily modified to change this to radians if needed. The degrees are converted to radians internally anyway before any processing is done. Degrees are easier to visualize though.
`double scale`	The scaling factor. Numbers between 0 and 1 will shrink the image, numbers greater than 1 will enlarge it.
`SizeF skew`	The number of pixels to skew each side of the image by. A size of (10,3) will cause the top side to move 10 pixels to the right, the bottom side moves 10 to the left. Then the left side moves up by 3 pixels and the right side down by 3.

The `GetBearingRadians()` method is not accessible to our programs but it is used by the component's `DrawWarpedPicture()` method; this is in accordance with the OOP's 'black box' principle. `GetBearingRadians()` calculates a 'compass bearing' from one point to another, returning this bearing as the angle expressed in radians.

The warping operations are applied in a specific sequence in `DrawWarpedPicture()`. First an array of `PointF` objects called `temp` is defined and this is where the skewing operation takes place. It is little more than adjusting the corners of the image to reflect the skew and storing these points in an array. Once that is done, a loop is used to iterate through the array and do the following things:

- Calculate the angle from the `sourceAxle` point to each point in the array.
- Calculate the distance between the same points and multiply that distance by the scale factor.
- Finally, convert this angle and distance back into a rotated and scaled point relative to the `destAxle`.

Once the array has been converted from the three image corners to skewed, rotated, and scaled points, the `Graphics.DrawImage()` method is called. Here we simply supply the image and the array of `PointF` objects. Then the GDI+ engine springs into action and does the hard work of drawing our image in its new position. All of this appears complex but it is very efficient and executes very quickly at run time.

When you execute the project, each picture's centre is aligned to the mouse pointer. This is because of the `pivotOnImage` variable, which is set to half the width and half the height of the original image. The `pivotOnTarget` point is simply set to the mouse coordinates, so the pivoted image appears aligned to the mouse. This coordinate doesn't even have to be within the image's area; you can supply any coordinates to it and the image will appear offset by the correct amount. Keep clicking on the form to see more and more warped images appear

Why go to all this trouble to draw images in such a strange way? Well let's say you wanted to design a control that looks like a volume control dial from your car stereo. Maybe you want to have your company logo on the dial control that rotates along with the turning of the dial. Using conventional methods this might mean capturing dozens of images of the logo at varying angles and drawing the appropriate image at the right time, or writing a complicated way to draw the logo manually, which would involve storing lots of coordinates, and colors. Both of these methods are far from ideal because of the time and effort it would take to implement them. With this method all you need to do is store a single image and just rotate it with a given angle. It's a great solution to a difficult problem.

One notable aspect of the GDI+ drawing methods is that they support transparencies and images that can provide transparent pixel data. You could use a partially transparent GIF image instead of our `CreatePicture()` method and the image would display properly. To use the dial analogy, you could make a circular logo to fit inside your dial area but make all the pixels outside the circle transparent so we cannot see the actual rectangular outline of the whole image. We'd only see the opaque logo inside the dial.

The ImageWarperControl

Based on the example above, let's now create a control named `ImageWarperControl`. This control will create an image and it will be able to scale, rotate, and skew this image. First, we will create an application that will be a typical Windows form and then we will create the `ImageWarperControl` that will create and draw a picture at certain scaling, rotating, and skewing factors provided by the application through control properties.

Time for Action—Creating the ImageWarperApp and the Image WarperControl

1. The first step is to create a new Windows Application project in Visual C# Express 2005 named `ImageWarperApp`.
2. Then add a control to the project. In the Solution Explorer, right-click on the project name and select Add | User Control and name the control `ImageWarperControl`.

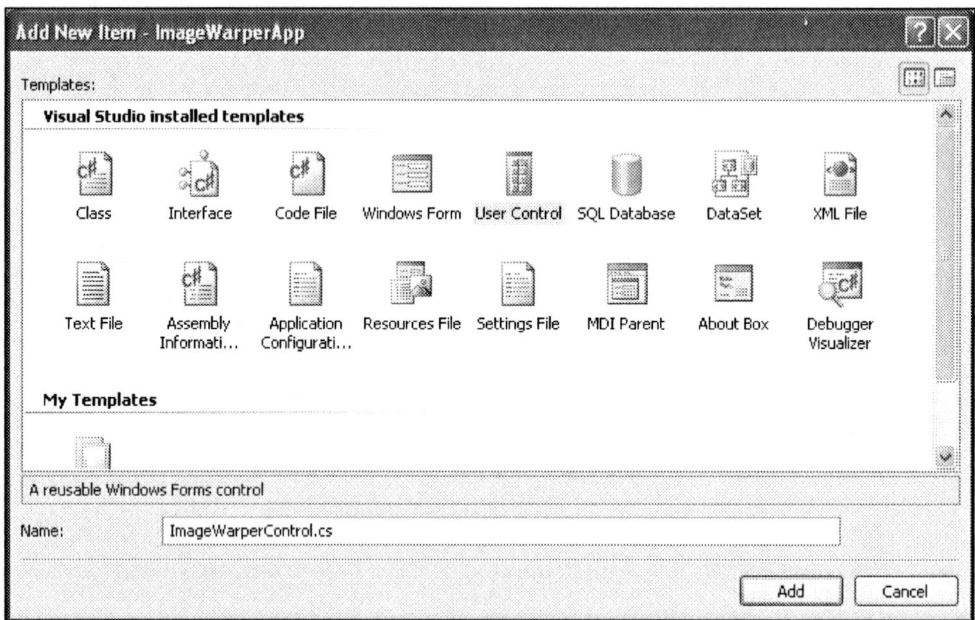

3. You have created a new control that looks like the following:

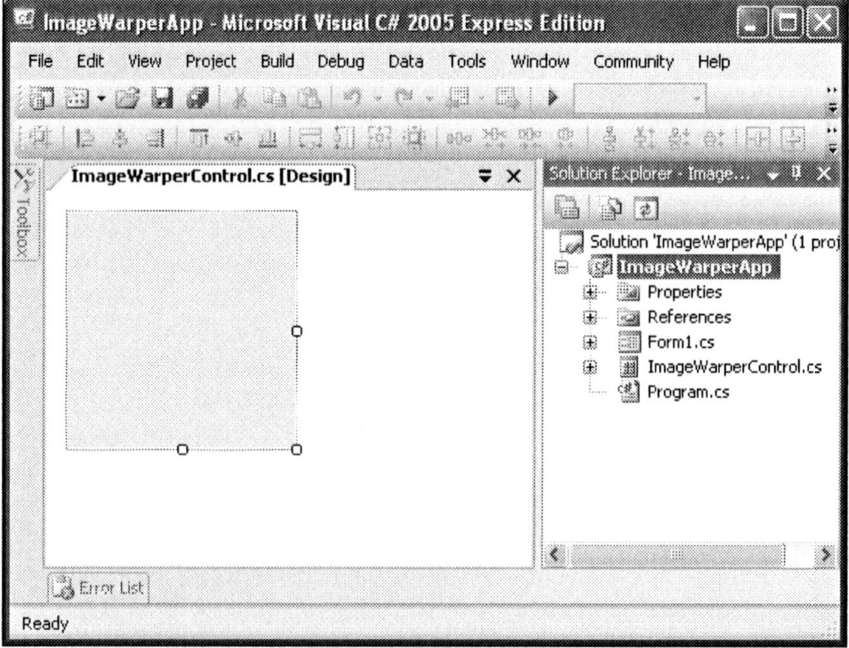

4. Right-click the control and choose Properties. Go to the Events tab.
5. Double-click the `Load` event. The resulting method will be `ImageWarperControl_Load`. Here we will create a picture and store it in `img` variable.

```
Image img,     // the image to draw
private void ImageWarperControl_Load(object sender, EventArgs e)
{
  img = CreatePicture();
}
```

6. Click on the Form and press *F4* to view the Properties window. Click on the Events tab and then double-click the `Paint` event. The result will be the `ImageWarperControl_Paint()` method. The picture will be rendered in this method.

```
private void ImageWarperControl_Paint(object sender, PaintEventArgs e)
{
  // set up all our parameters first before calling DrawWarpedPicture.
  Graphics target = this.CreateGraphics(); //draw onto the form's surface
  PointF pivotOnImage = new PointF(img.Width / 2, img.Height / 2);
  PointF pivotOnTarget = new PointF(this.Width / 2, this.Height / 2);
  double rotate = imageAngle;
  double scaleFactor = imageScale;
  SizeF skewing = imageSkew;
  DrawWarpedPicture(target, img, pivotOnImage, pivotOnTarget, rotate,
                    scaleFactor, skewing);
}
```

7. Add the `CreatePicture()` function to the class:

```
private Image CreatePicture()
{
  // Create a new Bitmap object, 50 x 50 pixels in size
  Image canvas = new Bitmap(50, 50);
  // create an object that will do the drawing operations
  Graphics artist = Graphics.FromImage(canvas);
  // draw a few shapes on the canvas picture
  artist.Clear(Color.Lime);
  artist.FillEllipse(Brushes.Red, 3, 30, 30, 30);
  artist.DrawBezier(new Pen(Color.Blue, 3), 0, 0, 40, 15, 10, 35,
  50, 50);
  // now the drawing is done, we can discard the artist object
  artist.Dispose();
  // return the picture
  return canvas;
}
```

8. Add the `DrawWarpedPicture()` method:

```
public void DrawWarpedPicture(
Graphics surface,    //the surface to draw on
Image img,     //the image to draw
PointF sourceAxle,   //pivot point passing through image.
PointF destAxle,   //pivot point's position on destination surface
double degrees,   //degrees through which the image is rotated clockwise
double scale,      //size multiplier
SizeF skew       //the slanting effect size, applies BEFORE scaling or
                 // rotation
)
{
  //give this array temporary coords that will be overwritten in the
  // loop below
```

```
    //the skewing is done here orthogonally, before any trigonometry is
    // applied
    PointF[] temp = new PointF[3] {  new PointF(skew.Width, -skew.Height),
                  new PointF((img.Width - 1) + skew.Width, skew.Height),
                  new PointF(-skew.Width,(img.Height - 1) - skew.Height) };
    double ang, dist;
    //convert the images corner points into scaled, rotated, skewed and
    // translated points
    for (int i = 0; i < 3; i++)
    {
      //measure the angle to the image's corner and then add the rotation
      // value to it
      ang = GetBearingRadians(sourceAxle, temp[i], out dist) + degrees;
      dist *= scale; //scale
      temp[i] = new PointF((Single)((Math.Cos(ang) * dist) + destAxle.X),
              (Single)((Math.Sin(ang) * dist) + destAxle.Y));
    }
    surface.DrawImage(img, temp);
  }
```

9. Also insert the following method:

```
  private static double GetBearingRadians(PointF reference, PointF target,
                                          out double distance)
  {
    double dx = target.X - reference.X;
    double dy = target.Y - reference.Y;
    double result = Math.Atan2(dy, dx);
    distance = Math.Sqrt((dx * dx) + (dy * dy));
    if (result < 0)
      result += (Math.PI * 2); //add  the negative number to 360 degrees to
                               // correct the atan2 value
    return result;
  }
```

10. Declare the following member variables in `ImageWarperControl.cs`:

```
  private double imageAngle;
  private double imageScale;
  private SizeF imageSkew;
  private Image img = null;
```

11. These members are accessed through properties. Add the following properties code in `ImageWarperControl.cs`:

```
  public double ImageAngle
  {
    get
    {
      return imageAngle;
    }
    set
    {
      if (imageAngle != value)
      {
        imageAngle = value;
        Invalidate();
      }
    }
  }
  public double ImageScale
  {
    get
    {
      return imageScale;
```

```
        }
        set
        {
          if (imageScale != value)
          {
            imageScale = value;
            Invalidate();
          }
        }
      }
      public SizeF ImageSkew
      {
        get
        {
          return imageSkew;
        }
        set
        {
          if (imageSkew != value)
          {
            imageSkew = value;
            Invalidate();
          }
        }
      }
```

12. Build the project by clicking Build | Build Solution. Now, when opening `Form1` in the designer, you should see the new `ImageWarperControl` in the toolbox:

13. Drag an `ImageWarperControl` control to the form.
14. Drag four `TextBox` controls to the form and name them angleBox, scaleBox, skewHorizontalBox, skewVerticalBox.
15. Drag a button to the form and name it applyButton and set the text to Apply new settings. After resizing the controls and inserting some label text controls for each edit control, your form should look as in the following screenshot:

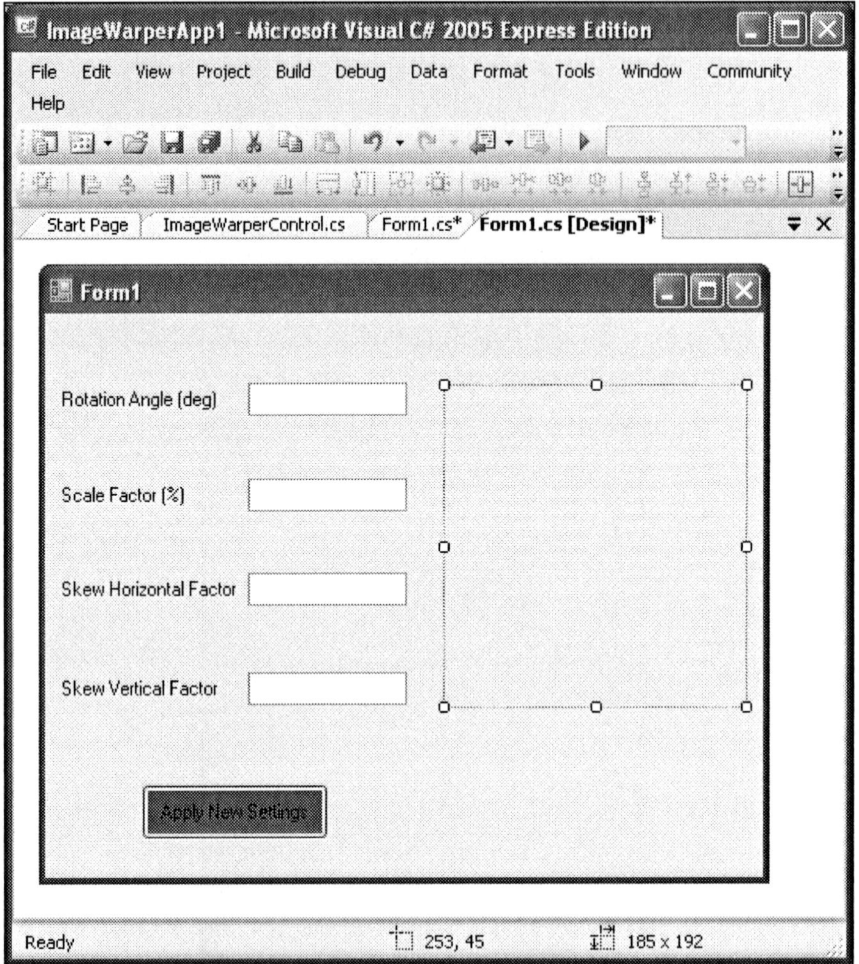

16. Double-click the button. This will generate the `applyButton_Click()` method. Here the values for rotate, scale, and skew are set through control properties.

```
private void applyButton_Click(object sender, EventArgs e)
{
  imageWarperControl1.ImageAngle = Double.Parse(angleBox.Text) *
                                   System.Math.PI / 180;
  imageWarperControl1.ImageScale = Double.Parse(scaleBox.Text) / 100;
  imageWarperControl1.ImageSkew =
  new SizeF(float.Parse(skewHorizontalBox. Text),
  float.Parse(skewVerticalBox.Text));
}
```

17. Now build your application and enjoy working with the `ImageWarperControl`.

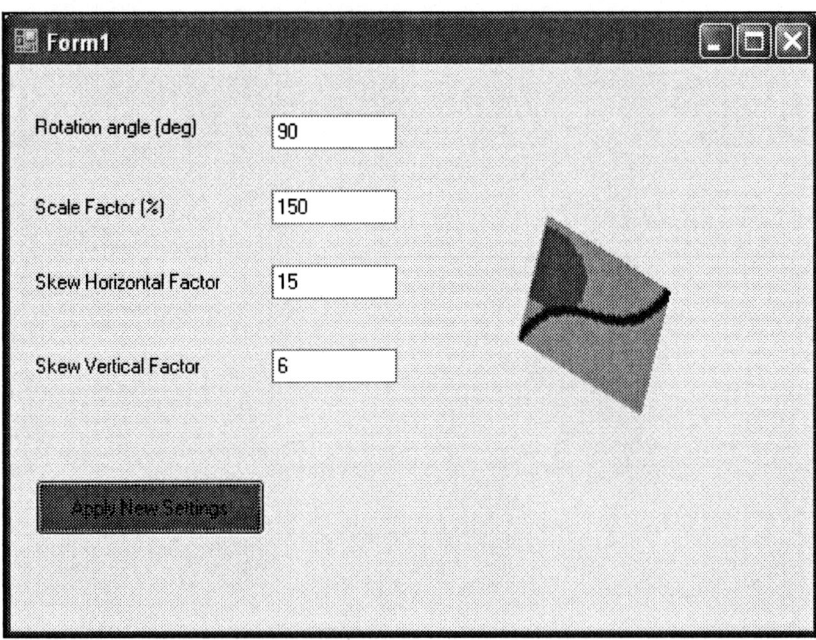

What Just Happened?

You have successfully written and used the `ImageWarperControl`. This control creates an image and exposes it to image's processing functions. You have used in this example the three most important functions that you can apply on an image: rotation, scaling, and skewing.

Summary

In this chapter you explored the area of the GDI+ that deals with various kinds of images. The `Image` and `Bitmap` classes were used to load, and save an image and create a brand new image from scratch through code. With our `ImageWarper` component we looked at the GDI+ coordinate system in great detail, and learned how to combine skewing, rotation, and scaling in high resolution. That component is invisible to the user but can enable us to create some impressive graphical effects that have negligible effect upon our program's performance. We also briefly visited the quality control features of the `Graphics` class. Graphics under .NET is a massive subject and we have only skimmed the surface here, but now we have a sound basis upon which to build deeper knowledge later on.

Finally, you have created a custom control named `ImageWarperControl` that can apply different functions to an image. This can be the start for you to create image handling custom controls.

7 Printing

There are a lot of reasons to use a computer and digital documents, but there are also many reasons to use scripted documents. Years ago all documents were hand-written; in some cases they were created by a typewriter. One mistake and you needed to start over. Today half of the jobs of writing are done on the computer. This is awesome because you can make lots of mistakes and correct them without involving an eraser. Just a click and your mistake will be undone.

When it comes to putting your document on paper, you talk about printing. There are many printer families and brands in the market, but they all have drivers that .NET knows how to use (through the operating system), making your interaction with the printer painless. Printing something onto paper is technically almost the same as printing graphics onto the screen. The same code can be used for both of these operations.

If this sounds pretty radical then you'd be right to think so. Older languages with no support for Object-Oriented Programming, such as VB6, separated screen and printer functionality so much that it was often necessary to effectively duplicate graphical routines. With .NET, printing belongs firmly under the category of GDI+, a fact that is often overlooked by many. In this chapter, we'll examine how we can implement true, 100% "*what you see is what you get*" printing and we'll dismiss the "black art" reputation that Windows printing has unfairly earned.

In the first part of this chapter you'll learn the general concepts about printing with .NET, and in the second part you'll see how to apply these concepts to enhance your custom controls.

.NET Printing Explained

GDI+ wraps up its printing technology in the `System.Drawing.Printing` namespace. The `Printing` namespace is within the GDI+-related `Drawing` namespace. You can begin to see how closely related screen and hardcopy are. We shall be using this namespace throughout this chapter so you'll need to remember to add its `using` statement to each of your projects' code files. Naturally, you should have a printer set up and working properly before we start, so you can reap the full benefits of this chapter.

Printing in .NET is accomplished by using a few specialized classes; the main ones are:

- `PrintDocument`
- `PrintDialog`
- `PageSetupDialog`
- `PrintPreviewDialog`

`PrintDocument` is in charge of actually sending data to the printer; `PrintDialog` and `PageSetupDialog` are provided to let the user supply information regarding the printing procedure, and `PrintPreviewDialog` can be used to let the user see what the finished output will look like before it is actually committed to paper.

Before we get into the specifics of these classes, you should understand how printing can be so similar to drawing on a computer screen. Since a sheet of paper is basically rectangular, flat, and white, it seems perfectly sensible to think of it as equivalent to a computer's screen image. There should be no reason to separate them simply because one is physically tangible and the other is hidden away inside a computer's memory. Both can abide by X and Y coordinates, both are two-dimensional. If we can draw a circle on the center of the screen then what's different about drawing that same circle on a piece of paper?

This brings us back to the `Graphics` class. You saw how it lets you draw on a multitude of objects including forms, controls, and even memory bitmaps that are not even visible at run time. What if you had access to a `Graphics` object that is bound to a real sheet of paper? That would be very useful indeed.

As luck would have it, this is exactly what the `PrintDocument` class gives you.

Using the PrintDocument Class

`PrintDocument` is your primary means of producing graphical output for a printer. It is a highly versatile class that does not restrict the nature of what you can print. In other words you can draw on paper what you draw on screen. The actual laying out of your graphics on the page is performed within (or called from) an event handler. The event will fire exactly once per page of the print-out. The event in question is:

```
PrintDocument.PrintPage(object sender, PrintPageEventArgs e)
```

The `PrintPageEventArgs` parameter is all-important to us here. It supplies us with all the information that we need in order to coordinate our printing operations. Some of its important members are listed here:

- `Cancel`: A Boolean value that defaults to `false`. If you wish to cancel the current print job at any point set this property to `true` and exit the event handler. The `PrintDocument` object will halt and cancel the printing process.
- `Graphics`: This is the `Graphics` object that is bound to a sheet of paper. It is a fully functional `Graphics` object just like the ones we used in previous chapters to draw on things like forms and bitmaps. Anything drawn on with this `Graphics` object (within the printable page area) will be put onto paper by the printer.

- `MarginBounds`: This is a property that we will be using a lot. It is a rectangle that represents the printable area of our page. That is to say, the part of the page that our printer is physically able to print on, which is usually smaller than the physical size of our paper.
- `PageBounds`: This is the actual size of the paper itself, and as such will feature much less in our code, because we must cater for all kinds of printers. Only very few printers can print right up to the very edges of a page. It is often useful to know the exact dimensions of a page though.
- `PageSettings`: This is our main source of information on our users' preferences. For example, we can find out further details about our page, if we are in Portrait or Landscape mode, if we are able to print in color. One particular member of this `PageSettings` object is `PrinterSettings`, which tells us a lot about the hardware that we are printing to, such as if the printer is the default one, if it supports duplexing or collating (neither of which will affect our code), and other things like what different resolutions and paper sizes this printer supports.

Using this event and its parameters we can generate some very impressive and professional-looking hardcopy without slaving over our code for weeks on end.

Your First Print Job

Let's start with a simple print job, writing "*Hello Printer!*" in middle of our page. You will create a simple application that prints a string using the `System.Drawing.Printing` namespace.

Time for Action—Creating the "Hello Printer!" Application

1. Start a new C# Windows Application project and name it `HelloPrinter`.
2. Add `using System.Drawing.Printing;`
3. Add the next member variable in the `Form1` class:
   ```
   PrintDocument _prtDoc = null;
   ```
4. Now, override the `Load` event of the form:
   ```
   private void Form1_Load(object sender, EventArgs e)
   {
     _prtDoc = new PrintDocument();
     _prtDoc.PrintPage += new PrintPageEventHandler(_prtDoc_PrintPage);
   }
   ```
5. Insert the next function that implement actually the printing:
   ```
   void _prtDoc_PrintPage(object sender, PrintPageEventArgs e)
   {
     Graphics tapeMeasure =
         e.PageSettings.PrinterSettings.CreateMeasurementGraphics();
     Single left = e.MarginBounds.Left;
     Single top = e.MarginBounds.Top;
     Single width = e.MarginBounds.Width;
     Single height = e.MarginBounds.Height;
     string message = "Hello Printer!";
     Font messageFont = new Font("Times New Roman", 30,
                             FontStyle.Bold | FontStyle.Italic);
     SizeF messageSize = tapeMeasure.MeasureString(message, messageFont);
     PointF messagePosition = new PointF(
   ```

```
                ((width - messageSize.Width) / 2) + left,
                ((height - messageSize.Height) / 2) + top);
        e.Graphics.DrawString(message, messageFont,
                            Brushes.Black, messagePosition);
        e.HasMorePages = false;
    }
```

6. Add a button to your form and set its Text property to Print. Double-click the button to override the `Click` event:

```
private void button1_Click(object sender, EventArgs e)
{
    _prtDoc.Print();
}
```

What Just Happened?

First we declare a `PrintDocument` object called `_prtDoc`. We initialize this object in the form's `Load` event handler, using `PrintDocument`'s default constructor. Immediately after that we assign an event handler to the object's `PrintPage` event, giving us a place to put our printing code.

While typing in this particular line of code, Visual Studio's IntelliSense feature gives us the opportunity to add the body of the event handler automatically by hitting the *Tab* key, which is extremely handy as it saves us having to write out the method signature by hand.

```
_prtDoc.PrintPage += new PrintPageEventHandler(_prtDoc_PrintPage);
```

This will create a stub of code that will throw an error if it is called; this is a reminder to us that we need to write the code for this event (it's all too easy to forget when writing many event handlers). So we need to remove the line of code that throws the error, leaving us with an empty event handler. Go ahead and fill the event handler with the code as shown on the previous page. Whenever the `PrintDocument` object is asked to print a page, this method is triggered by the `PrintDocument`'s `PrintPage` event.

The final piece of the jigsaw is the button's `Click` event handler, in which we simply place a call to our `PrintDocument's Print()` method. This sets in motion the whole printing process.

Try it now. Turn on your printer and run the program: your printer should output a single page with the words "***Hello Printer!***" written at the center of the page in 30 point font size. Let's examine the `PrintPage` handler in more detail.

The first line

```
Graphics tapeMeasure =
e.PageSettings.PrinterSettings.CreateMeasurementGraphics();
```

declares a `Graphics` object, but this one isn't used to do any drawing. We use `tapeMeasure` to measure how large a piece of text will appear on the page once it is printed. We use this `Graphics` object rather than the one accessed by `e.Graphics` because it's based on the printer's own resolution and settings and is not just a generic `Graphics` object. This makes our drawing of text much more accurate.

The next piece of code

```
Single left = e.MarginBounds.Left;
Single top = e.MarginBounds.Top;
Single width = e.MarginBounds.Width;
Single height = e.MarginBounds.Height;
string message = "Hello Printer!";
Font messageFont = new Font("Times New Roman", 30,
                            FontStyle.Bold | FontStyle.Italic);
```

caches a few values that will be used several times. Then it creates a string and a font that will be used for the measuring and drawing processes.

Now we need to measure the actual dimensions of the text we are going to draw:

```
SizeF messageSize = tapeMeasure.MeasureString(message, messageFont);
```

This is done by calling `MeasureString()`, a member of the `Graphics` class. We need to pass in the string that we need to measure and the font that we plan to use. Behind the scenes, the `Graphics` object determines the bounding rectangle for this text and returns the size of this rectangle to our calling code. Now that we know the size of our text we can apply arithmetic so that we can place the text accurately, anywhere on the page. For this demonstration we'll center the text both horizontally and vertically on the page

```
PointF messagePosition = new PointF(
        ((width - messageSize.Width) / 2) + left,
        ((height - messageSize.Height) / 2) + top);
```

Here we have subtracted half the text's width from half the page's width, leaving the centers of both aligned. This is also applied vertically in a similar fashion. That is all the setting up that we need to do; now all that's left is to draw the text and complete the print job.

```
e.Graphics.DrawString(message, messageFont, Brushes.Black, messagePosition);
e.HasMorePages = false;
```

Now we see the `Graphics` object that we use for the actual drawing procedures. It is a member of the `PrintPageEventArgs` object and it represents the current page in the print job. So we call its `DrawString()` method and pass our values to it and here we use a standard black `Brush`.

Last but not least, we set a flag to `false`. The `PrintDocument` queries the `HasMorePages` member of the `PrintPageEventArgs` parameter after each `PrintPage` event has fired. If this value is `true` then the event is fired again immediately, this is where we would take the opportunity to print the second page of our print job (if there was one), but we only have one page to print for now. Shortly, we will discuss multi-page printing.

That concludes our first demonstration of basic printing techniques. We have seen how we can use the `PrintDocument` to build up our page behind the scenes in code and we have watched the event-based printing system in action. It may seem like a lot of work just to print a few characters, but we have actually done the majority of the groundwork required to print anything. If you wanted to add many more things to your page you would only have to concentrate on those new features rather than do much more to the printing "engine" that you have created. Most of the further adjustments would be dependent on the way your particular application works.

Let's go up a gear now and tackle some more sophisticated, and more importantly, useful printing ideas.

The SimpleReportPrinter

Let's say you are required to create a program that prints out simple text-based reports, which features a corporate logo on the front page and a watermark across each page. This is a fairly typical use in many print-enabled programs and is the problem we shall address in this section, by the end of which we'll be producing quality output like this:

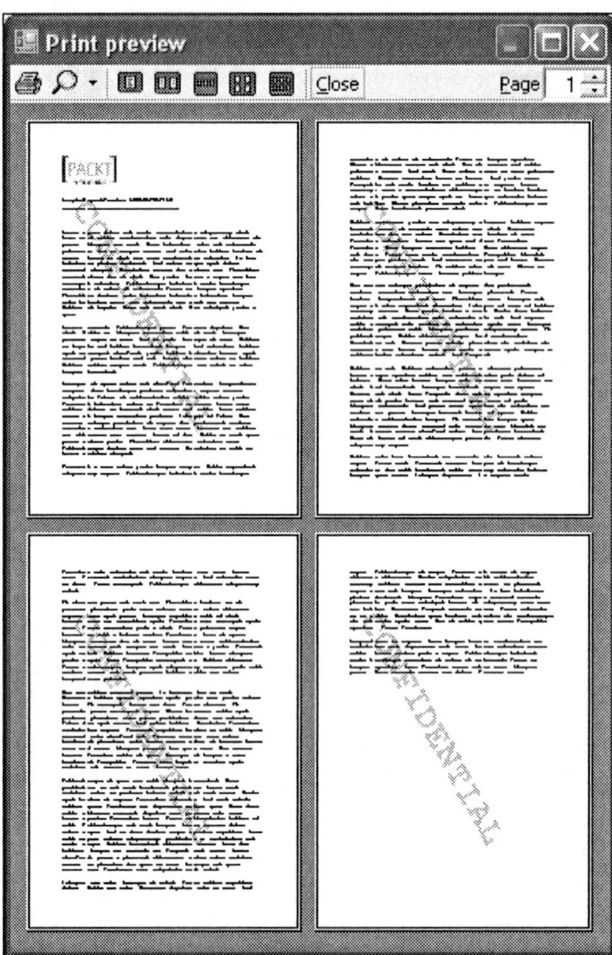

Building the SimpleReportPrinter and TextDispenser Classes

Here we will learn how to use OOP's features to our advantage in designing a class that can completely handle the entire printing process itself. Let's take a sneak preview of this class's constructor so we know what to expect:

```
public SimpleReportPrinter(Image header, string text, Font fnt)
```

That's all the data we need to supply from our program, the rest of the printing information is collated and handled internally. The parameters are simple: the `header` parameter is simply our company's corporate logo passed in as an image object, the `text` parameter is the main body of our document, and `fnt` is the font we'll use for our main text. In this case we will be using a long text file as our source of data. Any substantial (say three or four pages) sample of plain text (`*.txt`) will be fine; it should be non-formatted though, so don't use a document from a word processor.

So once we have instantiated our `SimpleReportPrinter` class and passed in an image and a string containing our data, all we need to do is produce a printed copy.

```
SimpleReportPrinter.Print(bool hardcopy);
```

This will either show us a preview of our printed document (if `hardcopy` is false) or actually send the document to the printer (when `hardcopy` is true). Both ways will enable us to choose what printer we wish to use and what page settings (orientation, margins, and so forth) we want.

That's the full extent of the class's exposed methods. Everything else is hidden away, encapsulated, in the "black box".

The `SimpleReportPrinter` class that we shall build here will teach us how to approach the following concepts:

- Obtaining user preferences for page settings and printer selection
- Previewing our output before optionally printing it
- Multiple page printing
- Using a private class to handle spanning text over multiple pages seamlessly, regardless of font or paper size
- Drawing images and transformed text on our printouts

Before we enter any code we should visualize how the `SimpleReportPrinter` (SRP for short) is put together. SRP uses instances of the important classes mentioned earlier: `PrintDocument`, `PrintDialog`, and `PrintPreviewDialog`. The first is a member instance, which persists between print jobs, and the other two are instantiated as and when required.

SRP also contains the event handler for the `PrintDocument's` `PrintPage` event. It is here (as in the previous example) that the printing operation is coordinated. Since this is a multiple-page print job, the number of pages depends upon the length of our text—something we will not know in advance until printing has started. So we need to do a bit of extra programming to overcome this difficulty. To this end, you will build a helper class for SRP called `TextDispenser`, which dispenses and draws just enough text to fill a known rectangle; we keep an eye on this class because it tells us when all the text has been printed and we can successfully end the print job. `TextDispenser` makes more advanced use of the `CreateMeasurementGraphics()` method that we visited briefly in the "Hello Printer!" example.

The `PrintPreviewDialog` will also come into play; it is one of the most powerful tools in the .NET printing arsenal because it enables us to preview our printed output on-screen exactly as it will look on paper. Remember the first paragraph of this chapter? Now we get to realize this for ourselves!

Without further ado, let's get coding, starting with the `TextDispenser` class.

Time for Action—Building the TextDispenser Class

1. Start a brand new C# Windows Application and name it `PrintApp`.
2. Add a new class called `TextDispenser`.
3. Insert the following `using` clause:

   ```
   using System.Drawing;
   ```

4. And add this code to the newly created class:

```
public class TextDispenser
{
int _start = 0;
string _text = null;
Font _fnt;

public TextDispenser(string text, Font fnt)
{
  _start = 0;
  _text = text;
  _fnt = fnt;
}

public bool DrawText(Graphics target, Graphics measurer, RectangleF r,
                     Brush brsh)
{
  if (r.Height < _fnt.Height)
    throw new ArgumentException(
"The rectangle is not tall enough to fit a single line of text inside.");
  int charsFit = 0;
  int linesFit = 0;
  int cut = 0;
  string temp = _text.Substring(_start);
  StringFormat format = new StringFormat(StringFormatFlags.FitBlackBox|
                        StringFormatFlags.LineLimit);
  //measure how much of the string we can fit into the rectangle
  measurer.MeasureString(temp, _fnt, r.Size, format, out charsFit,
                         out linesFit);
  cut = BreakText(temp, charsFit);
  if (cut != charsFit)
    temp = temp.Substring(0, cut);
  bool h = true;
  h &= true;
  target.DrawString(temp.Trim(' '), _fnt, brsh, r, format);
  _start += cut;
  if (_start == _text.Length)
  {
    _start = 0; //reset the location so we can repeat the document
    return true; //finished printing
  }
  else
    return false;
}
private static int BreakText(string text, int approx)
{
  if (approx == 0)
    throw new ArgumentException();
  if (approx < text.Length)
  {
    //are we in the middle of a word?
    if (char.IsLetterOrDigit(text[approx]) &&
       char.IsLetterOrDigit(text[approx - 1]))
    {
```

```
                int temp = text.LastIndexOf(' ', approx, approx + 1);
                if (temp >= 0)
                  return temp;
              }
            }
            return approx;
          }
        }
```

What Just Happened?

The sole purpose of this class is to return accurately measured chunks of text, one chunk at a time. Why is this necessary? Well, since our document must be split up into an unknown number of pages (maybe one, possibly hundreds!) we need to print one page's worth of text onto each page because a single drawing operation cannot span more than one page. We get a new `Graphics` object for each page so we must handle all pages separately.

This is easier than it might at first sound because we have some key information available to us before printing starts. For this `SimpleReportPrinter` walkthrough, the number of pages in our printout is dependent on only three things:

- The length of the string data that makes up our main text
- The font that we will use to print this text
- The margins of our page

Lots of text and large fonts both mean an increase in the pages required. The page count also increases if we use margins that are further in from the edges of the page, because we get less space per page to arrange text inside.

Fortunately, we know all of this information before we commence the print run.

So how does this tie into the `SimpleReportPrinter`? The SRP instantiates `TextDispenser` by passing in the text that we want to print and also the font we want to print it in. When the time comes to call `TextDispenser.DrawText()`, we also pass in a reference to the `Graphics` object that is 'bound' to our page; we will use the `Graphics` object to measure text width, and the rectangle that defines how much space we have left on the current page.

This gives us all the data that we need to calculate the right amount of text to submit for this page. In `TextDispenser.DrawText()`, this line of code is used to find out how many characters will fit into the rectangle:

```
measurer.MeasureString(temp, _fnt, r.Size, format, out charsFit, out linesFit);
```

At this point, `temp` is the entire remaining part of the string that has not been printed yet; then the font and rectangle size are specified. The important parameter is `out.charsFit`, because this is the basis of how much text we will dispense into this page.

But, simply counting characters is not enough: what if we end the page halfway through a word? That would look a little untidy so we call `BreakText()`, which searches the text nearby to find the nearest word boundary before the `charsFit` value. It's a subtle detail but it is very noticeable if ignored.

Once all the text has been dispensed, `TextDispenser` signals that printing should cease (`DrawText()` returns true).

The complex bit is now out of the way. Now on to the main `SimpleReportPrinter` class.

Time for Action—Building the SimpleReportPrinter Class

1. Add another new class to the `PrintApp` project and name it `SimpleReportPrinter`.
2. Make sure you add the following `using` clauses:

```
using System.Drawing;
using System.Drawing.Printing;
using System.Windows.Forms;
```

3. Then enter this code to the `SimpleReportPrinter` class:

```
public class SimpleReportPrinter
{
  Image _header = null;
  string _text = null;
  int _pageNumber = 0;
  PrintDocument _prtdoc = null;
  TextDispenser _textDisp = null;
  public SimpleReportPrinter(Image header, string text, Font fnt)
  {
    _header = (Image)(header.Clone());
    _text = text;
    _prtdoc = new PrintDocument();
    _prtdoc.PrintPage += new PrintPageEventHandler(_prtdoc_PrintPage);
    _textDisp = new TextDispenser(_text, fnt);
  }

public void Print(bool hardcopy)
{
  // create a PrintDialog based on the PrintDocument
  PrintDialog pdlg = new PrintDialog();
  pdlg.Document = _prtdoc;
  // show the PrintDialog
  if (pdlg.ShowDialog() == DialogResult.OK)
  {
    // create a PageSetupDialog based on the PrintDocument and
    // PrintDialog
    PageSetupDialog psd = new PageSetupDialog();
    psd.EnableMetric = true; //Ensure all dialog measurements are
                             // in metric
    psd.Document = pdlg.Document;
    // show the PageSetupDialog
    if (psd.ShowDialog() == DialogResult.OK)
    {
      // apply the settings of both dialogs
      _prtdoc.DefaultPageSettings = psd.PageSettings;
      // decide what action to take
      if (hardcopy)
      {
        // actually print hardcopy
        _prtdoc.Print();
      }
      else
      {
        // preview onscreen instead
        PrintPreviewDialog prvw = new PrintPreviewDialog();
        prvw.Document = _prtdoc;
```

```
                prvw.ShowDialog();
              }
            }
          }
        }

        private void _prtdoc_PrintPage(object sender, PrintPageEventArgs e)
        {
          e.Graphics.Clip = new Region(e.MarginBounds);
          // this method does all our printing work
          Single x = e.MarginBounds.Left;
          Single y = e.MarginBounds.Top;
          // draw the header image
          if (_pageNumber++ == 0)
          {
            e.Graphics.DrawImage(_header, x, y);
            y += _header.Height + 30;
          }
          RectangleF mainTextArea = RectangleF.FromLTRB(x, y,
                            e.MarginBounds.Right, e.MarginBounds.Bottom);
          // draw the main part of the report
          if (_textDisp.DrawText(e.Graphics,
             e.PageSettings.PrinterSettings.CreateMeasurementGraphics(),
             mainTextArea, Brushes.Black))
          {
            e.HasMorePages = false; //the end has been reached
            _pageNumber = 0;
          }
          else
            e.HasMorePages = true;
          // watermark
          e.Graphics.TranslateTransform(200, 200);
          e.Graphics.RotateTransform(e.PageSettings.Landscape ? 30 : 60);
          e.Graphics.DrawString("CONFIDENTIAL",
                              new Font("Courier New", 75, FontStyle.Bold),
                              new SolidBrush(Color.FromArgb(64,
                                                       Color.Black)),
                              0, 0);
        }
      }
```

4. Now, in the form designer drag a button from the Toolbox and set the text Print.
5. Double-click this button and override the `click` event:

```
private void button1_Click(object sender, EventArgs e)
{
  Image imageHeader = new Bitmap(50, 50);
  Graphics img = Graphics.FromImage(imageHeader);
  img.DrawEllipse(Pens.Black, 0, 0, 45, 45);
  img.DrawString("LOGO", this.Font, Brushes.Black, new PointF(7, 16));
  img.Dispose();
  string textDocument;
  textDocument = "";
  for (int i = 0; i < 60; i++)
  {
    for (int j = 0; j < i; j++)
    textDocument += " ";
    textDocument += "The quick brown fox jumps over the lazy dog\n";
  }
  SimpleReportPrinter printDocument =
                           new SimpleReportPrinter(imageHeader,
                                      textDocument, this.Font);
  printDocument.Print(false);
}
```

6. Run the application, click the Print button, and after selecting the printer and page setup, the Print preview dialog will occur. Print the document!

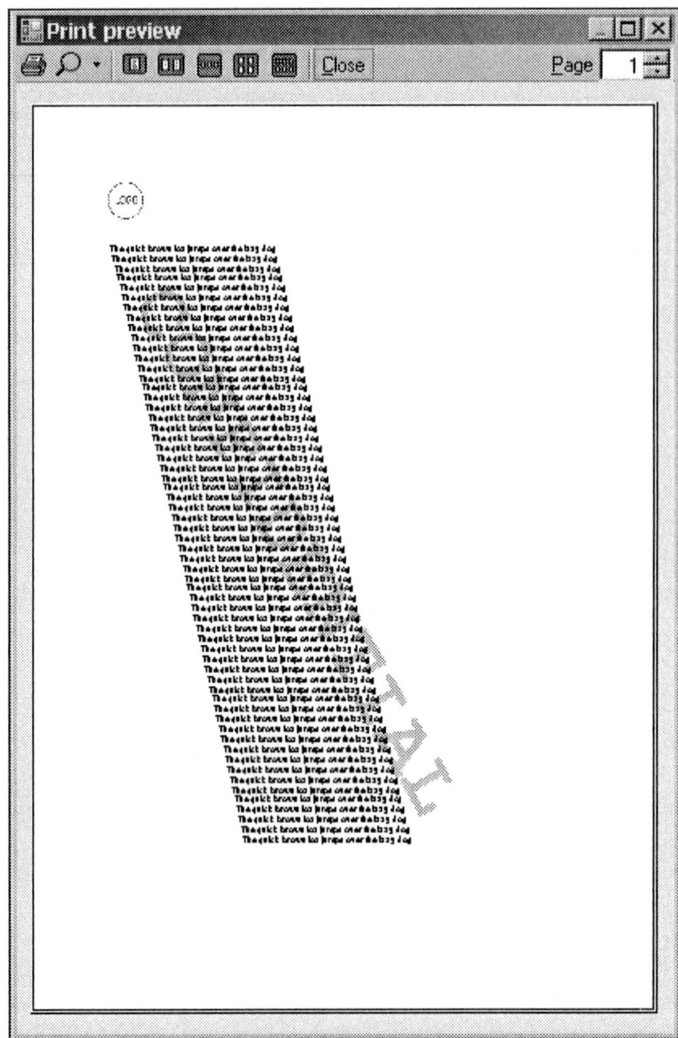

What Just Happened?

You have printed the document that contains the text, a logo, and a confidential marker on the background. Let's take a look at the code and how things work.

The code in the `_prtdoc_PrintPage()` method defines the way the printed document looks on the page; we can see how each line affects the output. The first thing that happens is that we set the `Clip` property on the `e.Graphics` object; this enforces the real margins of the page. This means that even if part of a drawn object falls just outside the page margins it will not be shown. If we do not do this then it would be possible that the objects are drawn outside the margins that the user may specify, but only if they are too large to fit on the page. With this property set to the margins of the page, any drawing operations that affect the page outside this area will be cropped.

A little further down the code we query the page number. We only want to draw our corporate logo onto the first page of the printout so we draw it only if `_pageNumber` equals zero. Then the `_pageNumber` variable is incremented; because it won't be queried again until the next page, postfix incrementing here is convenient. The image is then drawn.

We need to position the text below the image so we increment the Y variable to set a gap between the bottom of the drawn image and the top of the text area.

Now we start drawing the main body of text using `TextDispenser`. We need to do that only on the first page because all the following pages do not have images to get in the way. In order to tell `TextDispenser` what area it can print in, we create a rectangle object and pass it to the `TextDispenser.DrawText()` method, along with the two `Graphics` objects (one we'll use for drawing, the other for measuring). Then `TextDispenser` calculates how much of the remaining text to draw and draws it within our rectangle and using the desired font.

The `TextDispenser` will sit dormant until next time the `PrintPage` event fires and then it will give us the next batch of characters. This event loop will repeat until there is no text left, at which point it will signal the end of the print job.

Finally, we want to draw a watermark, to let readers know that our document is secret. We shall print the word "CONFIDENTIAL", but other commonly used watermarks are "Draft", "Superseded", and so on. Since it is a watermark, we still want to see everything that was drawn underneath it. To accomplish this we can use a semi-transparent `Brush`. As programmers, we are familiar with the RGB color system, which mixes colors on screen as a ratio of Red, Green, and Blue. .NET uses a fourth channel called "Alpha" which is a measure of how much of the underlying color is allowed to show through. Alpha, just like R, G and B, is denoted by a value in the range 0 to 255, zero being completely transparent and 255 being totally opaque.

We don't want our watermark to dominate the page so we will use the value 64, which is fairly subtle but should show up well on all kinds of printers. To create a transparent brush we use this line of code:

```
new SolidBrush(Color.FromARGB(64, Color.Black))
```

The `SolidBrush` class is basically the same as the normal `Brush` class, but it lets us define exactly what color we want rather than making us choose one from a shortlist of common colors. The `Color.FromArgb()` method lets us supply an alpha value and a solid color; these are combined to make a black brush that is partially see-through, so it will effectively show up as light gray on our white paper, while letting the black of the main text show through unaltered.

Then it's just a simple matter of applying translation and rotational transforms (see Chapter 4) to the `Graphics` object to position and orientate the text to the right coordinates. Note also that we are using the Landscape property to designate through what angle we want our watermark to be rotated. Landscape makes the page wide and short so we can only rotate the text by about 30 degrees before it starts to slide off the edge of the page. Conversely portrait mode requires the large text to be rotated by around 60 degrees so it fits onto the output area.

A final call to the `Graphics` object's `DrawString()` method finishes off this page of our printout. If there were more pages to print then the `PrintDocument` would know this by querying its `e.HasMorePages` property. A true value would cause the `PrintPage` event to fire again, false would be the end of the print job and operations would conclude.

User Involvement

In our example "Hello Printer!" we missed out an important step in Windows printing. We did not ask our user to tell us which printer to use, nor what page settings he/she preferred us to abide by. The users may have more than one printer available to them (for example, on an office network) and they may prefer us to use A3 paper instead of A4.

Luckily, for us, the provision of these features is very straightforward, and assuming our `PrintPage` handler is well designed to take its lead from our page's margin size, we will not have to rewrite it for each paper size.

To demonstrate adding these features let us look at the code again. One particular method interests us here.

```
public void Print(bool hardcopy)
{
  // create a PrintDialog based on the PrintDocument
  PrintDialog pdlg = new PrintDialog();
  pdlg.Document = _prtdoc;
  // show the PrintDialog
  if (pdlg.ShowDialog() == DialogResult.OK)
  {
    // create a PageSetupDialog based on the PrintDocument and PrintDialog
    PageSetupDialog psd = new PageSetupDialog();
    psd.EnableMetric = true; //Ensure all dialog measurements are in metric
    psd.Document = pdlg.Document;
    // show the PageSetupDialog
    if (psd.ShowDialog() == DialogResult.OK)
    {
      // apply the settings of both dialogs
      _prtdoc.DefaultPageSettings = psd.PageSettings;
      // decide what action to take
      if (hardcopy)
      {
        //actually print hardcopy
        _prtdoc.Print();
      }
      else
      {
        // preview onscreen instead
        PrintPreviewDialog prvw = new PrintPreviewDialog();
        prvw.Document = _prtdoc;
        prvw.ShowDialog();
      }
    }
  }
}
```

At the start of the chapter we alluded to three new dialogs, `PrintDialog`, `PageSetupDialog`, and `PrintPreviewDialog`. In this code we bring those all together in one go. The method shown above belongs to `SimpleReportPrinter` and is a wrapper for the `PrintDocument's Print()` method, but with a twist. It lets us choose whether we want to print our data onto paper or show it on-screen instead, we simply pass in a Boolean value indicating our choice.

First a PrintDialog is shown, allowing the user to select a printer:

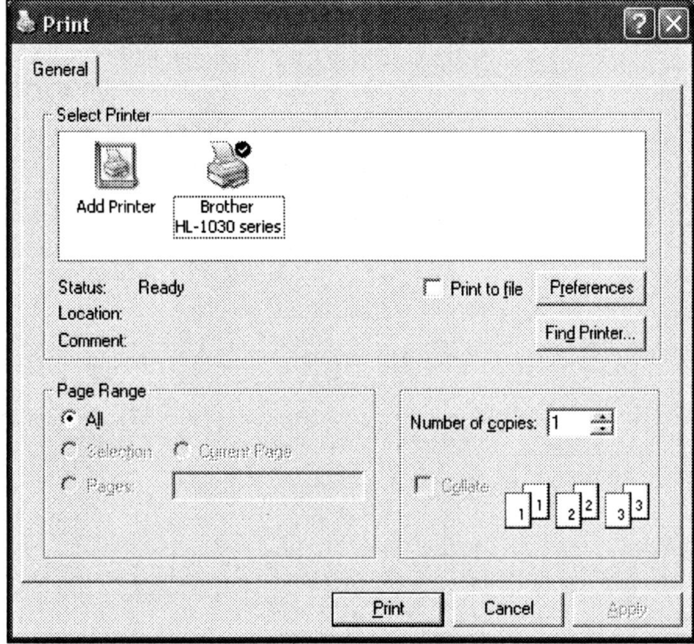

If the user clicks the Print button in the dialog, then it is followed by the PageSetupDialog:

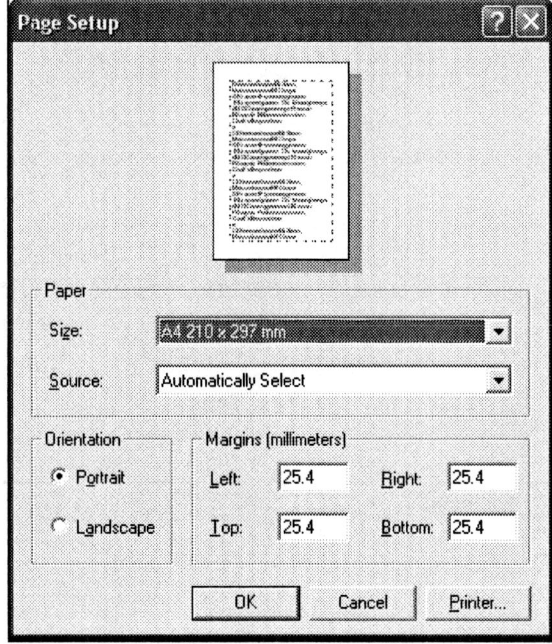

Here, the user can alter page margins or paper sizes, and orientation. If the user clicks Cancel to either of these two dialogs then the code returns without taking any further action; the settings in the `PrintDocument` remain unchanged. Otherwise, clicking OK here will take us to the final stage.

Depending on our `bool hardCopy` parameter, either the printer will kick into life and hand us a neatly pressed rendition of our document (`hardcopy == true`), or the third and final dialog will be displayed (`false`).

The PrintPreviewDialog is a real lifesaver (as well as a paper saver). It lets us browse a likeness of the as yet unprinted document on-screen. We can zoom in, pan around, and generally inspect the document, making sure it is to our liking before we decide to immortalize it on paper.

Here is an actual screenshot of PrintPreviewDialog displaying the output of the `SimpleReportPrinter` class:

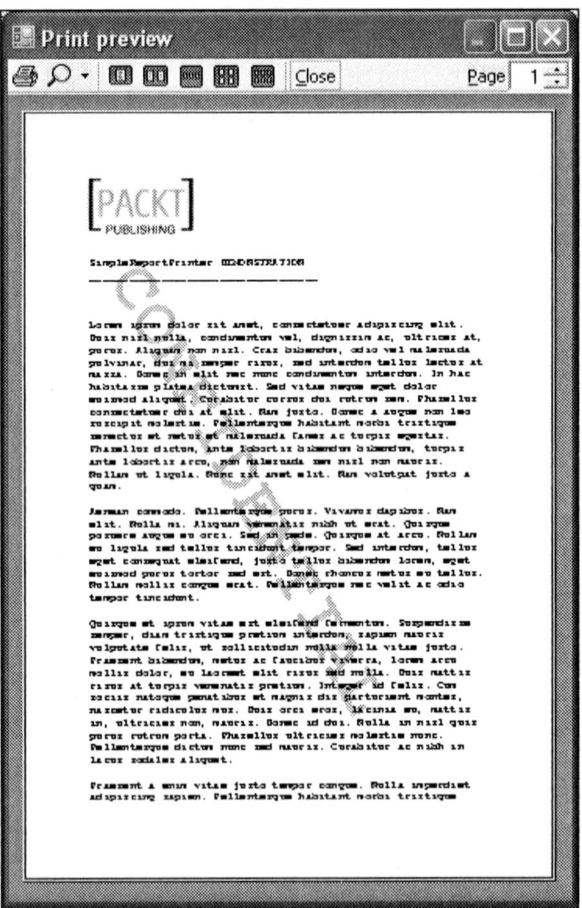

Our Responsibilities as Programmers

Printing program information is an intricate procedure at times; often the best way to learn is to get our hands dirty and try it for ourselves. With the .NET approach, it is easy to think "*Have I missed something?*" when perusing code samples because of the small number of methods that these classes expose to us. We just need to remember that .NET puts us 100% in the driving seat; we need to keep a tight ship and write printing code that is logical, and methodical. For example, we must manually keep track of how many pages we have printed by declaring our own variable for that purpose. We need to manually lay out our text, using regions, rectangles, and so forth. Where necessary we need to set our variables and reset them at the right times. This is something we must realize early on.

Things are this way because of the sheer breadth and varied nature of all the different things people need to commit to paper. Anything from accounting tables to Zoo trip photographs, corporate reports to fingerprint records, the scope is literally endless. This means that we as programmers must define absolutely everything that appears on our pages no matter how small or how obvious.

> It is tempting to start creating complex printout routines that draw very intricate pages. There is nothing wrong with this at all, .NET makes it easy to do so. But herein lies a problem, the more numerous the graphics you draw and the more page area you cover with your drawing, the more time is required to send the data to the printer. It's something to keep in mind at least; on today's computers this will seem insignificant but it may be more of a problem for users with older machines.

Printing Custom Controls

As always, we'll put all that theory into practice by teaching you how to apply it to use controls. In this case, you'll learn how to add printing features to existing custom controls.

More specifically, in the next pages you will learn how to create a custom control that prints itself. I have chosen for this demonstration a custom control derived from `RichTextBox` that will print text.

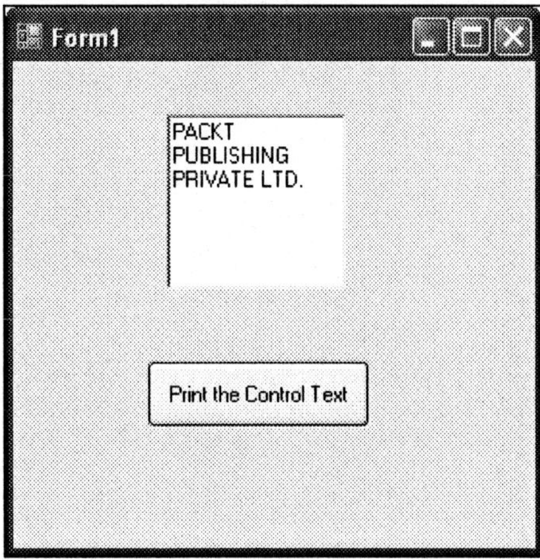

Time for Action—Creating the PrintableRichTextBox

1. Create a typical Windows Application named `PrintingCustomControlsApp`.
2. Add a UserControl to the project and name this `PrintableRichTextBox`.
3. Switch to code by right-clicking the control and choose View Code.
4. Modify the control so it derives from `RichTextBox` and not from `UserControl`.

```
public partial class PrintableRichTextBox : RichTextBox
{
    public PrintableRichTextBox()
    {
        InitializeComponent();
    }
}
```

5. Insert `using System.Drawing.Printing;`
6. Insert the following member variables:

```
string _text = null;
int _pageNumber = 0;
int _start = 0;
PrintDocument _prtdoc = null;
```

7. Add an event handler for the printing operation in the constructor, so it looks like:

```
public PrintableRichTextBox()
{
   InitializeComponent();
   _prtdoc = new PrintDocument();
   _prtdoc.PrintPage += new PrintPageEventHandler(_prtdoc_PrintPage);
}
```

8. Add the `DrawText()` and `BreakText()` functions used also in `TextDispenser` classes:

```
private bool DrawText(Graphics target, Graphics measurer,
                      RectangleF r, Brush brsh)
{
   if (r.Height < this.Font.Height)
   throw new ArgumentException("The rectangle is not tall enough to fit a
                              single line of text inside.");
   int charsFit = 0;
   int linesFit = 0;
   int cut = 0;
   string temp = _text.Substring(_start);
   StringFormat format = new StringFormat(StringFormatFlags.FitBlackBox
                       | StringFormatFlags.LineLimit);
  // measure how much of the string we can fit into the rectangle
   measurer.MeasureString(temp, this.Font, r.Size, format,
                       out charsFit, out linesFit);
   cut = BreakText(temp, charsFit);
   if (cut != charsFit)
   temp = temp.Substring(0, cut);
   bool h = true;
   h &= true;
   target.DrawString(temp.Trim(' '), this.Font, brsh, r, format);
   _start += cut;
    if (_start == _text.Length)
     {
       _start = 0; //reset the location so we can repeat the document
        return true; //finished printing
     }
```

```
        else
            return false;
    }

    private static int BreakText(string text, int approx)
    {
      if (approx == 0)
      throw new ArgumentException();
      if (approx < text.Length)
       {
        // are we in the middle of a word?
           if (char.IsLetterOrDigit(text[approx]) &&
              char.IsLetterOrDigit(text[approx - 1]))
            {
              int temp = text.LastIndexOf(' ', approx, approx + 1);
              if (temp >= 0)
              return temp;
            }
       }
        return approx;
    }
```

9. Add the `Print()` method. This is declared public so it can be called from outside the control. This method will be called from the form code to trigger the printing.

```
    public void Print(bool hardcopy)
    {
      _text = this.Text;
     // create a PrintDialog based on the PrintDocument
     PrintDialog pdlg = new PrintDialog();
     pdlg.Document = _prtdoc;
    // show the PrintDialog
    if (pdlg.ShowDialog() == DialogResult.OK)
    {
    // create a PageSetupDialog based on the PrintDocument and PrintDialog
     PageSetupDialog psd = new PageSetupDialog();
     psd.EnableMetric = true; //Ensure all dialog measurements are in
                               // metric
     psd.Document = pdlg.Document;
     // show the PageSetupDialog
     if (psd.ShowDialog() == DialogResult.OK)
      {
       // apply the settings of both dialogs
      _prtdoc.DefaultPageSettings = psd.PageSettings;
      // decide what action to take
      if (hardcopy)
       {
        //actually print hardcopy
        _prtdoc.Print();
       }
      else
       {
       // preview onscreen instead
       PrintPreviewDialog prvw = new PrintPreviewDialog();
       prvw.Document = _prtdoc;
       prvw.ShowDialog();
       }
      }
     }
    }
```

10. Insert the `_prtdoc_PrintPage()` method:

```
    private void _prtdoc_PrintPage(object sender, PrintPageEventArgs e)
    {
      e.Graphics.Clip = new Region(e.MarginBounds);
      // this method does all our printing work
```

```
    Single x = e.MarginBounds.Left;
    Single y = e.MarginBounds.Top;
    if (_pageNumber++ == 0)
     y += 30;
     RectangleF mainTextArea = RectangleF.FromLTRB(x, y,
                                e.MarginBounds.Right,
                                e.MarginBounds.Bottom);
    // draw the text
    if (DrawText(e.Graphics,
            e.PageSettings.PrinterSettings.CreateMeasurementGraphics(),
                 mainTextArea, Brushes.Black))
    {
      e.HasMorePages = false; //the end has been reached
      _pageNumber = 0;
    }
    else
     e.HasMorePages = true;
  }
```

If you build now you will get one error:

\PrintingCustomControlsApp\PrintableRichTextBox.Designer.cs(32,18): error CS0117: 'PrintingCustomControlsApp.PrintableRichTextBox' does not contain a definition for 'AutoScaleMode'

11. Go to `PrintableRichTextBox.Designer.cs` and delete the line

    ```
    this.AutoScaleMode = System.Windows.Forms.AutoScaleMode.Font;
    ```

12. Build the application. You will get no errors.
13. Open the Form1 in the designer and drag a `PrintableRichTextBox` control from the ToolBox to the form.
14. Drag a button to the application form. Set its text to "Print the control text".
15. Double-click the button so you will override the `Click` event.

    ```
    private void button1_Click(object sender, EventArgs e)
    {
        printableRichTextBox1.Print(false);
    }
    ```

16. Run the application. Write text to the control and hit the button when you are ready to print.

What Just Happened?

You have successfully created a control that prints the text found inside it. The control knows how to dispense the text and how to print on multiple pages. The `Print()`, and `_prtdoc_PrintPage()` methods are similar to the ones in the `SimpleReportPrinter` class. The `DrawText()` and `BreakText()` methods are similar to the ones in the `TextDispenser` class.

The `PrintableRichTextBox` control inherits the `RichTextBox` functionality and this is how you can draw text on multiple lines, or you can copy-paste text. At this moment if you click the form button, the method `Paint()` is called. This takes the text within the control and triggers a `Print` event that is handled by `_prtdoc_PrintPage()`. Here the text forwarded as string is passed to the `DrawText()` method. The text will be wrapped so that it will be printed on one or several lines or pages.

The `PrintableRichTextBox` control provides the printer selection and page setup dialogs. To ensure that the printing is all right, the control will display a print-preview window.

Summary

This chapter has thrown us into printing in .NET. We have seen how a small amount of well-structured code can bring about some impressive graphical results; we saw its numerous parallels with on-screen drawing and used many of the same techniques. Starting with drawing a short message in the center of a page and then moving on to much more advanced techniques.

We tackled a thorny issue of typographics, where we laid out a long string across several separate printed pages, how to treat pages differently from within the same routine. Our exploration then took us into using more advanced transparent colors to create a watermark effect.

Finally, we added the ability to let our users actively participate in the process by selecting how and where they wanted their printouts delivered. All these professional features are well within the reach of C#. With a little time and effort we can produce truly world-class quality output using .NET.

8
Collections

Building custom controls frequently implies working with collections of items. The `System.Collections` namespace contains many specialized classes that facilitate implementing tasks such as adding, sorting, and managing different groups of items. You are already familiar with some of these classes used in the previous chapters. Now you'll investigate them in more detail, and then you'll build a custom control that uses collections.

As you saw earlier in Chapter 1, a **Collection** is what its name implies: a group of items that have one or more things in common. The `System.Collections` namespace contains several classes useful for collecting objects together. Version 2.0 of the .NET Framework comes with a new approach to collections, adding support for strongly-typed generic collections (simply called *generics*). In this chapter, you will learn how to work with both generic and non-generic classes.

All collection classes accept, hold, and return their elements as objects. By using a collection you can write code that performs iterative processing on items within that collection. Think of iterative processing as an operation that uses a loop to perform an action on multiple objects instead of writing the code for each object.

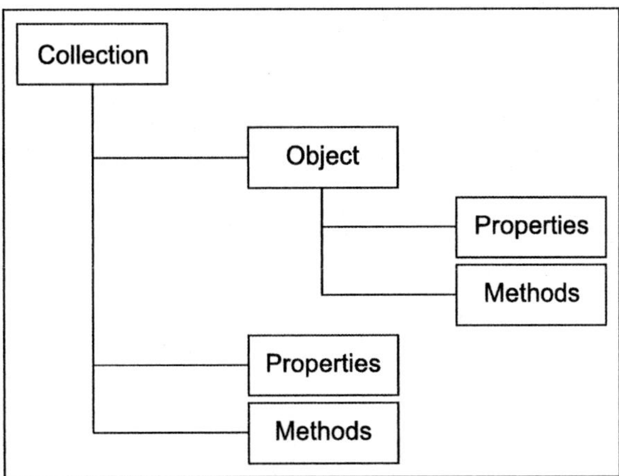

Each collection contains an indexed set of objects, properties, and methods. In other words, a collection is basically a class that has an inner collection, and methods like `Add()`, `Retrieve()`, and `Remove()` for manipulating its objects. The objects have properties and methods of their own.

So, a collection is a set of consistent objects, but how do we manage them? The management of all collection classes is done through the interface of a `Container` class. The `Container` class is the default implementation for the `IContainer` interface. A `Container` is an object that is used to encapsulate and track zero or more components. You can use `Containers` in both logical and visual scenarios, although in the case of collections, it is used in a logical sense.

Collections in the .NET Framework

The .NET Framework comes with a series of collection types for different scenarios, each of which maps to a different kind of data structure: `list`, `stack`, `queue`, `Hashtable`, and some specialized ones, like `string collection`, or `string dictionary`. Having so many choices can confuse us, but the truth is that it's beneficial to know your options:

1. `ArrayList`: This is an array-like resizable alternative to the fixed size arrays that can store any type of object. This collection class is very useful in a scenario where you do not know the exact size of your collection and you can use it to create a friendlier programming interface around it.
2. `Queue` and `Stack`: Perfect for the scenario where you receive data in a specific order, and need to process it one element at a time.
3. `SortedList`: This class should be used in the scenario where you need to maintain a sorted order, since `SortedList` behaves like a `Hashtable` when you access an element by key, and acts like an `Array` if you use an index.
4. `StringCollection`: As it uses a strongly typed interface, this is in most cases a better choice than the `ArrayList` for a dynamically sized array of strings.
5. `StringDictionary`: As it has strongly typed interface, this is a better choice than `Hashtable` if your collection will contain only strings.
6. `ListDictionary` and `Hashtables`: The choice between these two is made by the number of elements you need to use—in the case of 20 or fewer, use `ListDictionary`, otherwise opt for `Hashtable`. They are good options when key-based access is a must.
7. `NameValueCollection`: As it provides both indexed and key-based access to data, this is the slowest collection.

You can also build your own collections class for data binding purposes and even use the `System.Collections.Generic` namespace that contains interfaces and classes that define generic collections. Among the most useful non-generic collection classes are `ArrayList`, `Queue`, `Stack`, and `SortedList`, and we will briefly discuss each of them.

ArrayList

Generally, `Arrays` aren't always very permissive when it comes to removing an element or inserting one. `ArrayList` on the other hand is a great way for shuffling elements around in an `Array`. By using the `Remove()` method you can take away an element from the `ArrayList` and it automatically takes care of rearranging the elements. The only collection type that does not do this, is the `Array`, all other .NET collections are dynamic and take care of this operation. By using the `Add()` method you can insert an element at the end of the list. If we need to put an element at a certain position in the ArrayList we can use the Insert() method, which allows us to introduce the element at a specified position. In both cases the ArrayList will resize itself if necessary.

You can use the public properties of ArrayList to:

- Define the actual number of elements an ArrayList can contain: ArrayList.Capacity.
- Get the number of elements actually contained in the ArrayList: ArrayList.Count.
- Access the element at a specified index: ArrayList.Item.

Other useful methods are:

- ArrayList.Add: Add an object at the end of the ArrayList, if the collection's capacity is already filled, the size will double.
- ArrayList.AddRange: Add elements from an ICollection to the end of the collection.
- ArrayList.Clear: Removes all elements from the ArrayList.
- ArrayList.Contains: Determines whether an element is in the ArrayList.
- ArrayList.Insert: We can specify the index where we need our object inserted.
- ArrayList.InsertRange: Inserts the elements of a collection into the ArrayList at the specified index.

You are in complete control of where the elements are stored within an ArrayList, and you can choose the exact index where an element (or the elements from an ICollection) is inserted.

```
using System.Collections;
...
ArrayList colors = new ArrayList(4);
colors.Add(Color.Cornsilk);
colors.Add(Color.DarkOrange);
colors.Insert(1, Color.Blue);
```

We first created the colors as an ArrayList collection of four items, after we add the first two we use the Insert() method to insert Color.Blue at our desired place.

Queue

The Queue class implements the classic first-in first-out collection; any element that joins the queue at the back (enqueue) and leaves the queue at the front (dequeue).

```
using System.Collections;
...
Queue numbers = new Queue();
int numb = new int[4] { 4, 3, 9, 1};
foreach (int num in })
{
  numbers.Enqueue(num);
}
// the numbers are now inside the Queue, 4 is the first element
while (numbers.Count != 0)
{
  int num = (int)numbers.Dequeue();
}
// the output would now be 4, 3, 9, 1
```

Variables of type `object` can refer to any object of any reference type, and any instance of a class. Variables of type `object` can also refer to any value of any type. In our case we first set

```
num = 4;
numbers.Enqeue(num);
```

The second line creates an object inside our collection that references the value 4, in other words:

```
int num = 4;
object x = num;
/* although this is different from the code above, here we do the same thing,
but we don't include the object in the Queue */
```

The effect of the second initialization is subtle; the reference inside the variable `x` will not refer to the variable `num`. Instead an exact copy of `num` will be made on the heap and the reference inside `x` refers to that copy. This automatic copying is called **boxing**. If we modify the value of `num` (`num=3`) we will not modify the value on the heap, hence `x` will reference the same value.

You might expect to be able to access the boxed `int` value that a variable `x` refers to by using `int num = x`. This will get you a compile-time error.

```
object x = 4; // ok
int num = x;  // Compile time error
```

`x` could reference absolutely anything, so it's only normal for an error to be thrown. You must use:

```
object x = 4;
int num = (int)x;
```

This is called a **cast** and will work, if the value referenced by `x` is an `int`. The compiler checks what `x` is actually referring to and if it is a boxed `int`, and everything matches, the cast will succeed and the compiler will extract the value from the boxed `int` and initialize `num`. This is called **unboxing**. If `x` wasn't referring to an `int`, there will be a type mismatch causing the cast to fail and not to return causing an `InvalidCastException` to be thrown. The type from the unboxing cast must match exactly with the type actually in the box. For example, if the box contains an `int` and you try to unbox it in a `long`, you will get `InvalidCastException`. It doesn't matter that there is a built-in implicit conversion from an `int` to a `long`, the match must be exact.

Stack

The `Stack` class implements the classical last-in first-out collection. An element that joins the stack at the top using the `Push()` method will leave the stack at the top with the `Pop()` method.

We'll build a simple control that will add selected colors from a `ComboBox` to a `Stack`. Since it's the first full code example, we'll make it short:

```
using System;
using System.Collections;
using System.ComponentModel;
using System.Drawing;
using System.Windows.Forms;
namespace PacktCustomControls
{
  /// <remarks>
  /// The ComboBoxExample is a simple ComboBox adds
  /// colors to a stack
  /// </remarks>
  public partial class ComboBoxExample : UserControl
  {
```

```
        /// <summary>
        /// The stack of picked colors
        /// </summary>
        public Stack colors;
        /// <summary>
        /// The default ComboBoxExample constructor
        /// </summary>
        public ComboBoxExample()
        {
          colors = new Stack();
          InitializeComponent();
        }
        private void ComboBoxExample_Load(object sender, EventArgs e)
        {
          string[] knownColors = Enum.GetNames(typeof(KnownColor));
          try
          {
            foreach (string color in knownColors)
            {
              colorCombo.Items.Add(color);
            }
          }
          catch (ArgumentNullException ex)
          {
            MessageBox.Show(ex.Message);
          }
        }
        private void AddColor(object sender, EventArgs e)
        {
          colors.Push(colorCombo.SelectedItem);
          lstAddedColors.Items.Add("Added " + colorCombo.SelectedItem);
        }
      }
    }
```

There are some things that you might want to notice. First, we populate a `ComboBox` named `colorCombo` with every known color when the control is loaded in the system memory:

```
        private void ComboBoxExample_Load(object sender, EventArgs e)
        {
          string[] knownColors = Enum.GetNames(typeof(KnownColor));
          try
          {
            foreach (string color in knownColors)
            {
              colorCombo.Items.Add(color);
            }
          }
          catch (ArgumentNullException ex)
          {
            MessageBox.Show(ex.Message);}
          }
```

The `GetNames()` method might raise an `ArgumentNullException` when it gets all the names from the `KnownColor` enum and it's good programming practice to handle it.

The second thing that you should notice is the `AddColor()` method that was set as an event handler for the `SelectedIndexChanged` event of the `ComboBox`. Basically, it pushes the item onto the stack and adds a text in the `lstAddedColors` `ListBox`.

SortedList

The `ArrayList` type provides a way to map an integer index to an element; you can provide the integer index (say `[3]`), and you insert the item in the collection at the desired location (which actually is the 4th spot in our case because it's a zero-based list). `SortedList` provides a way of mapping items by other types like `string`, `double`, or `Time` (this is called an **associative array**). It provides this by maintaining two object arrays:

- One for the keys you are mapping from
- One for the values you are mapping to

Just as the name says, the key array is always sorted; this means that elements held inside the keys array must be comparable. Each element is a key/value pair that can be accessed as a `DictionaryEntry` object. The capacity of a `SortedList` is the number of elements the `SortedList` can hold. The default initial capacity for a `SortedList` is 0. As elements are added to a `SortedList`, the capacity is automatically increased as required through reallocation. The capacity can be decreased by calling `TrimToSize` or by setting the `Capacity` property explicitly.

This collection can be sorted either by a specific `IComparer` implementation specified when the collection is first created, or according to the `IComparer` implementation provided by the keys themselves, in both cases, the `SortedList` does not allow duplicate keys. If you allow the `Add()` method to add a key that is already present in the keys array, you will get an exception.

In contrast to the other collection classes, you are not in control of where the elements live within the `SortedList` and when you use the `foreach` statement to iterate through a `SortedList`, you get back a `DictionaryEntry`. This class provides access to the elements in both the arrays through the `key` property and the `Value` property.

We'll build on the last example, adding some functionality to our controls, like filling the `ComboBox` `Items` collection with an existing `ArrayList` so we'll automatically have a list with color names.

```
using System;
using System.ComponentModel;
using System.Drawing;
using System.Windows.Forms;
using System.Collections;
namespace PacktCustomControls
{
  /// <remarks>
  /// The ArrayList combobox example user control
  /// </remarks>
  public partial class ArrayListExample : UserControl
  {
    Color selectedColor;
    ArrayList colors;
    /// <summary>
    /// Gets the selected color from the
    /// </summary>
    public Color SelectedColor
    {
      get
      {
        return selectedColor;
      }
    }
    /// <summary>
    /// The default ArrayListExample constructor generated by VS 2005
```

```
        /// plus the initialization of the selectedColor to Black.
        /// </summary>
        public ArrayListExample()
        {
          selectedColor = Color.Black;
          colors = new ArrayList();
          string[] knownColors = Enum.GetNames(typeof(KnownColor));
          foreach (string knownColor in knownColors)
          {
            if (!Color.FromName(knownColor).IsSystemColor)
              colors.Add(knownColor);
          }
          InitializeComponent();
        }
        private void colorCombo_SelectedIndexChanged(object sender, EventArgs e)
        {
          selectedColor = Color.FromName(colorCombo.Text);
        }
        private void ArrayListExample_Load(object sender, EventArgs e)
        {
          foreach (object item in colors)
          {
            colorCombo.Items.Add((string)item);
          }
        }
      }
```

The trick is done by the

```
if (!Color.FromName(knownColor).IsSystemColor)
```

line that will simply skip the so called system colors, like `HightlightText`.

As you can see, these are very simple examples of collections just to give you an idea of what they are all about. If you need to use a collection for your project, you will need to know all the details concerning the collection before choosing one. We presented some scenarios with the same goal, so you know what they are all about.

Unfortunately, the data is not checked when an object enters the collection and because a collection can have any kind of objects we can get errors that are hard to detect and correct. Let's take as an example the case where we have an `ArrayList` named `list` where we want to add three objects:

```
ArrayList list = new ArrayList();
list.Add("something ");
list.Add(23);              // no exception
list.Add(new ArrayList());    // no exception
```

If we do not use the `ToString()` method when we add them and try to use them as strings (since the first member was a string) we'll get an exception :

```
foreach (string t in list)
{
  comboBox.Items.Add(t);  // exception
}
```

We have to work around this exception by using a strongly typed collection, but they are not easily modified and the code is not easily reused. Fortunately, with .NET 2.0 a new breed of classes was introduced, one that simplifies working with many items and provides a lot of useful features.

Generics

In the non-programming world, the word generic means something that is not related to any brand name. If we buy a hammer, we don't need to know who made the hammer, and what chemical composition the head of the hammer has. So without really knowing much about it, we can use it the way it was intended.

The same idea is behind the concept of **Generics**, when we refer to a collection of items whose type isn't known at compile time, but that are strongly typed at run time, being initialized to store a specific type. We can still add or remove items, iterate through it, and use it in a type-safe manner. The support for Generics is a new programming language feature that is implemented in .NET 2.0. Generics are completely Common Language Specification (CLS)-compliant. (The CLS defines what features a .NET language must support, and being CLS-compliant is the minimum that a .NET language must meet.)

The features of Generics include:

- **Type Safety**: If any of the type-checking rules are broken going into or coming out of a Generic Collection class, the compiler will not be happy and will tell us that.
- **Performance**: It eliminates the boxing/unboxing, and casting procedure by building the generics directly into the runtime.
- **Efficiency**: There is no need for run-time type checks.
- **Clarity**: The code is cleaner by having to perform fewer explicit conversions.
- **Ease of reading**: Due to the intuitive syntax of generics, the code is easy to read

All the Generic collections are in System.Collections.Generic. Below is a table providing a few Generic classes, along with a short description, and the corresponding non-generic class:

Generic class	Description	Non-generic equivalent
List<T>	Strongly typed ordered list of objects of the same type, or with a shared base class	ArrayList
Queue<T>	Strongly typed queue of objects of the same type, or with a shared base class	Queue
Stack<T>	Strongly typed stack of objects of the same type, or with a shared base class	Stack
SortedList<K,V>	A collection of key/value pairs	SortedList
Collection<T>	Provides the base class for a generic collection	CollectionBase
ReadOnlyCollection<T>	The base class for a generic read-only collection	ReadOnlyCollectionBase
Dictionary<K,V>	A collection of key/value pairs	Hashtable
LinkedList<T>	A doubly linked list (each node knows about the previous and next node)	none
BindingList<T>	List that supports complex data-binding scenarios	none

As you can see each class has a type placeholder `T`, which represents the type of the generic collection. Dictionaries that take a key and a value type as parameters use `K` and `V` respectively to represent those types, as in `Dictionary<K,V>`.

In the previous example, we used an `ArrayList` to hold the names of the colors in the `KnownColor` enumeration. The truth is anybody could have added any kind of item to the colors `ArrayList`. Instead, we could use a generic `ArrayList` only for objects of the string type.

```
using System;
using System.ComponentModel;
using System.Drawing;
using System.Windows.Forms;
using System.Collections.Generic;
namespace PacktCustomControls
{
  /// <remarks>
  /// The ArrayList combobox example user control
  /// </remarks>
  public partial class ArrayListExample : UserControl
  {
    Color selectedColor;
    List<string> colors;
    /// <summary>
    /// The SelectedColorChanged event that is fired every time the
    /// selected color changed.
    /// </summary>
    public event SelectedColorChangedEvent SelectedColorChanged;
    /// <summary>
    /// Gets the selected color
    /// </summary>
    public Color SelectedColor
    {
      get
      {
        return selectedColor;
      }
    }
    /// <summary>
    /// The default ArrayListExample constructor generated by VS 2005
    /// plus the initialization of the selectedColor to Black.
    /// </summary>
    public ArrayListExample()
    {
      selectedColor = Color.Black;
      colors = new List<string>();
      foreach (string knownColor in Enum.GetNames(typeof(KnownColor)))
      {
        if (!Color.FromName(knownColor).IsSystemColor)
          colors.Add(knownColor);
      }
      InitializeComponent();
    }
    private void colorCombo_SelectedIndexChanged(object sender, EventArgs e)
    {
      selectedColor = Color.FromName(colorCombo.Text);
    }
    private void ArrayListExample_Load(object sender, EventArgs e)
    {
      foreach (string item in colors)
      {
        colorCombo.Items.Add(item);
      }
    }
  }
```

As you can see, using `Generics` makes the code a lot more intelligent than using plain objects—the `Add()` method will work only for the string type or it will throw an exception.

Building the Font Picker

So far, we've talked about collections and listed some recommendations related to what type of collection you should use and when. It might seem a bit awkward to use generics in a simple custom control, but we'll show you that it's simple and efficient to use them. There are thousands of examples but it would be more fun to build a custom font picker. We figured that almost every application that requires user input could provide a font picker.

The following figure shows a screenshot of what the control could look like:

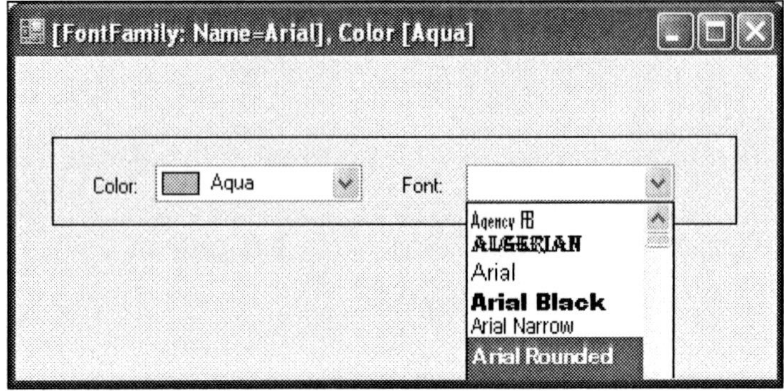

Our first `FontPicker` will also have a color picker that will show all the predefined colors.

After taking a quick peek at the screenshots and the code listing, it's probably best to start with the project one step at a time.

Time for Action—Building Font Picker

1. Start by creating a Windows Application project named HostApplication.

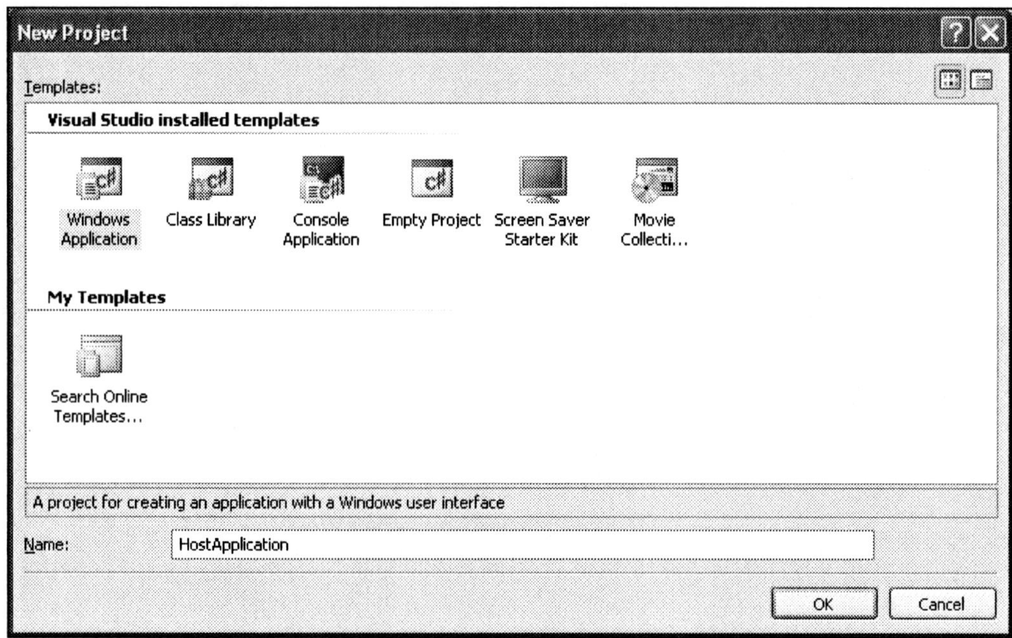

2. Right-click on the project name in the Solution Explorer to add a UserControl.

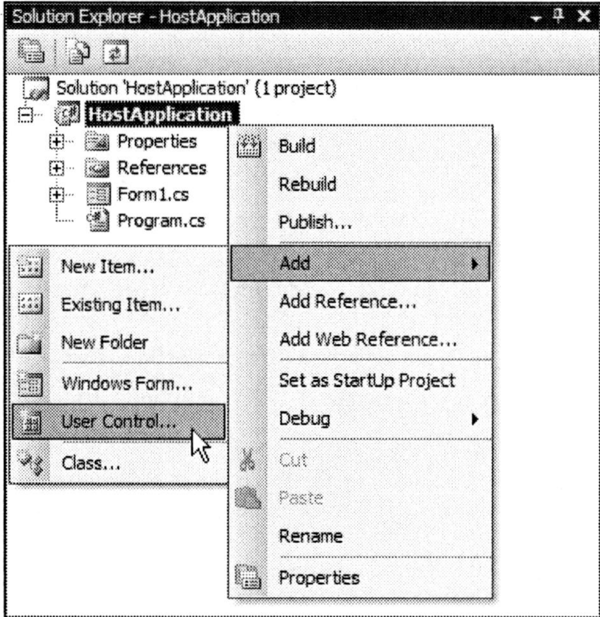

3. Name the new control `FontPicker.cs` (or simply `FontPicker`).

4. Add two labels and two ComboBoxes on the surface of the user control. After following steps five through nine, your user control will look like this:

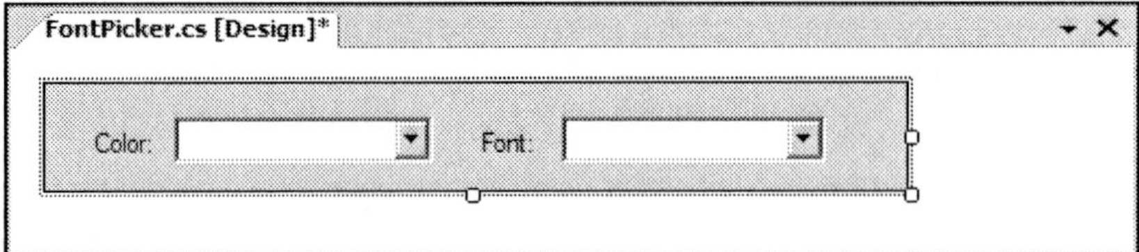

5. Set the properties of your user control like this:

Property	Value
Size	400, 50
BorderStyle	FixedSingle

> `FontPicker` is your control. To set its properties, simply select an empty part of the control in the designer, and open up its Properties window with *F4*. Then to set the properties of the individual controls inside your user control, simply highlight them by clicking on their surface on their designer.

6. Modify the default property values of the first label like this:

Property	Value
(Name)	`colorLabel`
Text	Color:
Location	20, 20

7. Modify the properties of the first combo box like this:

Property	Value
(Name)	`colorCombo`
Location	60, 15
DropDownStyle	DropDownList
DrawMode	OwnerDrawFixed

8. Modify the properties of the second label like this:

Property	Value
(Name)	`fontLabel`
Text	Font:
Location	200, 20

9. Modify the properties of the second combo box like this:

Property	Value
(Name)	fontCombo
Location	240, 15
DropDownStyle	DropDownList
DrawMode	OwnerDrawFixed

10. Switch FontPicker.cs to Code View by selecting View | Code (or pressing the default shortcut *F7*). The default code that was generated for you should look like this:

```
using System;
using System.Collections.Generic;
using System.ComponentModel;
using System.Drawing;
using System.Data;
using System.Text;
using System.Windows.Forms;
namespace HostApplication
{
  public partial class FontPicker : UserControl
  {
    public FontPicker()
    {
      InitializeComponent();
    }
  }
}
```

11. Add a reference to the System.Collections namespace:

```
using System;
using System.Collections;
using System.Collections.Generic;
using System.ComponentModel;
using System.Drawing;
using System.Data;
using System.Text;
using System.Windows.Forms;
```

12. Modify the FontPicker class like this:

```
/// <remarks>
/// The Font Picker user control
/// </remarks>
  public partial class FontPicker : UserControl
  {
    Color selectedColor;
    FontFamily selectedFont;
    List<string> colors;
    List<FontFamily> fontFamilies;
    /// <summary>
    /// The FontPicker creates a generic list with known colors
    /// and populates the combobox Items collection.
    /// </summary>
    public FontPicker()
    {
      // prepare the fields
      selectedColor = Color.Black;
      selectedFont = new FontFamily("Arial");
      colors = new List<string>();
      fontFamilies = new List<FontFamily>();
```

```
            // initialize the list of colors
            foreach (string knownColor in Enum.GetNames(typeof(KnownColor)))
            {
              if (!Color.FromName(knownColor).IsSystemColor)
              {
                colors.Add(knownColor);
              }
            }
            // initialize the list of font families
            foreach (FontFamily fontFamily in FontFamily.Families)
            {
              if (fontFamily.IsStyleAvailable(FontStyle.Regular))
              {
                fontFamilies.Add(fontFamily);
              }
            }
            // perform control initialization tasks
            InitializeComponent();
          }
        }
```

At this point we have a pretty generic custom control that does virtually nothing. We see that we expose two properties called `SelectedColor` and `SelectedFont`. We also prepared the necessary fields that will store the color names and font families in two generic lists. You can also see that `FontPicker` is a partial class, which means that another part of this class can be found in another file. In our case, the other part of the class can be found in the `FontPicker.Designer.cs` file, which contains the code generated by Visual C# Express to build the controls that you've created using the designer. Feel free to take a look into that file to find the definitions of the labels and combo boxes you've created and set up using the designer.

Why did we choose to create a `FontFamily` list instead of a `Font` list? The answer is that in order to define a font, you need a `FontFamily`, and a size. The so called fonts, like *Times New Roman* or *Arial*, are actually font families. We'll filter the fonts that cannot be used with the Regular font style (the font styles are Regular, *Italic*, **Bold**, and ***Bold Italic***). Also, when building the colors we'll remove the *system colors* (such as *Control* or *MainText*), whose values depend on the settings of the system.

The typical colors like red or green are easy to pick because everybody knows what they look like. Still, there are some lesser known colors like `AliciaBlue`. To give the user a hand, add a small colored rectangle near the name of the color in the color combo box.

13. Let's use the designer to have Visual C# Express generate the `DrawItem` event handler (`colorCombo_DrawItem`) for the color combo for us. Select `colorCombo`, press *F4* to open its Properties window, click the little lightning symbol to display the control's events, and double-click the `DrawItem` entry (shown in the figure opposite) to generate the event handler.

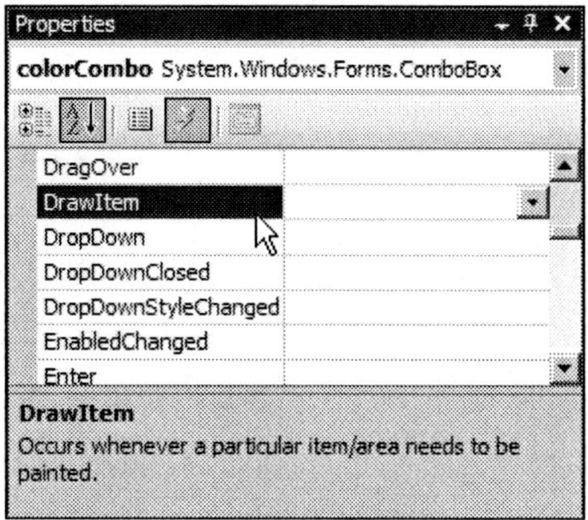

14. Complete the code of the `colorCombo_DrawItem()` method as shown in the following code snippet, and add the `ColorItem` (which draws each combo box item) and the `DrawColorBoxHightlight` (which draws the selection rectangle) helper methods:

```
void colorCombo_DrawItem(object sender, DrawItemEventArgs e)
{
  if (e.Index != -1)
  {
    bool hasFocus = false;
    if ((e.State & DrawItemState.Selected) != 0)
    {
      hasFocus = true;
      DrawColorBoxHighlight(hasFocus, e.Graphics, e.Bounds);
    }
    else
    {
      DrawColorBoxHighlight(hasFocus, e.Graphics, e.Bounds);
    }
    ColorItem(e.Graphics, e.Bounds, e.Index, hasFocus);
  }
}
void ColorItem(Graphics graphics, Rectangle rectangle, int p, bool
              hasFocus)
{
  SolidBrush text =
            new SolidBrush(Color.FromKnownColor(KnownColor.MenuText));
  SolidBrush color = new SolidBrush(Color.FromName(colors[p]));
  Pen pen = new Pen(Color.Black, 1);
  if (hasFocus)
  {
    text.Color = Color.FromKnownColor(KnownColor.HighlightText);
  }
  graphics.FillRectangle(color, rectangle.Left + 2, rectangle.Top + 2,
                   20, rectangle.Height - 4);
  graphics.DrawRectangle(pen, new Rectangle(rectangle.Left + 1,
                   rectangle.Top + 1, 21, rectangle.Height - 3));
  graphics.DrawString(colors[p], colorCombo.Font, text, rectangle.Left
                 + 28, rectangle.Top);
}
void DrawColorBoxHighlight(bool isSelected, Graphics graphics,
                     Rectangle rectangle)
{
  if (!isSelected)
  {
```

```
        graphics.FillRectangle(new SolidBrush(SystemColors.Window),
                               rectangle);
    }
    else
    {
        Pen borderPen =
                    new Pen(Color.FromKnownColor(KnownColor.Highlight));
        SolidBrush backgroundBrush =
               new SolidBrush(Color.FromKnownColor(KnownColor.Highlight));
        graphics.FillRectangle(backgroundBrush, rectangle);
        graphics.DrawRectangle(borderPen,
                               rectangle.Left, rectangle.Top,
                               rectangle.Width - 1, rectangle.Height - 1);
        borderPen.Dispose();
        backgroundBrush.Dispose();
    }
}
```

15. At this point the visual part of the color picker part is done. Let's continue dealing with the font picker. Something that we would like to provide is a sort of preview of the font. The simplest way is to draw each item ourselves, just like in the color combo box example, but using the font family stored in the `fontFamilies` list. Follow the same steps as before to generate the `fontCombo_DrawItem` event handler, and then type this code:

```
private void fontCombo_DrawItem(object sender, DrawItemEventArgs e)
{
  if (e.Index != -1)
  {
    bool hasFocus = false;
    if ((e.State & DrawItemState.Selected) != 0)
    {
      hasFocus = true;
      DrawFontBoxHighlight(hasFocus, e.Graphics, e.Bounds);
    }
    else
    {
      DrawFontBoxHighlight(hasFocus, e.Graphics, e.Bounds);
    }
    DrawFontItem(e.Graphics, e.Bounds, e.Index, hasFocus);
  }
}
private void DrawFontBoxHighlight(bool isSelected, Graphics graphics,
                                  Rectangle rectangle)
{
  if (!isSelected)
  {
    graphics.FillRectangle(new SolidBrush(SystemColors.Window),
                           rectangle);
  }
  else
  {
    Pen borderPen =
                new Pen(Color.FromKnownColor(KnownColor.Highlight));
    SolidBrush backgroundBrush =
           new SolidBrush(Color.FromKnownColor(KnownColor.Highlight));
    graphics.FillRectangle(backgroundBrush, rectangle);
    graphics.DrawRectangle(borderPen,
                           rectangle.Left, rectangle.Top,
                           rectangle.Width - 1, rectangle.Height - 1);
    borderPen.Dispose();
    backgroundBrush.Dispose();
  }
}
```

```
void DrawFontItem(Graphics graphics, Rectangle rectangle, int p, bool
                  hasFocus)
{
  float fontSize = 10;
  Font font = new Font(fontFamilies[p], fontSize);
  SolidBrush text = new SolidBrush(SystemColors.ControlText);
  SolidBrush color = new SolidBrush(SystemColors.ControlText);
  Pen pen = new Pen(Color.Black, 1);
  if (hasFocus)
  {
    text.Color = Color.FromKnownColor(KnownColor.HighlightText);
  }
  graphics.DrawString(fontFamilies[p].Name, font, text, rectangle);
}
```

The code looks similar to that which displayed the list of colors. The most notable difference is the use of `fontFamilies[p].Name` as a parameter for the `graphics.DrawString()` method.

16. You need to make one more step to reach the first milestone. Switch `FontPicker.cs` to Design View and double-click an empty part of the form to have its `Load` event handler generated. Then complete the generated code as given below:

```
private void FontPicker_Load(object sender, EventArgs e)
{
  foreach (string item in colors)
  {
    colorCombo.Items.Add(item);
  }
  foreach (FontFamily font in fontFamilies)
  {
    fontCombo.Items.Add(font.Name);
  }
}
```

17. Let's do a quick test for our brand-new control before continuing to develop it further. Compile the project, and then open the form of your host application (Form1) in the designer, and also open the Toolbox. You should see your new control as shown below:

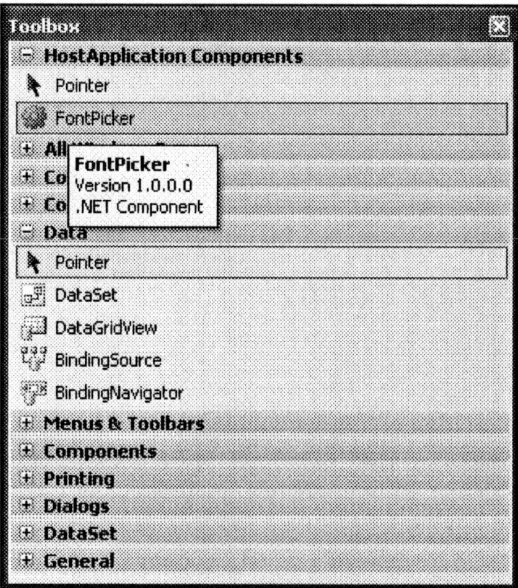

18. Add a new `FontPicker` control to `Form1`:

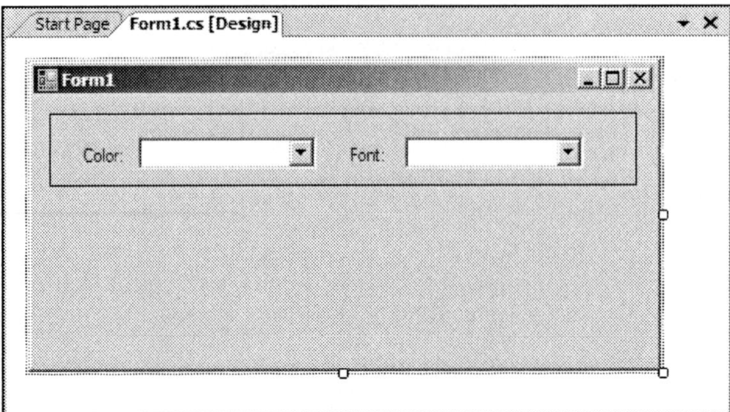

19. Execute the project and verify that both combo boxes work correctly, as shown in figure below. If they work, feel free to continue with the exercise, otherwise go back to make sure you typed everything correctly.

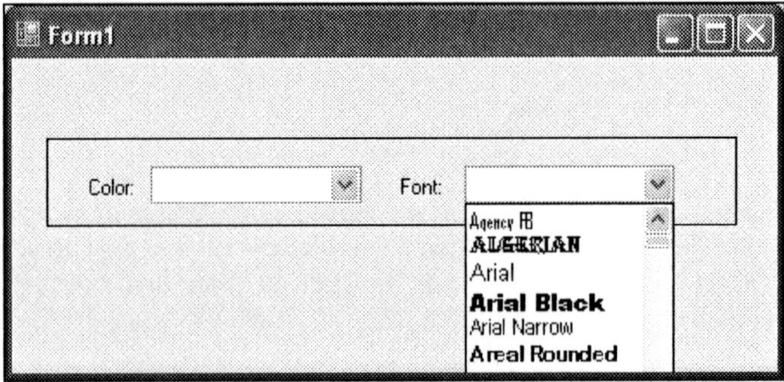

20. In order to make any real use of such a control, you need to expose the selected values somehow. Add the `SelectedColor` and `SelectedFont` properties to the `FontPicker` control:

```
/// <summary>
/// Gets the selected color from the color dropdown list.
/// </summary>
public Color SelectedColor
{
  get
  {
    return selectedColor;
  }
}
/// <summary>
/// Gets the selected font from the font dropdown list.
/// </summary>
public FontFamily SelectedFont
{
```

```
    get
    {
      return selectedFont;
    }
  }
```

21. Using these properties is useful, but adding events to have the control signal when the values change would be even more useful. We need a class that inherits from the `EventArgs` class, a `delegate`, and an event for the custom events to work. We can start by adding the `ControlChangedEventArgs` class, and the `SelectedControlChangedEvent` delegate to the same namespace as the `FontPicker` (`HostApplication` in this case), next to the `FontPicker` class. Normally their location shouldn't make a difference, but the Visual C# designer requires you to add these members after the `FontPicker` class.

```
/// <remarks>
/// The SelectedColorChangedEvent delegate
/// </remarks>
public delegate void
   SelectedControlChangedEvent(ControlChangedEventArgs e);
/// <remarks>
/// The custom event args for the SelectedColorChanged event
/// </remarks>
public class ControlChangedEventArgs : EventArgs
{
  private Color changedColor;
  private FontFamily changedFont;
  /// <summary>
  /// The new color.
  /// </summary>
  public Color ChangedColor
  {
    get
    {
      return changedColor;
    }
  }
  /// <summary>
  /// The new font family.
  /// </summary>
  public FontFamily ChangedFont
  {
    get
    {
      return changedFont;
    }
  }
  /// <summary>
  /// The ColorChangedEventArgs are custom event args
  /// for the SelectedControlChanged event.
  /// </summary>
  /// <param name="changedColor">The new color.</param>
  /// <param name="changedFont">The new font.</param>
  internal ControlChangedEventArgs(Color changedColor, FontFamily
                                   changedFont)
  {
    this.changedColor = changedColor;
    this.changedFont = changedFont;
  }
}
```

22. Add the following members to the `FontPicker` class:

```
/// <summary>
/// The SelectedColorChanged event is fired when the selected color
/// changes.
/// </summary>
public event SelectedControlChangedEvent SelectedControlChanged;
private void OnSelectedControlChanged(ControlChangedEventArgs
                                      controlEventArgs)
{
  if (SelectedControlChanged != null)
  {
    SelectedControlChanged(controlEventArgs);
  }
}
```

23. We can now change the `SelectedIndexChanged` event handlers for both combo boxes to raise the `SelectedControlChanged`. Use Visual C# Express to generate their `SelectedIndexChanged` event handlers, and then type this code:

```
private void colorCombo_SelectedIndexChanged(object sender, EventArgs e)
{
  selectedColor = Color.FromName(colorCombo.Text);
  ControlChangedEventArgs controlEventArgs =
    new ControlChangedEventArgs(selectedColor, selectedFont);
  OnSelectedControlChanged(controlEventArgs);
}
private void comboFonts_SelectedIndexChanged(object sender, EventArgs e)
{
  selectedFont = fontFamilies[fontCombo.SelectedIndex];
  ControlChangedEventArgs controlEventArgs =
    new ControlChangedEventArgs(selectedColor, selectedFont);
  OnSelectedControlChanged(controlEventArgs);
}
```

24. This about wraps it up. Save the project using File | Save All, and select these options:

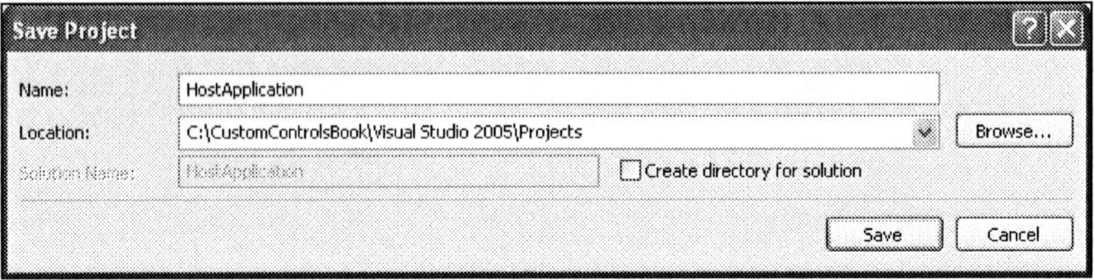

25. The only thing left to do is to test the new functionality! Open `Form1.cs` in the designer, select the `FontPicker` control, and use the Properties window to generate the event handler for the `SelectedControlChanged` event:

```
private void
        fontPicker1_SelectedControlChanged(ControlChangedEventArgs e)
{
  Text = e.ChangedFont.ToString() + ", " + e.ChangedColor.ToString();
}
```

Execute your application and notice the information being updated on the form's status bar when you change the values:

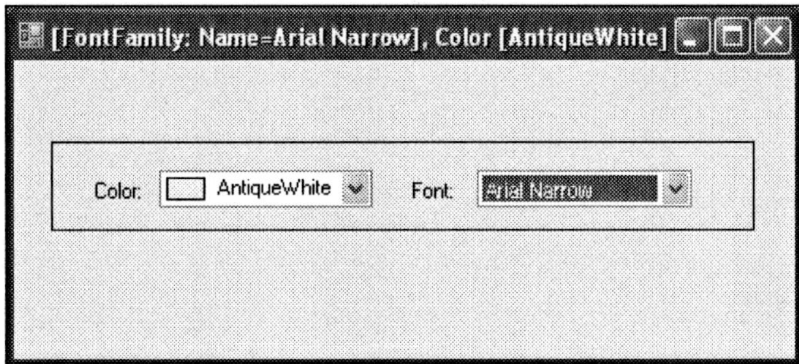

What Just Happened?

Your Font Picker control is functional, and easily customizable to fit a wide range of usage scenarios. Feel free to continue playing with it, and try using it in a real project.

The core functionality for selecting colors is performed by the `colorCombo_DrawItem()`, `ColorItem()`, and `DrawColorBoxHighlight()` methods, and the functionality for selecting font families happens in the `fontCombo_DrawItem()`, `DrawFontItem()`, and `DrawFontBoxHighlight()` methods. These are the first methods that you'll want to change in order to customize your control's behavior. We'll leave the task of using this control in a real project that needs font and color selection for you, as an exercise.

Summary

By understanding the building blocks of `System.Collections` you can build any collection you need, and be relaxed about using any available collection. You can now understand what collections really mean and how to choose the type of collection we need for our goal. The .NET 2.0 Framework comes with new and interesting collections that actually give you more freedom and permits you to skip the hard (and somewhat weird) part of boxing/unboxing/casting, and by making the code easier to read and reuse.

Using collections in your custom controls may be a necessity if you want to store some dynamic data or if you want to have easier access to some already available data, like font families or predefined colors. In many cases, it's really simple to implement and the code tends to look cleaner.

With a little bit of practice you'll find really easy to pick which collection you should use for a certain situation.

9

Double Buffering

Usually, developers have really fast machines: computers packed with the latest processors and lots of memory. This way they shorten the development cycle by getting the most out of their hardware.

However, it's not the performance of the programmer's workstation that matters, but the performance your application will have on the end user's machine. Performance is a very important aspect to keep in mind while developing software and this becomes a critical area when building processor-intensive applications.

What might surprise you is that even simple GDI+ applications consume lots of resources. You may think that you shouldn't require a fast video card or processor in order to run a text editor or accounting application. It goes without saying, right? Actually, it doesn't. Many applications draw a large number of items at once, especially if the end user works at a high resolution. While it may not seem so obvious at the beginning, drawing the application may sometimes require a tenth of a second or so, when the human eye can observe the so-called "flickers" at a speed as high as 70 Hz or 0.014 seconds. Wow, that's fast!

In this chapter we'll talk about how we can optimize the painting speed of Windows applications in general and our own controls in particular. Usually, the technique employed is called **double-buffering** and it has been called that since the golden days of MFC and COM.

Now, the new .NET Framework 2.0 can do much of the work for you, and we'll see how it happens by going through a little control that scrolls text using a scrollbar.

Introduction to Double Buffering

Before you start painting with performance in mind, it's good to learn a couple of things about how Windows and the .NET Framework manage drawing under the hood.

If your application contains graphic-intensive controls that consume significant resources to be drawn, the user is likely to start noticing the flicker effect. Among the techniques you can implement to improve your application's performance, there's one GDI+ specific, called double-buffering that can make quite an impact. Double-buffering implies drawing the graphical output into a memory buffer instead of drawing it directly on the screen; after the image is finally composed in that memory buffer, you quickly copy it into the display buffer. This way updating the user's output is done very quickly, and the flickering problems are gone.

If we look deep into the Windows core, we'll see that there is a WM_PAINT message handler that will eventually call OnPaintBackground() and OnPaint() delegates, in that specific order. By default, .NET Framework 2.0 applications will use double-buffering because the OptimizedDoubleBuffer property is set to true (the same effect is achieved by setting the DoubleBuffer, UserPaint, and AllPaintingInWmPaint properties to true). The class that does all the double-buffering tricks is called BufferedGraphicsContext, and a special object called BufferedGraphics manages a memory buffer, as you might have guessed.

If you develop applications that involve intensive graphics you practically have to create your own BufferedGraphics object and handle all the display logic by yourself. But most of the time, you'll be safe as long as you have the OptimizedDoubleBuffer and the AllPaitingInWmPaint flags of your form set to true. These are the default settings so you normally shouldn't do anything to have them enabled, but if you want to set their values yourself, you can do so with the following code:

```
private void Form1_Load(object sender, EventArgs e)
{
  this.SetStyle(ControlStyles.AllPaintingInWmPaint, true);
  this.SetStyle(ControlStyles.OptimizedDoubleBuffer, true);
}
```

One of the things you might want to do by yourself is to write custom code for the OnPaintBackground() and OnPaint() methods, usually by overriding the default methods. A typical scenario when such techniques can bring benefits is the scenario when you have scrolling text (or scrolling anything) on your form, because scrolling is a particularly intensive operation that implies lots of drawing.

Before writing some code, let's talk a bit about scrollbars. We'll use them in our example later on.

The Scroll Bar

Most of the time, your custom controls will be large enough to accommodate their contents. Sometimes, as in the case of word processors, text or any kind of item might overflow, either sideways or downwards. Due to this, some knowledge about scroll bars and how to use them is essential.

While scroll bars are used in almost every Windows application, the .NET way of doing things might require some explanations. The ScrollBar class is derived from the more general Control class, but most of the time you will be working with two descendants from the ScrollBar class, called HScrollBar and VScrollBar. These are, as you might have guessed, the horizontal and the vertical scrollbars, but they don't really add new properties or methods.

The scrollbars are represented by the ScrollBar class. The following picture shows a vertical scrollbar and a horizontal scrollbar and shows a few of their properties.

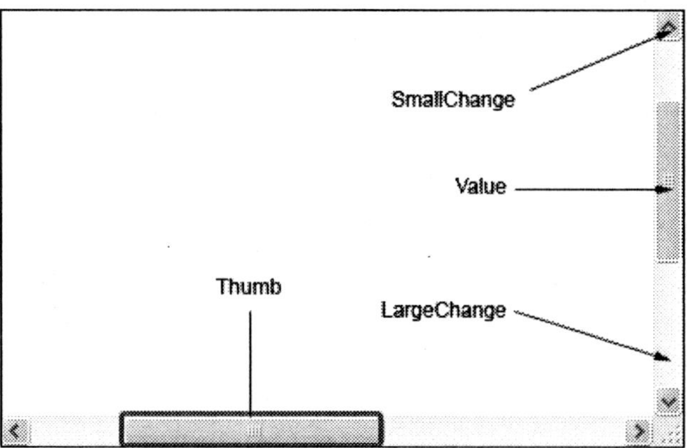

The `ScrollBar` class brings some new properties to the table that will help you a lot when dealing with scrollbars:

Property	Description
`Value`	Used to get or set the current position of the scrollbar
`Minimum`	Used for the lower limit of the scrollable area
`Maximum`	Used for the upper limit of the scrollable area
`SmallChange`	Used to show how much the scrollbar will move if one of the directional keys is pressed or if the user clicks on the scrollbar arrows
`LargeChange`	Used to show how the *Page Up* or *Page Down* keys will cause the scrollbar to change its position with a LargeChange value upwards or downwards

But these are just properties. It's the events that do all the scrolling magic by telling you when the scrollbars are being moved and by how much. The `ScrollBar` class has two specialized events you could use: `ValueChanged` and `Scroll`. And there really isn't a big difference between the two events apart from the number of times the event is raised and the information received by the event handler.

The `ValueChanged` event is more comfortable to work with, as it is raised only when the scrollbar is being moved, either by the user or programmatically, and provides just the new position. That's enough most of the time and since the event doesn't occur very often, the `ValueChanged` event is quite performance-friendly.

Sometimes you might want more information when dealing with the scrolling event: was it a `SmallChange` or `LargeChange`? Did the user click on the scrollbar arrows or is he or she moving the thumb? That's where the `Scroll` event is really useful. Besides being raised more often than `ValueChanged`, the event handler receives the new position and a special type of object: the `ScrollEventArgs` object.

The `ScrollEventArgs` object contains information about the new position of the scrollbar, and a `ScrollEventType` property, that basically is just an enumeration with the following values:

Value	Description
`SmallIncrement`	Used for a `SmallChange` downwards
`SmallDecrement`	Used for a `SmallChange` upwards
`LargeIncrement`	Used for a `LargeChange` downwards (the *Page Down* key was pressed)
`LargeDecrement`	Used for a `LargeChange` upwards (*Page Up*)
`ThumbTrack`	Used when the thumb is currently being moved
`ThumbPosition`	Used when the thumb was moved
`First`	Used when the *Home* key is pressed
`Last`	Used when the *End* key is pressed
`EndScroll`	Used when the scrolling operation has completed

But wait, why is a `SmallIncrement` used for a change downwards? The answer is quite simple: the `Value` property ranges from the minimum value to somewhere near the maximum value. Since the minimum is used for the top of the area and since minimum usually is smaller than maximum, increasing the `Value` property actually moves the scrollbar downwards.

Scroll that Text!

We introduced scrollbars because you will need them in many custom controls. Most of the time you will have to scroll something and it's very likely that you will employ double-buffering techniques.

In the following example, we'll use two trackbars, which are a special kind of scrollbars, to set the scrolling interval and the scroll amount. Because we want to show you as many interesting things as possible, we will end up not just using the default double-buffering property but our own `OnPaintBackground()` and `OnPaint()` methods.

Before we go any further, the following is a screenshot of the application:

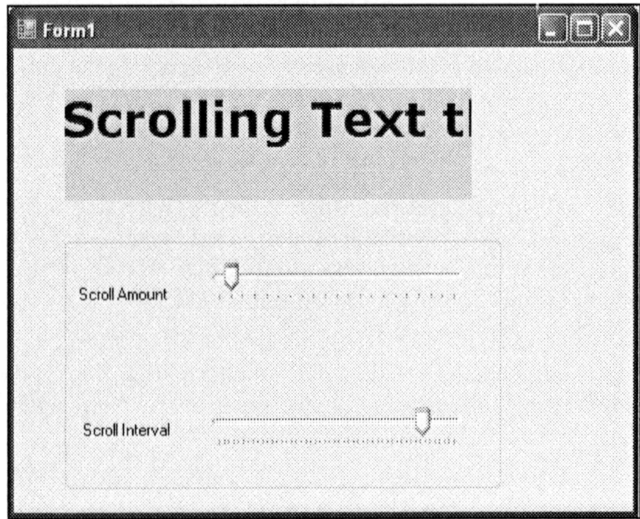

Time for Action—Building FlickerFree Control

1. Start by creating a Windows Application project named FlickerFree.

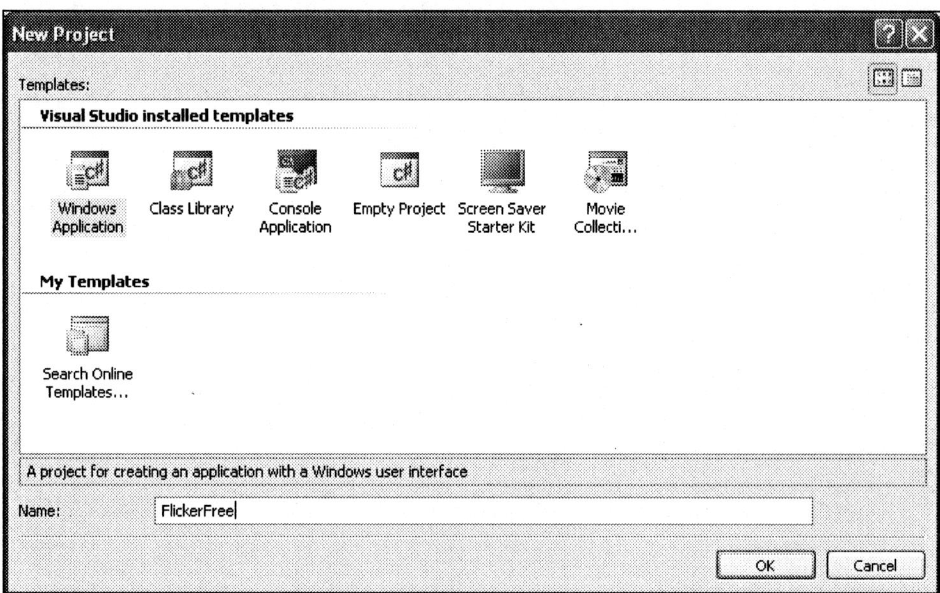

2. Add a UserControl to the project, by right-clicking the project name in Solution Explorer, and selecting Add | User Control from the context menu. Name the new control ScrollingText so you will get a new file named `ScrollingText.cs` in the Solution Explorer.
3. Change the control size so it will have the following properties:

Property	Value
(Name)	`ScrollingText`
Size.Width	400
Size.Height	100

4. Drag a Timer control from the Components tab of the Toolbox to the ScrollingText control and name it scrollTimer. Also, set its Modifiers property to Internal. We will use the timer's tick event to scroll the text. At this moment your control should look like this, when opened in the designer:

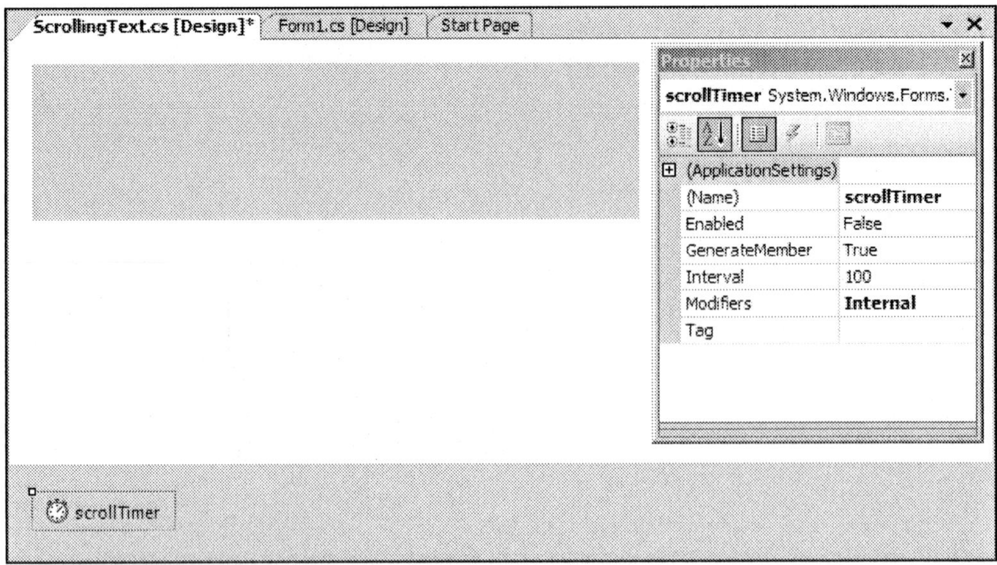

5. Create a new event handler for the `Load` event of the control by selecting **Events** in the **Properties** tab, scroll down to `Load`, and double-click on the empty space next to `Load`.

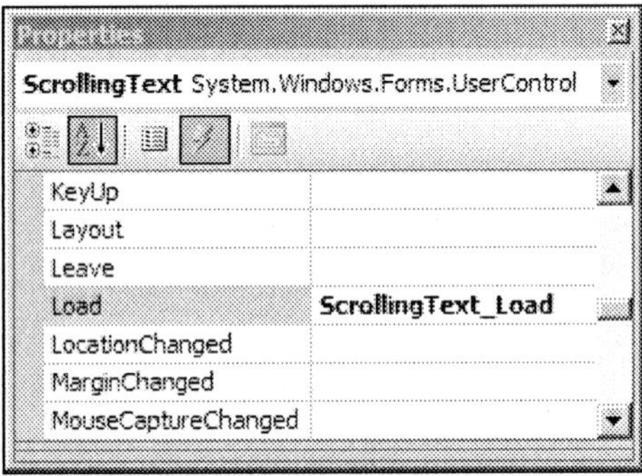

Visual C# Express will automatically create a `ScrollingText_Load()` method and it will open the code viewer where it created the event handler.

6. Set the control to redraw itself each time it is resized and enable the timer control. The code should look like this:

```
private void ScrollingText_Load(object sender, System.EventArgs e)
{
  this.ResizeRedraw = true;
  if (!this.DesignMode)
  {
    scrollTimer.Enabled = true;
  }
}
```

7. While you are in the code viewer, add the following fields to the `ScrollingText` class:

```
private string text;
private int scrollAmount = 10;
private int position = 10;
```

8. Using the same procedure as the one at point 5, add an event handler for the timer's `Tick` event that increments the position field and forces a refresh using the `Invalidate()` method.

```
private void scrollTimer_Tick(object sender, System.EventArgs e)
{
  position += scrollAmount;
  this.Invalidate();
}
```

9. Now we have to create three control properties: an overridden `Text` property, `ScrollTimeInterval`, and `ScrollPixelAmount`. Overriding the `Text` property allows us to specify the attributes required to make the property visible from the applications that use the control. Add the following code to the `ScrollingText` class:

```
[Browsable(true), DesignerSerializationVisibility(
                        DesignerSerializationVisibility.Visible)]
public override string Text
{
  get
  {
    return text;
  }
  set
  {
    text = value;
    this.Invalidate();
  }
}

public int ScrollTimeInterval
{
  get
  {
    return scrollTimer.Interval;
  }
  set
  {
    scrollTimer.Interval = value;
  }
}

public int ScrollPixelAmount
{
  get
  {
    return scrollAmount;
  }
  set
  {
    scrollAmount = value;
  }
}
```

10. The next step is to use GDI+ to create a scrolling text effect without using a Label control. We will use a bitmap to hold the text, and we'll implement the fastest draw method available for our drawing, `DrawImageUnscaled()`. For this to work we must override the `OnPaint()` method. The following code shows what it looks like:

```
protected override void OnPaint(System.Windows.Forms.PaintEventArgs e)
{
  // to avoid a design-time error we need to add the following line
  if (e.ClipRectangle.Width == 0)
  {
    return;
  }

  base.OnPaint(e);
  if (position > this.Width)
  {
    // Reset the text to scroll back onto the control.
    position = -(int)e.Graphics.MeasureString(text, this.Font).Width;
  }

  // Create the drawing area in memory.
  // Double buffering is used to prevent flicker.
  Bitmap bufl = new Bitmap(e.ClipRectangle.Width,
                e.ClipRectangle.Height);
  Graphics g = Graphics.FromImage(bufl);
  g.FillRectangle(new SolidBrush(this.BackColor), e.ClipRectangle);
  g.DrawString(text, this.Font, new SolidBrush(this.ForeColor),
               position, 0);
  // Render the finished image on the form.
  e.Graphics.DrawImageUnscaled(bufl, 0, 0);
  g.Dispose();
}
```

Notice the `g.Dispose()` method that will free the system memory from the `Graphics` object, which is no longer needed.

11. Build the project. Open Form1 in the designer, and you should see the `ScrollingText` control in the toolbox. Add the following controls from the toolbox to Form1:

A ScrollingText control with the following properties:

Property	**Value**
(Name)	`scrollingText`
BackColor	LightGray
Text	Scrolling text that scrolls
ForeColor	Navy
Font	Verdana; 26,25pt; style=Bold
ScrollPixelAmount	10
ScrollTimeInterval	100
Size.Width	300
Size.Height	80

A GroupBox (from the Containers tab) named grpTrackerBars, and change its text to an empty string.

Inside the GroupBox add two labels one having the text property Scroll Amount and the other Scroll Interval

Drag and drop two TrackBar controls from the Toolbox to the GroupBox, one named `tbAmount` and the other `tbInterval` with the following properties:

Property	Value
(Name)	`tbAmount`
Maximum	20
Minimum	0
Size.Width	200
Size.Height	45
TickFrequency	1
Value	1

Property	Value
(Name)	`tbInterval`
Maximum	500
Minimum	10
Size.Width	200
Size.Height	45
TickFrequency	10
Value	100

At this moment your form should look like this:

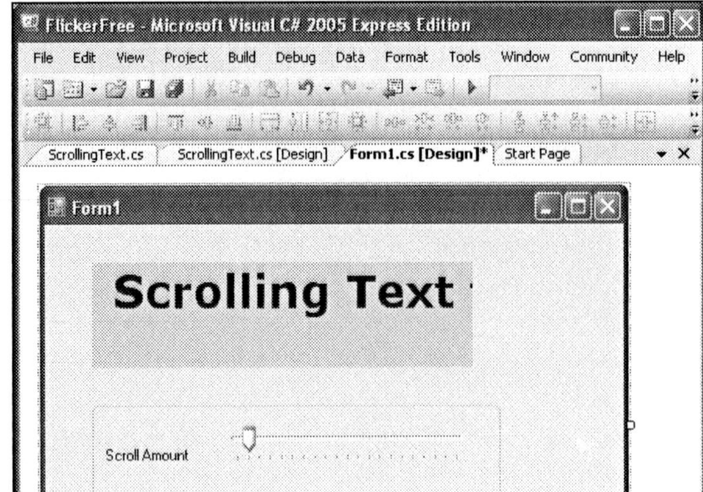

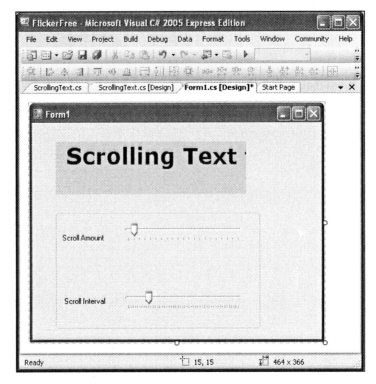

12. From the visual designer, if you double-click each of the `TrackBar` controls, Visual Studio will create Scroll event handlers. We will use these event handlers to change the ScrollingText controls' `ScrollPixelAmount` and `ScrollTimeInterval` properties:

```
private void tbInterval_Scroll(object sender, System.EventArgs e)
{
  scrollingText.ScrollTimeInterval = tbInterval.Value;
}

private void tbAmount_Scroll(object sender, System.EventArgs e)
{
  scrollingText.ScrollPixelAmount = tbAmount.Value;
}
```

13. At this point, you can execute the project and see that it works. You can reduce flickering even more by disabling the control from keeping redrawing its background. Because the output you're producing contains a background color anyway, there's no need to let the control redraw its own background too. (If you don't redraw the background too, the original content remains underneath the new content.)

    To disable background painting, all you need to do is override the `OnPaintBackground()` method. In other words, you won't call the base `OnPaintBackground()` method. Add this code to the `ScrollingText` class:

```
    protected override void OnPaintBackground
    ( System.Windows.Forms.PaintEventArgs pevent)
{
}
```

By overriding the `OnPaintBackground()` method to do nothing, we prevent it from redrawing its background, improve performance. We are painting the background ourselves with a filling method from the `Graphics` class, in the `OnPaint()` method. Note that this method by itself does reduce the flickering effect, but to eliminate it completely we used the double-buffering technique. This way, the image is built in memory instead of on the surface of the form (or control), and after the image is composed, it's drawn directly on the control.

What Just Happened?

The heart of our control, where the double-buffering technique is implemented, is the `OnPaint()` method. Here, instead of drawing directly on the display buffer using `e.Graphics`, we created our own `Graphics` object:

```
// Create the drawing area in memory.
// Double buffering is used to prevent flicker.
Bitmap bufl = new Bitmap(e.ClipRectangle.Width, e.ClipRectangle.Height);
Graphics g = Graphics.FromImage(bufl);
```

We then fill this virtual buffer with a `SolidBrush` rectangle, building the background color. Because we're drawing the background ourselves we also could prevent the control redrawing its own background, as you saw in the final step of the exercise.

```
g.FillRectangle(new SolidBrush(this.BackColor), e.ClipRectangle);
```

On the top of the background we draw the text:

```
g.DrawString(text, this.Font, new SolidBrush(this.ForeColor), position, 0);
```

The final two steps are important. The first is to finally paint the user's view by copying the temporary buffer into the display buffer. We used the `DrawImageUnscaled()` method for this purpose:

```
// Render the finished image on the form.
e.Graphics.DrawImageUnscaled(bufl, 0, 0);
```

Finally, we're disposing the temporary graphics buffer, to ensure it's cleaned out of memory as soon as possible:

```
g.Dispose();
```

Summary

This concludes our discussion about double buffering and how this can be used to improve performance. Hopefully, you'll use it carefully and decide when you can leave the .NET Framework to do most of the work by setting the `SetStyles` property, and when you have to write your own painting logic by overriding the `OnPaintBackground()` and `OnPaint()` methods.

However, be careful about how you handle drawing optimization, because while the application will be faster, you can end up with more complex code that can become harder to maintain and extend.

10
Handling Mouse Events

One of the first customer support calls my company received for our latest software product was from a customer who was having a hard time pasting a text into a textbox because when he right-clicked the control there was no "Paste" option. At the time of development we thought it was easier to paste by just pressing *CTRL+V* and that the context menu for the right-click wasn't needed; but we learned the hard way that many customers thought differently.

Don't make the same mistake when building your own programs. Since the mouse became such an essential way to interact with Windows applications, you can no longer afford to disregard correctly handling the mouse events that customers expect to be handled.

Nowadays, the operating system does most of the work for you: think about Tablet PCs, for example, where using a stylus or the old-fashioned mouse makes no difference from a developer's point of view as you still get a left click, a right click, and an (X,Y) position.

The pointing device is seen by the system as a pixel coordinate, and when the user moves the mouse, the OS moves the pointer coordinate, called the **hot spot**. Each time the mouse buttons are clicked or the mouse is moved, the control that contains the hot spot raises the appropriate mouse events that you can handle.

When creating a Windows Forms control you will have a large number of inherited events. The two most important events concerning this chapter are the `Click` and `DoubleClick` events:

```
public event EventHandler Click
public event EventHandler DoubleClick
```

Yes, you saw the bad news: there are no `LeftClick` or `RightClick` or `DoubleLeftClick` events. You must handle `Click` and `DoubleClick` and use the event arguments to check which mouse button was pressed.

However, by inheritance a lot of features are available to us. Let's take the `Cursor` class, which allows us to reshape the mouse cursor when hovering over a control. The `Cursor` class represents the image used to paint the mouse pointer. A cursor is actually a small picture whose location on the screen is controlled by the pointing device (like the mouse or a trackball). When the user moves the pointing device, the operating system moves the cursor accordingly. Among these class members you can find:

Class Member	Description
Arrow	Gets the arrow cursor
Hand	Gets the hand cursor
IBeam	Used to show where the text cursor appears when the mouse is clicked
Help	A combination of the question mark and the arrow
No	A cursor that indicates an invalid region for the operation, the user is trying to do
NoMove2D, NoMoveHoriz, PanEst, PanNorth, PanNW, PanSE, PanS, PanW	Cursors used during wheel operations when the mouse is performing scrolling-like operations
UpArrow	The up arrow cursor
WaitCursor	The hourglass shape cursor, used when the user must wait, typically for loading times

Different shapes can be used to inform the user of the operations the mouse will perform. For example, when another thread is running in the background and processing data, or when your form is waiting for a certain event, the mouse could turn into the `WaitCursor`. If you build your own text processor you might want to enable some visual indicators of scrolling, like `PanEst`, `PanNorth`, or other wheel-related cursors.

Handling Mouse Events

The best part about the mouse is that most of the time you won't have to worry about it: the mouse, as a `Cursor` object is hardly used, as apart from for changing the appearance. Instead you will look for the mouse-control interactions that will fire one of the following events: `MouseDown`, `MouseEnter`, `MouseHover`, `MouseLeave`, `MouseMove`, and `MouseUp`.

Let's talk about each one and see what each event looks like and what it does:

Mouse Event	Description
MouseDown	Will occur when the mouse pointer is over the control and any mouse button is pressed.
MouseUp	Occurs when the mouse button is released while the pointer is over the control or the pointer leaves the region of the control.
MouseEnter	Occurs when the mouse pointer (`HotSpot`) enters the control.
MouseMove	Occurs when the mouse pointer is moved over the control.
MouseHover	Occurs when the mouse pointer rests on the control.
Click	When a mouse button is pressed, before the `MouseUp` event, the `Click` event occurs.
MouseClick	When the user clicks the control with the mouse. Since a click can be generated by pressing the enter key, handle this event when you need to get information about the mouse when a click occurs.
MouseLeave	When the mouse pointer leaves the border or client area of the control.
MouseWheel	When the user rotates the mouse wheel while the control has focus, the handler for this event receives an argument of type `MouseEverntArgs`; from which you could use the `Delta` property to determine how far the mouse has been scrolled.

Each event handler will have the proper .NET Framework method signature: an object sender, and in this case, a `MouseEventArgs` object. The `MouseEventArgs` object contains information like:

- `Button`: If you want to check if the left or right button was pressed, you'll have to compare the `Button` property with one of the `MouseButtons`.
- `Location`: Contains data about the location where the event happened.
- `Delta`: The number of notches the mouse wheel was rotated.

Working with Coordinates

When writing applications that work with mouse coordinates, you may need to convert a point from the client area coordinates to the screen coordinates, or the other way round. Some location information can be received or stored in client coordinates, or some might be in your screen coordinates. To convert these coordinates you can use the `PointToClient()` and `PointToScreen()` methods available in the `Control` class.

The `Control.PointToClient()` method will compute the location of the specified screen point into client coordinates; the syntax is:

```
public Point PointToClient ( Point p )
```

The input parameter is the screen coordinate point and the return value is the same point represented in client coordinates.

The `Control.PointToScreen()` method will compute the location of the specified client point into screen coordinates:

```
public Point PointToScreen ( Point p )
```

Here `p` is the client coordinate point; the return value will be another `Point` that represents the converted value of the point `p` in screen coordinates.

Dragging and Dropping

The examples in this chapter cover a very common mouse-related feature: drag and drop. This is one of those features you're so used to, that (as a user) you're always taking it for granted. In Windows, people use features like drag and drop without thinking. And they even expect this kind of behavior from almost every program they'll ever use. So, to be consistent with the functionality the operating system is offering, you'll quite frequently want to implement such functionality in your programs as well.

The first example will consider simply dragging. You will have a control that contains an image, and you'll be able to change the location of that image by dragging it (using a mouse) inside its container.

In the second example, you'll implement real drag-and-drop functionality, where you actually "move" an object from one form (or application) to another. In this case, the user would "drag" an object from an application, and move it over another container. At this moment, if the container can accept the type of content the mouse is "carrying", the mouse cursor will change into a drag-and-drop icon. If the control cannot accept this type of information, the mouse cursor will become a circle with a line drawn through it, meaning that the operation cannot be completed. Provided that the control accepts the dragged object and the user releases the mouse button, the control will receive the information the mouse was carrying, and it will decide what to do with it.

Dragging

In this first example we will drag an image around our form. This does not imply any drag-and-drop logic, and we'll focus only on mouse movement functions. Here's how the first application will look:

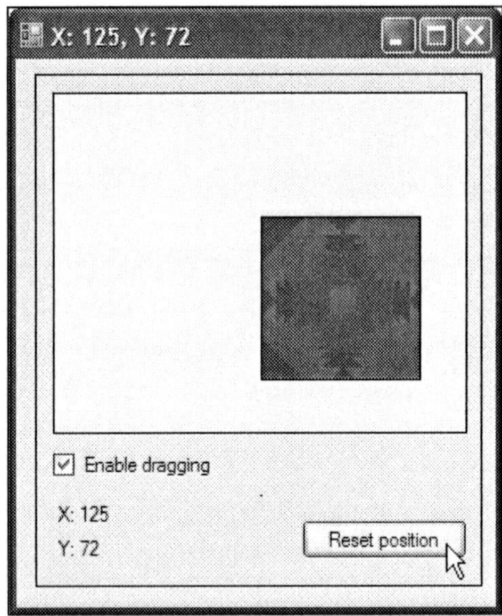

Time for Action—Dragging

1. Create a new Windows Application project named SimDrag.

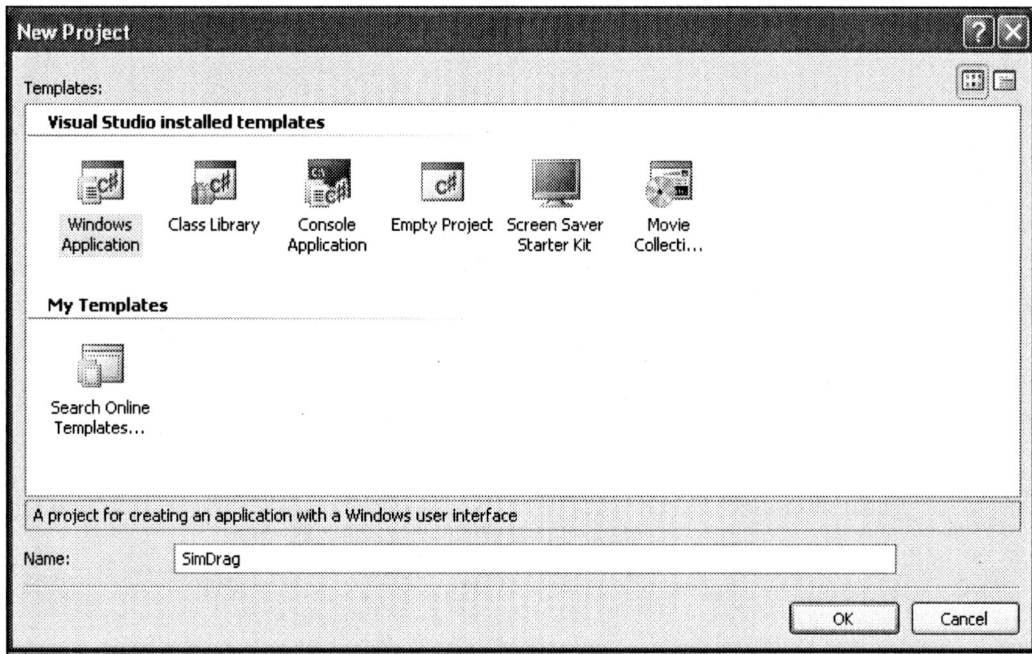

2. Rename `Form1` to `MainForm` and set the following properties:

Property	Value
(Name)	`MainForm`
Size.Width	300
Size.Height	350
Text	Sim Drag

3. Right-click on the project name in Solution Explorer and add a new User Control named DragArea, and then set these properties:

Property	Value
(Name)	`DragArea`
BorderStyle	FixedSingle
Size.Width	270
Size.Height	300

4. Add a Panel from the Containers tab of the Toolbox to your `DragArea` control. This panel will be used as the main dragging zone. Set these properties for the panel:

Property	Value
(Name)	`panelDraggingZone`
BackColor	WhiteSmoke
BorderStyle	FixedSingle
Location.X	10
Location.Y	10
Size.Width	250
Size.Height	200

5. Add a PictureBox control (which is going to be dragged around) to the center of the panel, and then set these properties for it (you may want to change the size depending on the image you're displaying):

Property	Value
(Name)	`draggingIcon`
BackColor	WhiteSmoke
BorderStyle	FixedSingle
Image	Select Local Resource, click Import, then choose an image of your choice. We'll assume you choose c:\Windows\Zapotec.bmp
Size.Width	96
Size.Height	96

At this moment your control should look like this:

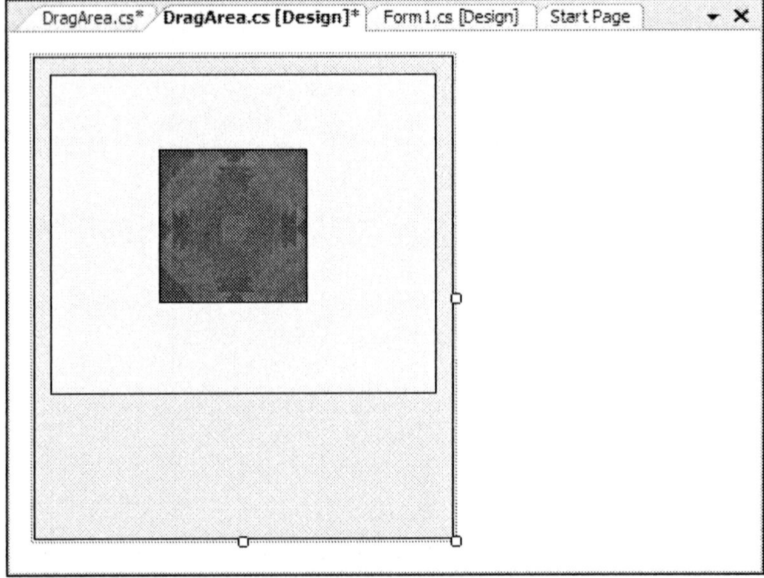

6. Let's continue by adding a few more controls to `DragArea`. Add these directly to your custom control, and don't place them inside the panel:

   A **Checkbox** to enable and disable dragging.

Property	Value
(Name)	`chkDragging`
Checked	True
CheckedState	Checked
Location.X	10
Location.Y	220
Text	Enable dragging

   Another two **Labels** to display the X and Y values of the draggable image:

   The **Label** to display the X value of draggable image.

Property	Value
(Name)	`lblX`
Location.X	10
Location.Y	250
Text	X:

   The **Label** to display the Y value of draggable image.

Property	Value
(Name)	`lblY`
Location.X	10
Location.Y	270
Text	Y:

   A **Button** to reset the position.

Property	Value
(Name)	`btnReset`
Location.X	160
Location.Y	260
Size.Width	100
Size.Height	23
Text	Reset position

Now your control should look like that in the following picture:

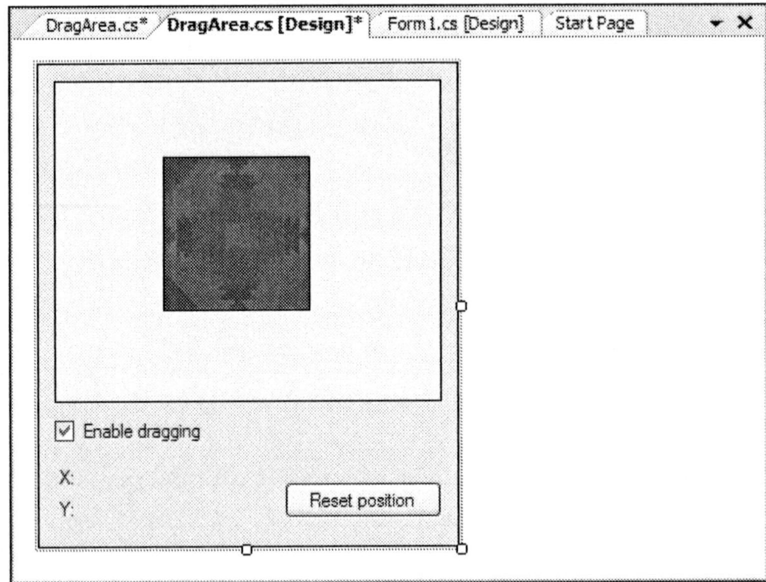

7. Select the `draggingIcon` control, select the **Events** list from the **Properties** window, and add three event handlers for the following events:
    - `LocationChanged`
    - `MouseDown`
    - `MouseMove`

And add the following code:

```
private void dragginIcon_LocationChanged(object sender, EventArgs e)
{
  lblX.Text = "X: " + draggingIcon.Location.X.ToString();
  lblY.Text = "Y: " + draggingIcon.Location.Y.ToString();
}

private void dragginIcon_MouseDown(System.Object sender,
  System.Windows.Forms.MouseEventArgs e)
{
  if (chkDragging.Checked)
  {
     clickOffsetX = e.X;
     clickOffsetY = e.Y;
  }
}

private void dragginIcon_MouseMove(System.Object sender,
  System.Windows.Forms.MouseEventArgs e)
{
  if (e.Button == MouseButtons.Left &&  chkDragging.Checked)
  {
    draggingIcon.Left = e.X + draggingIcon.Left - clickOffsetX;
    draggingIcon.Top = e.Y + draggingIcon.Top - clickOffsetY;
  }
}
```

8. Add the following members to the `DragArea` class:

```
private int clickOffsetX, clickOffsetY;
```

9. Add a new method called `ResetPosition()` to the `DragArea` class:

```
private void ResetPosition()
{
  draggingIcon.Left = (panelDraggingZone.Width - draggingIcon.Width) / 2;
  draggingIcon.Top = (panelDraggingZone.Height - draggingIcon.Height)
                     / 2;
}
```

10. Add a new delegate and a helper `EventArgs` class that we will use to create our own `LocationChanged` event. Add them directly in the `SimDrag` namespace (don't place them inside the `DragArea` class!). Theoretically the location of these new structures isn't important as long as they are located in the `SimDrag` namespace, but the Visual C# Express designer requires the `DragArea` class to be the first in the namespace, so add this code after the `DragArea` class:

```
public delegate void LocationChangedEvent(LocationChangedEventArgs e);
public class LocationChangedEventArgs : EventArgs
{
  int x;
  int y;

  public int X
  {
    get
    {
      return x;
    }
  }

  public int Y
  {
    get
    {
      return y;
    }
  }

  internal LocationChangedEventArgs(int x, int y)
  {
    this.x = x;
    this.y = y;
  }
}
```

11. In the `DragArea` class, add a new `LocationChanged` event that will hide the control's `LocationChanged` event using the `new` keyword:

```
public new event LocationChangedEvent LocationChanged;
```

12. Modify `dragginIcon_LocationChanged()` to fire the new event:

```
private void dragginIcon_LocationChanged(object sender, EventArgs e)
{
  lblX.Text = "X: " + draggingIcon.Location.X.ToString();
  lblY.Text = "Y: " + draggingIcon.Location.Y.ToString();
  // fire the event if anyone's listening)
  if (LocationChanged != null)
  {
    LocationChangedEventArgs lcea =
      new LocationChangedEventArgs(draggingIcon.Location.X,
                                   draggingIcon.Location.Y);
```

```
            LocationChanged(lcea);
        }
    }
```

This way, the event will bubble up to the main form and we will be able to track the location of the dragged icon.

13. We now have to create an event handler for the button's `Click` event and add code so that when the user clicks the `Reset position` button the draggingIcon picturebox control will be nicely centered:

```
    private void btnReset_Click(object sender, EventArgs e)
    {
        ResetPosition();
    }
```

14. At this moment the project is compilable. Build the project and then switch to the designer of `MainForm`. You should see the `DragArea` control in the Toolbox. Drag a `DragArea` control from the Toolbox to your form, and resize the form so that the `DragArea` will fit nicely.

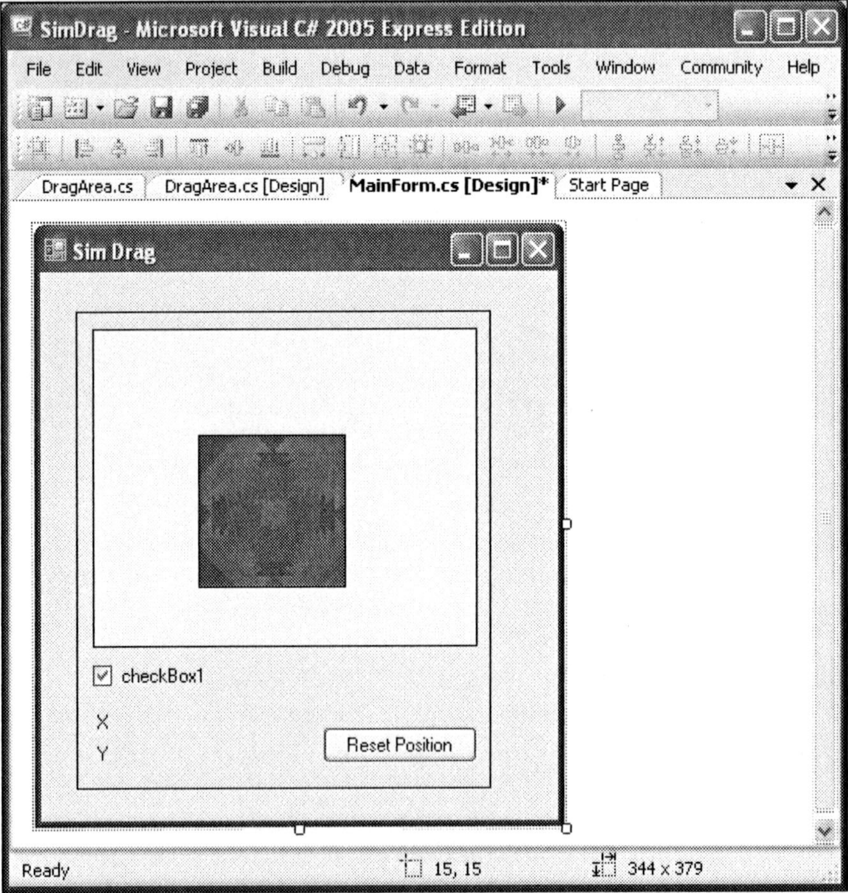

15. Select the `DragArea` object, and use its **Properties** window to generate the event handler for the `LocationChanged` event. Complete the code like this:

```
private void dragArea1_LocationChanged(LocationChangedEventArgs e)
{
  Text = "X: " + e.X + ", Y: " + e.Y;
}
```

16. Be sure to save the project. You will make changes to this project in the following chapter.

What Just Happened?

Build and run the application. If everything works as planned, you should be able to drag the image on the control, and its location will be displayed both by the control and by the form (in its title bar):

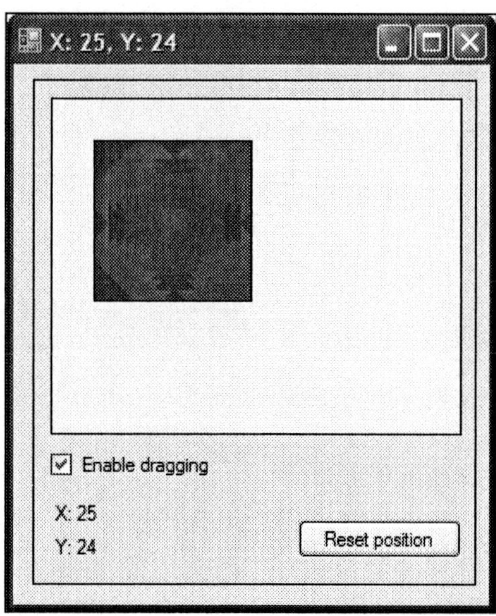

The members that hold mouse location when the user clicks the control are `clickOffsetX` and `clickOffsetY`, and their values are set in the `MouseDown` event handler of the `PictureBox`, which keeps firing as long as the mouse button is pressed:

```
private void draggingIcon_MouseDown(object sender, MouseEventArgs e)
{
  if (chkDragging.Checked)
  {
    clickOffsetX = e.X;
    clickOffsetY = e.Y;
  }
}
```

The `clickOffsetX` and `clickOffsetY` are used to move the picture according to the location that was clicked. The location is changed only if the **Enable dragging** checkbox is checked.

You may have noticed we have some duplicate functionality. The picture location is shown both in the control itself, and on the parent form. Both ways can work for your own projects, depending on what you want to do. You can see that it's easy and efficient to fire events from your control, and let the forms or controls using your control decide whether they want to implement an event handler for those events.

Dragging and Dropping

In this new example, we'll create a more general control: a picture drag-and-drop control with preview. We could use it later to send pictures using a web service or organize them on the hard disk.

We'll drag and drop pictures from the desktop and we'll resize them, if needed, so that we could see six of them at once. We won't do any extensive checking or error handling and we'll focus more on the actual drag and drop.

Time for Action—Dragging and Dropping.

1. Create a new Windows Application project and name it DragAndDrop.
2. Add a new User Control, just as you did in the previous exercises and name it DrawingPanel. Set the following properties:

Property	Value
Size.Width	360
Size.Height	180

3. While still in the custom control's designer window, add a Panel and set the following properties:

Property	Value
(Name)	drawingArea
AllowDrop	True
BackColor	WhiteSmoke
BorderStyle	FixedSingle
Dock	Fill

4. Switch the control to Code View, and add this method to the DrawingPanel class:

```
public partial class DrawingPanel : UserControl
{
  public DrawingPanel()
  {
    InitializeComponent();
  }

  public void Clear()
  {
    drawingArea.Controls.Clear();
    this.count = 0;
    this.left = 0;
    this.top = 0;
  }
}
```

5. Modify the constructor of `DrawingPanel` like this:

```
public DrawingPanel()
{
  InitializeComponent();
  picSize = new Size(90, 90);
  this.maxPictures = (this.Height / picSize.Height) *
                     (this.Width / picSize.Width);
}
```

6. That was the easy part. Everything is in place and we only have to add the control logic. Right-click the `DrawingPanel.cs` control in the Solution Explorer and select View Code. We will add some class fields that we'll use later on. We recommend that you add them just below the lines containing the `class` keyword and the opening brace. Add the following members to the `DrawingPanel` class:

```
public partial class DrawingPanel : UserControl
{
  int left = 0;
  int top = 0;
  int count = 0;
  int maxPictures = 0;
  Size picSize;
```

   The `top` and `left` fields will be used to set the location of new picture boxes that we'll create.

7. Build the project. Open the `Form1` form in the designer, and drag one `DrawingPanel` object from the Toolbox to the form. (Change the width of the form to 400 so the new control will fit.)

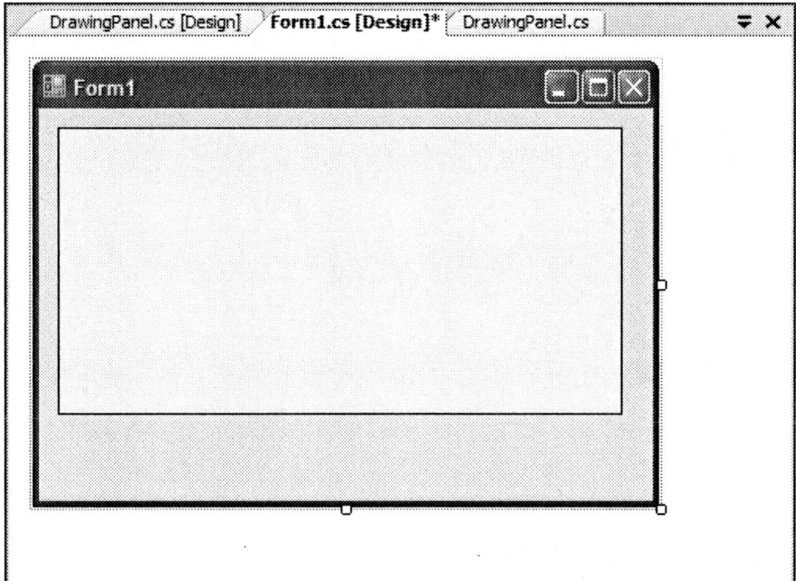

8. Add a Button below the control, name it `btnClear`, set its `Text` to Clear, and create an event handler for its `Click` event by double-clicking the button. Then complete the generated code like this:

```
private void btnClear_Click(object sender, EventArgs e)
{
  drawingPanel1.Clear();
}
```

9. There are two key events that you need to implement to enable dragging and dropping logic. The first one is `DragEnter` and we will create its event handler for the panel we added to the user control, which will enable us to drag pictures to the form. Open the `DrawingPanel` control in the designer, select the panel, and use the Properties window to generate the event handler for the `DragEnter` event. Then complete the code like this:

```
private void drawingArea_DragEnter(object sender, DragEventArgs e)
{
  if (e.Data.GetDataPresent(DataFormats.FileDrop) && count <
     maxPictures)
  {
    e.Effect = DragDropEffects.Copy;
  }
  else
  {
    e.Effect = DragDropEffects.None;
  }
}
```

10. When the image is ready to be copied we will have to handle the `DragDrop` event. Use the designer to create the event handler, and complete the code like this:

```
private void drawingArea_DragDrop(object sender, DragEventArgs e)
{
  if (e.Data.GetDataPresent(DataFormats.FileDrop))
  {
    string[] fileData = (string[])e.Data.GetData(DataFormats.FileDrop);
    try
    {
      Bitmap bitmap = new Bitmap(fileData[0]);
      AddPictureBox(bitmap);
    }
    catch (Exception ex)
    {
      MessageBox.Show( "An error has occurred: " + ex.Message,
        "Error",
        MessageBoxButtons.OK,
        MessageBoxIcon.Error);
    }
  }
}
```

11. Add the `PictureBox` helper method referenced in `drawingArea_DragDrop()`. This method should add a new `PictureBox` to the panel and position it nicely.

```
private void AddPictureBox(Bitmap bitmap)
{
  PictureBox pictureBox = new PictureBox();
  drawingArea.Controls.Add(pictureBox);
  if (bitmap.Width > picSize.Width - 20 || bitmap.Height >
     picSize.Height - 20)
  {
    bitmap = ResizeBitmap(bitmap);
  }

  pictureBox.BackgroundImage = bitmap;
  pictureBox.BackgroundImageLayout = ImageLayout.Center;
```

```
        pictureBox.Height = picSize.Height; pictureBox.Width = picSize.Width;
        pictureBox.Location = new Point(left, top);
        if (count < maxPictures)
        {
          this.left += picSize.Width;
          count++;
          if (left == drawingArea.Width)
          {
            this.top += picSize.Height;
            this.left = 0;
          }
        }
      }
```

Most of the code above handles creating the `PictureBox` control, such as setting `BackgroundImage` or `Height` and `Width`.

12. Let's now create yet another helper method, `ResizeBitmap()`, which we called in `AddPictureBox()` to resize the pictures that are too large. We're using a variable called `ratio` to avoid having pictures skewed:

```
      private Bitmap ResizeBitmap(Bitmap bitmap)
      {
        double ratio;
        int height;
        int width;
        Size size;
        if (bitmap.Height >= bitmap.Width)
        {
          ratio = (float)bitmap.Height / 70;
        }
        else
        {
          ratio = ((double)bitmap.Width) / 70.0;
        }
        height = Convert.ToInt32(bitmap.Height / ratio);
        width = Convert.ToInt32(bitmap.Width / ratio);
        size = new Size(width, height);
        Bitmap newBitmap = new Bitmap(bitmap, size);
        return newBitmap;
      }
```

13. Execute the project, and drag a few image files to your control:

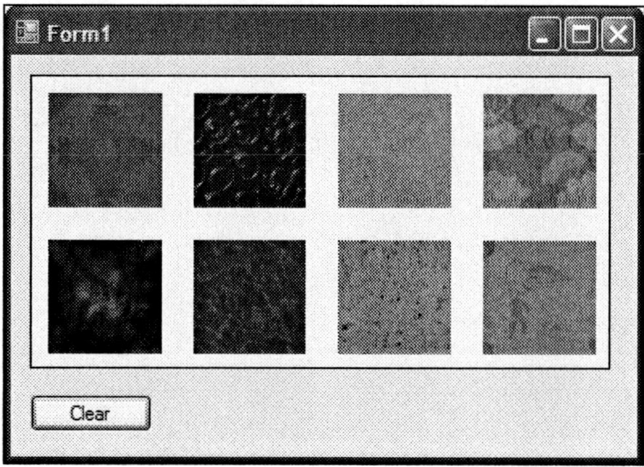

What Just Happened?

If you take another look at the code, you'll see that most of the work was done to resize and arrange the pictureboxes. The logic behind the drag-and-drop actions is built into the event handlers for `DragDrop` and `DragEnter`:

```
private void drawingArea_DragEnter(object sender, DragEventArgs e)
{
  if (e.Data.GetDataPresent(DataFormats.FileDrop) && count < maxPictures)
  {
    e.Effect = DragDropEffects.Copy;
  }
  else
  {
    e.Effect = DragDropEffects.None;
  }
}
```

The `DragEnter` event is fired when the dragged object enters a control that has the `AllowDrop` property set to `true`, as does the panel in our case. We use the `FileDrop` data format because we're dropping an entire image file. We're also counting the pictures in the panel, to forbid adding more than a maximum of `maxPictures`.

The drag-and-drop magic happens in the `drawingArea_DragDrop()` method. This method basically checks again to see if the file format is a `FileDrop` and will extract the information stored in the `DragEventArgs` object e into a `fileData` array. The path to the file is stored in the first element of the array and we will use the path to create a new `Bitmap` from that file.

```
private void drawingArea_DragDrop(object sender, DragEventArgs e)
    {
      if (e.Data.GetDataPresent(DataFormats.FileDrop))
      {
        string[] fileData = (string[])e.Data.GetData(DataFormats.FileDrop);
        try
        {
          Bitmap bitmap = new Bitmap(fileData[0]);
          AddPictureBox(bitmap);
        }
        catch (Exception ex)
        {
          MessageBox.Show( "An error has occurred: " + ex.Message,
            "Error",
            MessageBoxButtons.OK,
            MessageBoxIcon.Error);
        }
      }
    }
```

If things go wrong, a `MessageBox` is shown containing the error message.

Summary

The mouse plays a very important role in most Windows Applications, and learning how to deal with mouse events is an essential asset in your developer's skills. Data about mouse events comes in the form of the mouse position and the actions that triggered the event (such as mouse clicks), and you can handle these events to respond to users' actions.

One of the most powerful uses for the mouse is dragging and dropping text, images, files, and many other kinds of objects. This feature is one of the most commonly used features of the Windows operating system, and practically any user interface enables it through various methods; adding this kind of functionality to your applications can only be very well received by the users.

Taming the mouse usually won't bring any performance improvements, or add new features per se, but it will give your application that finished touch that separates a so-called "beta" application from a professional one.

11
Implementing Design-Time Support

How many times have you looked around your code, trying to find a special custom property or essential field? How many times have you opened the "Find and Replace" window to search for a certain comment?

If you have ever longingly looked at the properties of the .NET built-in controls and how they can be manipulated from Visual C# Express, then you'll love this chapter. It's all about taking custom controls to the next level by making them easier to use from Visual C# Express, just like the regular .NET Framework controls.

This theory is going to be really fun to explore because the .NET Framework 2.0 brought a lot of goodies to what the 1.1 version already had, such as:

- Your toolbox got smarter. There are a lot of new components in Visual C# Express, but there is room for user components too: more categories and a smart toolbox that gets automatically populated as soon as you create and compile new controls in your project.
- Do you like the Smart Tag available for some of the built-in controls? You can add similar functionality to your controls!
- Support for undo/redo features, allowing you to automatically accept or reject changes to your control's properties.
- The Visual C# Express designer can assist the user of your controls in positioning the controls through a feature called **snaplines** that you can add to your controls to provide this feature.

The complete list of new features is larger and the implications are more complex than can be covered in this short chapter. An excellent MSDN article called *What's New In Design-Time Support in the .NET Framework 2.0*, available at `http://msdn2.microsoft.com/en-us/library/ms171832.aspx`, will reveal more technical details.

For the rest of this chapter we'll get you started implementing design-time support for your custom controls.

Building Designer-Friendly Controls

Basically, the design-time support architecture of the .NET Framework allows you to develop custom controls that will expose certain properties through the Visual C# Express IDE. Allowing users to modify the properties of your controls through Smart Tags or the Property window will certainly be very beneficial and will make your controls look professional and behave professionally.

As you might have expected, there are certain interfaces or classes that you work with, which must be implemented if you want to enable customized design-time extensions. The design-time environment typically includes design-time services that can be accessed and used by the design-time mechanisms.

The main tools that allow you implement design-time support are **attributes**, **designers**, **type converters**, and **UI type editors**. Attributes are associated with types and type members in order to correlate the design-time support providers.

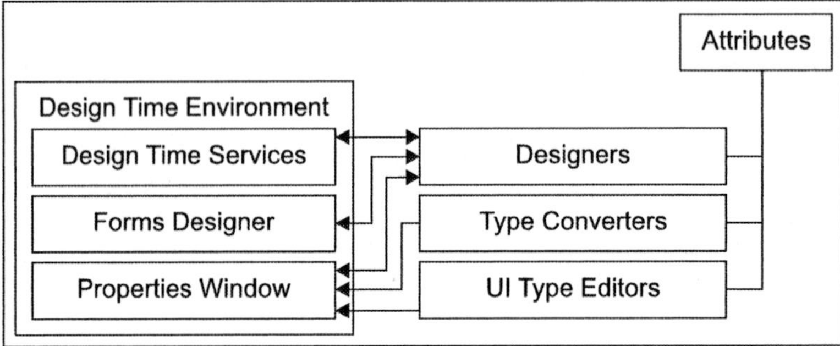

Attributes

Say you are working on a custom control that's going to be used as a feedback form for various projects developed by your shop. Because you are a really good programmer and you believe in the power of code reuse, you want to make your control as good as possible, so that it will require little or no modifications when using it in different projects. And you want to use design-time extensions.

The first step that you'll probably take is defining a default event to your control. This way you'd only need to double-click the control in the designer to have the designer generate the signature for that default event. That's where the `Type` attributes step in. Have a look at the following code:

```
[DefaultEvent("OnChange")]
public class FeedbackControl
{
  public FeedbackControl()
  {
  }
}
```

When you want to make various class properties editable through the Properties window, you'll need to use, guess what? Class member attributes. Here's an example:

```
[Browsable("True")]
public string Name
{
}
```

The following is the list of other attributes that might come in handy:

- `BrowsableAttibute`: Specifies if a property should be displayed in the Property browser
- `DescriptionAttribute`: Defines a small block of text to be displayed at the bottom of the Property browser
- `EditorAttribute`: Specifies the editor that will be used for editing a property in a visual designer
- `CategoryAttribute`: Specifies the name of the category in which a property or event is grouped
- `LocalizableAttribute`: Specifies that a property can be localized
- `TypeConverterAttribute`: Sets the type converter to use for converting the type of the property to another data type

When adding such an attribute to your code, you'll use a syntax similar to that used in the examples presented earlier. Basically attributes associate a type or type member with a class so that it extends design-time behavior. A `DesignerAttribute` associates a type with a designer: an `EditorAttribute` associates a type or type member with a UI type editor, a `TypeConverterAttribute` associates a type or type member with a type converter. We will see later in this chapter what `TypeConverters` are and what they are used for.

Designers

Suppose, you have a nice custom control that can be modified a bit using the Properties window. Can it be customized a bit more? Could we change the data bindings from child controls?

Sure we can! That's where Designers step in. They can be considered helper classes that can alter the way your control looks, how it is initialized, or how it interacts with the user. Designers customize the behavior of a control.

A Designer is assigned through a `DesignerAttribute`, just like in the following example:

```
[Designer("System.Windows.Forms.Design.DocumentDesigner,
          System.Windows.Forms.Design.DLL",
          typeof(IRootDesigner)), DesignerCategory("Form")]
public class MyForm : ContainerControl
{
    // Insert code here.
}
```

Type Converters

Let's go back to our feedback form project. The form is supposed to be used by different teams in their big projects, so that users can provide some kind of feedback regarding the software they bought. Some might require a larger font; others might require a certain color palette.

Your first reaction could be something along the lines "*let's open up the code and hack the control.*" Here is some good news: you don't have to do that anymore, since the .NET Framework brings some really interesting feature named **type converters**.

Type converters allow you to convert values between different types of data; they can be implemented to convert values between built-in types and custom types. Type converters also provide the infrastructure to enable configuring a property at design time through a **Property** browser, and produce the required initialization code. To write a type converter, you need to derive a class from the `TypeConverter` class, and override the `ConvertFrom()` and `ConvertTo()` methods. `ConvertFrom()` parses the specified string and converts it to an instance of the target type. It's actually easier than it looks:

```
[TypeConverterAttribute(typeof(StringArrayConverter))]
public string[] Items
{

}
```

Here we have a `TypeConverter` that will take `string[]` array `items` and will somehow convert its members to some values you might want to use in your program.

UI Type Editors

UI type editors allow you to build a custom interface for editing the value of a property of a control, and displaying the value of that property at design time. Type editors are classes that inherit from the base class `UITypeEditor`.

UI type editors are type-specific and provide a user interface that is used to configure properties of the type it is built to support. UI type editors can be displayed as a drop-down configuration interface, or as a Windows form for configuring a property. Using type editors you can implement design-time interfaces for complex property types.

Type editors can let you edit a property as a string, and then using a type converter, that string can be converted to the correct data type inside the control. For properties whose values need to belong in a fixed set, you could use a type editor to display a drop-down list with the possible values. For complex properties, you can use a type editor that displays a modal dialog box with various options that can be set.

When implementing a custom UI type editor, the following tasks must be completed:

1. Create a class that derives from `UITypeEditor`, and override its constructor for any initialization work.
2. Override the `GetEditStyle()` method to set the type of the editor style you want to use. Each time you select a control in the designer, the **Properties** window is repainted to show the property values of the selected control. When you select a property, the designer will query the `GetEditStyle()` method in order to determine how to represent the property entry. Our method will return a value that specifies the style, which can be `UITypeEditorStyle.None` (the property will be edited as a string), `UITypeEditorStyle.Modal` (modal dialog box), or `UITypeEditorStyle.DropDown` (drop-down window).

3. Override the `EditValue()` method, which is responsible for popping up the editing window and for any operation necessary to get and store the new value.
    - For a modal UI type editor, we need to query a service provider for the `IWindowsFormsEditorServices` interface; this will provide the position information for our dialog box. Our `EditValue()` method implementation will create a new instance of this form, initialize it with the current value property, and then pass it to the `ShowDialog()` method for execution by the designer.
    - For a drop-down UI type editor, we query a service provider for the `IWindowsFormsEditorService` interface that will provide information on the position and size of our UI. The `EditValue()` method implementation creates a new instance of our control, initializes it with the current property value, and passes it to the `DropDownControl()` method for execution.
4. Override `GetPaintValueSupported()` to indicate that the editor supports displaying the property value.
5. Override the `PaintValue()` method to implement the display of the value's representation. We can display a graphical representation of our property's value by overriding the `PaintValue()` method and use the provided `PaintValueEventArgs` to draw a representation in a small rectangle on the left side of the property's entry in PropertyGrid (you will need to pay attention to the `Bounds` property defined in the `PaintValueEventArgs` parameter).

Property Editors

Property Editors are displayed in the drop-down area inside the Properties window itself, and are also able to appear in modal windows.

`Dock` is one of these properties; it helps aligning the control to the edge of our form, and designates where the control resides in the form.

- `Bottom`: Docks to the bottom of the container.
- `Fill`: Fills all unused space in the container.
- `Left`: Docks to the left side of the container.
- `None`: Does not dock, but appears wherever we first set it. When arranging the control on the form (in the designer view) we actually are setting up the `System.Windows.Forms.Control.Location` that sets (or gets) the coordinates of the upper-left corner of the control relative to the upper-left corner of the container.
- `Right`: Docks to the right side of the container.
- `Top`: Docks to the top of the container.

Creating Property Editors

To show you an example for adding design-time support to a custom control, we'll extend the first example of Chapter 10—the SimDrag project. In the exercise that follows, you'll be adding two new properties to your `DragArea` control: `CanvasColor` and `PictureSize`.

The `CanvasColor` property allows you to edit the background color of the panel where you drag the image directly in the designer, using the Properties window. The `PictureSize` property will let you choose the size of the draggable color, using a slider. Follow the steps of the following exercise, and enjoy the effects!

Time for Action—Adding Design-Time Support

1. Open the `SimDrag` solution that you built in Chapter 10.
2. Open the `DragArea.cs` control and select View Code.
3. Let's change the code so that you can change the background of the panel from the host form. We must create a new property that will encapsulate the panel `BackColor` property. Add this property to the `DragArea` class:

```
public Color CanvasColor
{
  get
  {
    return panelDraggingZone.BackColor;
  }
  set
  {
    panelDraggingZone.BackColor = value;
  }
}
```

4. Add the following attributes to make the property browsable and set a default value. Add the highlighted code right above the property you just added:

```
[Browsable(true),
 DefaultValue(typeof(Color)),
 Description("The control background")]
public Color CanvasColor
{
  get
  {
    return panelDraggingZone.BackColor;
  }
  set
  {
    panelDraggingZone.BackColor = value;
  }
}
```

5. Build the project, and switch to the designer of the host form (`MainForm`). You will notice that the `CanvasColor` property has appeared in the Properties window, and that it can easily be modified using the editor:

6. Now let's add a new class. Right-click the project name (not the solution name) and select Add | New Item. Select the Class template, and name the class `PictureSizeUITypeEditor`. Then click Add.
7. Modify the template to add the required namespace references, and modify the class to inherit from `UITypeEditor`:

```
using System;
using System.Collections.Generic;
using System.Text;
using System.Drawing.Design;
using System.Windows.Forms.Design;
using System.Windows.Forms;
using System.Drawing;

namespace SimDrag
{
  class PictureSizeUITypeEditor : UITypeEditor
  {

  }
}
```

8. Add the following code to the `PictureSizeUITypeEditor` class:

```
class PictureSizeUITypeEditor : UITypeEditor
{
  public override UITypeEditorEditStyle
    GetEditStyle(System.ComponentModel.ITypeDescriptorContext context)
  {
    return UITypeEditorEditStyle.DropDown;
  }

  public override object
       EditValue(System.ComponentModel.ITypeDescriptorContext context,
               IServiceProvider provider, object value)
  {
    IWindowsFormsEditorService iwfes =
                (IWindowsFormsEditorService)provider.GetService(
```

```
                        typeof(IWindowsFormsEditorService));
        if (iwfes == null)
        {
          return null;
        }

        TrackBar trackB = new TrackBar();
        trackB.Orientation = Orientation.Vertical;
        trackB.SetRange(30, 90);
        trackB.Size = new Size(50, 100);
        trackB.TickFrequency = 15;
        iwfes.DropDownControl(trackB);
        Size picSize = new Size(trackB.Value, trackB.Value);
        return picSize;
      }
    }
```

9. Switch again to the code of `DragArea.cs`, and add an assembly reference to the beginning of the class:

```
using System.Drawing.Design;
```

10. Then add the `PictureSize` property to the `DragArea` class:

```
[Browsable(true),
 DefaultValue(90),
 Description("Picture size (width and height are equal)"),
 Editor(typeof(PictureSizeUITypeEditor), typeof(UITypeEditor))]
public Size PictureSize
{
  get
  {
    return draggingIcon.Size;
  }
  set
  {
    draggingIcon.Size = value;
  }
}
```

11. Build the project again, and open `MainForm` in the designer. Select your custom control, and see that it now has a property called `PictureSize` in the Properties window, which can be changed using a Trackbar:

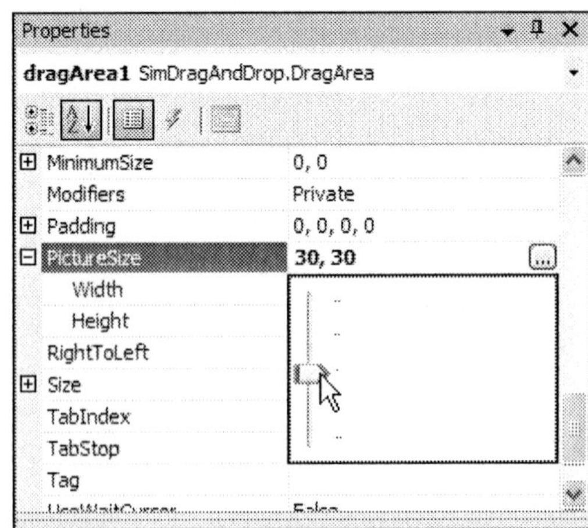

What Just Happened?

The newly added code is quite straightforward. The Editor takes two `System.Type` arguments: the first is the type editor and the second is the `UITypeEditor` type. Also, we've supplied a simple description.

That said, we needed to create the `PictureSizeUITypeEditor` class. This was inherited from the `System.Drawing.Design.UITypeEditor` class so we needed to override two methods: `GetEditStyle()` and `EditValue()`. We used a drop-down window to set the size of our rectangle. When the form designer paints the **Properties** window with the values of all the properties of the control, it calls the `GetEditStyle()` method. If we need a more complex way to control this property, we can use a modal dialog box in the place of the dropdown.

To display the control in the drop-down area we used the `IWindowsFormsEditorService`. We used a standard TrackBar and provided the configuration input for it: orientation, range, size, and frequency. As you can see, we used `iwfes` (so the `IWindowsFormsEditorService` class) to show our TrackBar in the drop-down window.

Summary

One of the true strengths of the .NET Framework custom control model is the design-time support: any of your custom controls could be used just like any regular .NET control and expose its internal workings so they could be changed during the design of the Windows Form. It could be actually covered in a whole book of its own—that's how many types of examples and situations you could encounter!

The design-time support's value will be critical if you want to provide custom controls for others without making the source code available for them to modify.

12

Designing Intuitive Interfaces

A common complaint leveled at modern software (or indeed old software for that matter) is the lack of "user friendliness", otherwise known as intuitiveness. It is often the case that the people who actually design software interfaces are those least suited to the job, at least from the user's perspective. A control can be the most stable and data-efficient one ever made, but if the user has difficulty using it then it has failed.

Programmers are already extremely competent in computing; few events happen on a day-to-day basis that we don't already understand, or know how to deal with. We often take simple things completely for granted. When we coders look at a computer screen, we see a thousand different things in the first few seconds. We can tell what version of what operating system is installed, we can guess the screen's resolution and color depth, we can imagine the countless event handlers behind the myriad controls on screen, and we can perceive the tiniest delays caused by hard disk accesses. The list goes on much further than you might think, and it makes programmers so much more in tune with our beloved computers than most other everyday computer users.

This, unfortunately, does not always make for good Graphical User Interface (GUI) design.

In this chapter we'll examine how the users see our interfaces. We'll think about users' needs and how we can cater for them. At the end of this chapter we will address some important aspects of our users' computing experience.

The Relationship between User and Computer

Computers are in an interesting position; they are highly complex tools that can be found both at home and at work. It is extremely rare to find a business that doesn't have at least one computer on its premises, and the large majority of homes also have one. This situation tends to breed two distinct kinds of users: those that learn just enough to get along on a day-to-day basis and those who decide to devote a huge amount of time to learning as much as they can. And of course there are many people starting in the former category and making their way towards the latter.

This is not to say that all home users are novices and all work users are experts, as this couldn't be further from the truth. Quite often home users voluntarily spend a lot of time doing a wide range of different activities with their computers: playing games, writing letters, doing homework, or doing their accounts. Conversely, work users tend to have a much more limited avenue of computer use that depends solely on their job. It's common for them to use only one or two programs all day and spend little time learning things that interest them about IT. A worker who has used a computer every day for several years may know less about computers than a home user would, who tinkers around with a PC at weekends.

People will learn faster if they enjoy what they are learning about, which is one reason why home users frequently have a wider knowledge than work users; they can pick and choose what they want to do.

This gives us a wide spectrum of talent that we must think about when we develop our software. This spectrum may not even affect the way our program works, but it should affect the way our program presents itself and our users' perception of what is actually going on "under the hood".

Since everyone that uses a computer could be labeled as a "user" (yes, even programmers) we will, for the duration of this chapter, define a "user" as someone that uses the software that we are designing. Programmers will not fall under this category unless otherwise stated.

Communicating with Users

The most important thing to think about during interface design is what the user might be expecting at any given time. Let's say a program has just loaded and is waiting for the user to do something, a good interface will make clear that it is waiting for user interaction. There are many ways to indicate this including:

- **Display a written message**: For example, "*Please select an option to begin working*".
- **Use images to denote program status**: For example, an egg timer icon to indicate that the program is still busy.
- **Use sound to notify**: A short sound sample can alert the user to what is happening; such as a sound played when a new email has arrived. Some programs even use sampled human speech to help the user decide what to do. However, this approach is rare now, but can be a very effective approach when designing software for children or people with disabilities such as visual impairment.

Let's say our user has just asked for a lengthy process to start; the user will probably wait a few seconds before starting to wonder if the process has finished or not. We want to avoid uncertainty at all costs, as this can (and will) lead to our users losing confidence in our software. We need to try to give positive feedback at all times even when something goes wrong.

Requests, Input Parsing, Fault Tolerance, and Feedback

The most unpredictable factor in software development is the user. We really have no idea who is going to use our software. OK, we know who our software is aimed at, but actual users never fit that specification exactly so we need to "overcompensate" just to be satisfied that our program won't fail at an important moment. Requests, Input Parsing, Fault Tolerance, and Feedback are all closely related. Indeed they are all links in a chain.

Requests are any kind of questions that we ask our user. There are many forms of request, among them are:

- "Please select an option"—This will prompt the user to click a button, type an option number, or maybe quit our program altogether.
- "Enter your email address"—This asks the user to type in a string that must conform to a very strict formatting policy; this can be fraught with problems.
- "Load a file"—This requires the user to know about the file system on the computer, and how to navigate it without getting lost.

Game controller (joystick) input, and biometrics data (fingerprint and iris scanning) also fall into this category, but these are usually tightly controlled by the hardware and require less in the way of on-the-fly validation.

Input Parsing is the largest of these four topics. Since the range of input varies so much, there must be at least as many provisions in place to make sure that the incoming data is in a format that our software can cope with and understand. For instance, if we ask our user to type in their date of birth, there are many different ways to do so. A British user might enter "3 February 1980"; an American user may type "02/03/80". This is a problem because both of these strings represent the same date. There are many situations like that and in this particular scenario we would need to refer to the country's local settings to determine which format the user entered. .NET has many ways to let us validate and parse user input of any kind.

Fault Tolerance is the fine art of handling unexpected occurrences, be they an error or omission in user data, or an event that happens out of the expected sequence. A program that throws up error messages at the slightest provocation will not inspire confidence or trust in its users. Software that can absorb such problems, and even suggest ways to fix them (or prevent them happening in the first place) will be impressive and will save the users a lot of time and stress.

Feedback affects all three other categories; communication should be consistent throughout the program. A system of warnings, hints, and notifications should be devised in order for users to quickly interpret the information presented to them. .NET already provides access to the normal Windows methods for warning users of program events, but it may still be necessary to develop one of your own.

Let's explore some of these principles with a practical exercise. Let's build a control that manages user input, gives visual information about important internal workings, and provides helpful features. A good candidate for this might be a simple drawing control that provides a few tools to let the user do basic sketches. Such a control could be used effectively when incorporated into Internet-based messaging programs, to allow two people to sketch out something they would normally have to describe at length in words.

The area of user input that we will be primarily interested in is the mouse. This is because the mouse can be used to quickly position the cursor accurately on the screen. We are helped by a range of events focused on mouse manipulation. We shall use these events to good effect along with a few OOP techniques to create a simple but effective UserControl that we will call `Sketcher`.

Examining the Sketcher Control

To keep things straightforward we will include just two drawing tools, a `FreeHand` tool and a `StraightLine` tool. Both of these are implemented as classes that inherit from a `DrawingTool` base class. There is a button on the UserControl for each of these two tools (`DrawingTool` is abstract and is itself unable to create any graphics directly, but it provides functionality for its derived classes). There is also a Clear button that our user can click if they want to start over from a clean page.

Our page is represented by a Picturebox that fills the majority of the UserControl's area. To the right of the FreeHand and StraightLine buttons there is a small Picturebox that is for displaying a preview of the current pen style that the user has selected.

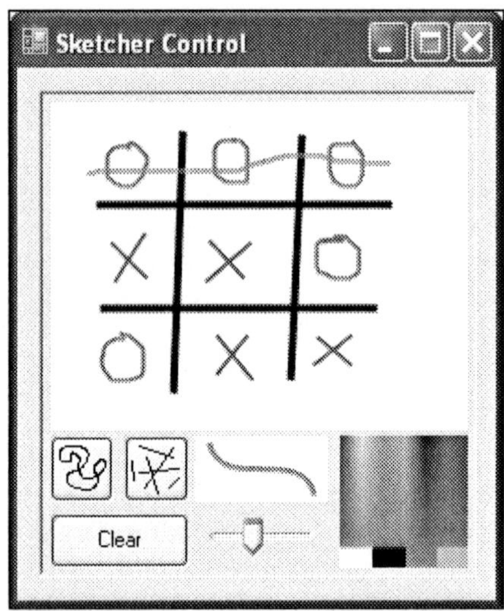

In this screenshot, our user has just finished an imaginary game of tic-tac-toe with a friend (our user won of course). The last line (the top line showing the winning circles) was drawn with the same pen that we can see in the preview, and this is our first example of communicating to the user what will appear when they draw on the page. It has a thickness that can be altered using the TrackBar control (below the preview); sliding it to the left makes the pen thinner, to the right makes it thicker. Our user can select a pen color by clicking in the colorful palette area in the lower right corner of `Sketcher`. So we end up with a realistic preview of the pen settings even before we apply them to paper.

This all seems very simple and easy, and for the most part it is, but there are some serious points to be made about interface design here; but first we should think about what we expect the user to do.

We could do this by looking at both sides of the interface, the user, and the code. On the code side we put all the mostly hidden topics that the user need not know about ("black boxes" again), and also the responsibilities of all our constituent controls. On the user side we should identify how our user is expected to fit into things. The code explanation on one side should reflect the user's needs on the other and address them as well as possible.

User	Code
1. **First appearance**: User should be able to quickly identify parts of the control and know that they can be used for drawing.	Set out constituent controls in a sensible manner. Grouping related controls together and using graphical cues where possible. The "page" should use up the majority of the space. The whole control should be manipulated using only the mouse.
2. **Intuitive Interface**: The user needs to have an intuitive interface to be able to predict what will happen when they click a button or perform similar actions.	Provide on-screen feedback when the user does something. For example, update the pen preview whenever the user changes tools, selects a different pen color, or line thickness. Also provide ToolTips for all controls apart from the page area. The preview area should reflect the shape of the tool being previewed. For example, `FreeHandTool` in the Sketcher control should be represented by a `Bezier` curve.
3. **Stability**: The user expects a rich and stable environment from our control.	Provide real-time graphical updating to the page and to all tool-related controls. Any drawing that occurs via captured mouse events should instantly be reflected on the interface. A **backbuffer** must be used in order for the artwork to be persisted after changes of working contexts, such as minimizing/restoring or changing to another program entirely. Use cursor clipping to restrict the movements of the mouse to within working areas and the palette.

The following are all the practical requirements of the users met by this UserControl:

1. **First Appearance**: We address item one of the above table through placement of controls. All controls that directly affect what happens on our page have been placed to the lower-left of the control. `FreeHand` is signified by the button featuring the smooth curve graphic. `StraightLine` is, of course, represented by the button sporting several straight lines. Using images on buttons in this way appeals to the eye in a much more natural way than text could. This is particularly important when dealing with users that are very young (have not yet learned to read well), or those with some level of visual impairment.

   Since this is a demonstration control, the Clear button has not used a graphical image, instead text is used. This change of tactics can be useful in delineating between a set of controls that do one thing (in this case create pixels), and another set of controls that perform other functions (for us the Clear button removes pixels). Although both the drawing tools and the Clear button affect our work, there is a division between them.

   Then we move along to the pen preview area, the user might click on this control experimentally to see what happens but no user events are used here. The user will tend to go and play with other controls instead. Directly below we find the TrackBar that controls the pen width. Changes on the TrackBar are reflected immediately in the thickness of the line on the preview area. This is made all the more obvious by the close proximity between the TrackBar and the preview. Then our user will continue experimenting by moving their attention to the colorful palette area. Once again, clicking on this region prompts changes on the preview. The line thickness will remain the same but the color of the line will alter to reflect the color currently under the users' cursor. This also occurs in real time so when the user drags the mouse over the palette, the preview quickly fades in and out of many colors. As soon as the user releases the mouse button the color is finally chosen.

2. **Intuitive Interface**: Once the items mentioned above are fresh in the user's mind we can keep them there by using subtle visual cues like altering the mouse pointer's shape depending on what tool they have selected. If the user picks the `FreeHand` drawing tool then the `FreeHandTool` class directs the page area to display a cursor that is shaped like a hand. Similarly, when `StraightLine` is chosen, the page will use a cross-hair cursor to make it easier for the user to accurately choose the starting and ending points of their lines.

   If the user changes between tools, then the current pen width and color settings are maintained. This means the user doesn't have to keep fiddling with the TrackBar and the palette each time.

   The `MessageBox` class is also used in `Sketcher`. If the user clicks the Clear button then a message box appears asking them about their intentions.

   This dialog contains three deliberate user-targeted ideas. The simplest is the "?" speech bubble image, which is one of the options selected when the message box is called. The second is the word ERASE in uppercase within the message itself, something as simple as this can remind the user that they will lose their work if they select the Yes button. Finally, the No button is set to be the default answer to this dialog. This makes it less likely that the user will accidentally delete their image.

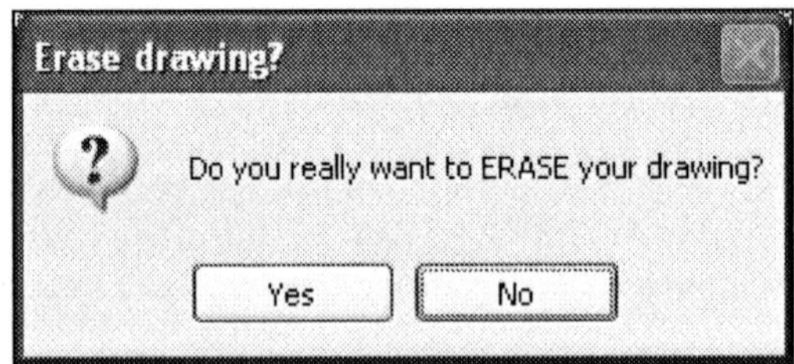

   This may seem obvious but it is common to find many applications that just use the default dialog settings for everything, regardless of the severity of the warning being given or the action being prompted. A well-designed interface uses a consistent approach to various situations.

   The `ToolTip` control is also used to good effect here: hovering the mouse over each control will give a short text description of what each control is responsible for. The exception to this is the page area itself; it does not show a `ToolTip` because the mouse will be occupying this area of the user control very frequently and having a `ToolTip` appearing all the time would be irritating.

3. **Stability**: Something as simple as restricting the mouse's movements to within a specific area can be of great benefit. This is used twice in `Sketcher`, once on the page area, and again within the palette. Clipping the mouse so it can only move within certain areas of the screen can enable your software to concentrate on the task at hand (selecting colors on the palette, or drawing on the page) rather than having to do all kinds of checks to make sure the mouse isn't doing anything on a different part of the form, or even on another program altogether. This is a preventative measure as it stops such problems arising in the first place; error trapping is a cure, not prevention.

   Back-buffering is also used in `Sketcher`. You may remember from previous chapters that if we drew something (for example, a circle, or a line), and then let another form pass in front of our own form, our drawn graphics would be lost. That is known as non-persistent graphics and it is the default mode for almost all operating systems and computers. We can easily overcome this hurdle by a special technique known as "back-buffering", or "double-buffering" (the terms are used interchangeably and are generally regarded as synonymous). There are a few different ways to implement this but the easiest and most common is to create a separate image in memory that is the same size and shape as our screen area. Then we re-direct all our drawing routines to draw to this back-buffer image instead of directly to the screen.

   This back-buffer is not affected by forms moving around on the screen, and will remain intact throughout our program unless we deliberately destroy it. So whenever our screen area wants to re-paint itself (like when one form moves out of its way), all we have to do is copy the contents of the back-buffer back onto the screen. The user will not even notice this effect because they wouldn't even realize that their on-screen work had been destroyed in the first place, the effect would be seamless. Back-buffers also offer the handy facility for us to manipulate the graphics as a solid object rather than a short-lived group of pixels in video memory. We could save the image, rotate it, re-color it, or do anything we want with it. It gives us a perfect opportunity to add extra, rich functionality while at the same time solving a GUI issue.

Go ahead and download the code for this control (from the URL mentioned below), and see how all this is implemented.

> The full code and project files are available for download at this URL:
> `http://www.packtpub.com/support`

So how does `Sketcher` deal with the four topics of Requests, Input Parsing, Fault Tolerance, and Feedback?

Requests are plentiful: tool and color selection, the `MessageBox`, and the mouse events captured on the drawing surface are all user responses to requests (implied or explicit).

Input Parsing is done at a simple level, by preventing the user making input that falls outside prescribed parameters. This is done by using mouse clipping, buttons that perform stand-alone operations, and a TrackBar, which deals with user input internally.

Fault Tolerance is one topic that `sketcher` handles by using its simple input parsing techniques, and also by the back-buffering code. If back-buffering did not take place then anything obscuring the drawing area would corrupt the user's work, which would be regarded as a fault.

Feedback is given through the pen preview, and the real-time drawing features. Changes to either the drawing or the tools are reflected instantly in the control's appearance.

Looking Further Into Input Parsing

A major ally in the war against bad user input is a thing called "Regular Expressions". **Regex** (as it is known for short, pronounced with a hard "g" by the way) is a cryptic name for an extremely powerful and sometimes complex technology. To put it simply, Regex's job is to analyse text, and perform many different operations based upon that data. Its capabilities include:

- Extraction of recognizable patterns of text, or numerical data (or both)
- "Find and Replace" based on these patterns
- Alteration of the data to make it conform to the specified patterns
- Even simple true/false results as to whether the data is OK or not; this is the most frequently used and the simplest to set up

Regex has its roots in the programming/scripting language Perl, and has a long history of different versions, revisions, rebuilds, and hybrids. It is used extensively in UNIX, Linux, and other related operating systems. Fortunately for us we don't have to learn all about its different varieties in order to use it in our code. .Net has its own built-in Regex engine ready for us to use.

Regex is such a massive topic that it could easily fill a large technical reference book on its own; it is almost a programming language in itself, such is its power. If your software needs really mandate a more extensive understanding of Regex then you can have a look at the website `http://www.regular-expressions.info/`.

How Can We Use Regex to Our Advantage?

Let's say we had to ask our user for a string that represented a serial number of a product, for example, it could be required for hardware technical support auditing. We already know the format for the serial numbers to be in, three letters followed by between four and seven digits, followed either by "A", or "B", and a final digit. So an example of a valid serial number would look like this:

RKU34910B8

To break it down:

Three letters: RKU

Followed by between four and seven (here 5) digits: 34910

"A" or "B": B

And a final digit: 8.

If we didn't have Regex at our disposal we would most likely need to manually check each character of the string to make sure it conformed to our required format. This could be very time consuming from a programmer's point of view, and if there are many different formats to consider, it would be quite difficult to keep the software up to date.

But with Regex things are a lot more straightforward and quicker.

Let's just wade in to it by creating a simple `bool` function that tells us whether or not a string is formatted correctly to the above standard.

```
private bool ParseSerialNumber(string userData)
{
  //create our parser that will do all our work for us
  Regex parser = new Regex(@"^[A-Z]{3}\d{4,7}[AB]\d$");
  //return the bool result of parser's findings
  return parser.IsMatch(userData);
}
```

"*Where's all the code?*" Well that is all the code we need to test a string. It is both simple and complex at the same time. The regular expression object `parser` is declared, and its constructor is supplied with what looks to the untrained eye like a load of random, garbage characters. In a moment we'll examine that garbage carefully because there is method in the madness. Let's see it in action.

Time for Action—Creating the Regex Application

1. Start a new Windows application in C#.
2. Add a textbox and a button to your form.
3. Add this `using` clause to the top of the code:
   ```
   using System.Text.RegularExpressions;
   ```

This enables you to access the `Regex` classes and methods.

4. In the button's `Click` event enter the following code (double-click the button in the form):
   ```
   private void button1_Click(object sender, EventArgs e)
   {
     if(ParseSerialNumber(textBox1.Text))
     MessageBox.Show("Serial Number is valid!", "Regex results:",
                     MessageBoxButtons.OK, MessageBoxIcon.Information);
     else
     MessageBox.Show("No match!", "Regex results:", MessageBoxButtons.OK,
                     MessageBoxIcon.Stop);
   }
   ```
5. And finally add the `ParseSerialNumber()` method code after the `click` event block; the string `@"^[A-Z]{3}\d{4,7}[AB]\d$"` must be entered exactly as seen here.
   ```
   private bool ParseSerialNumber(string userData)
   {
    // create our parser that will do all our work for us
    Regex parser = new Regex(@"^[A-Z]{3}\d{4,7}[AB]\d$");
    // return the bool result of parser's findings
    return parser.IsMatch(userData);
    }
   ```

What Just Happened?

Run the program and type in the serial number we used earlier (RKU34910B8). Then click the Test Button. If everything has gone to plan we will see something like this:

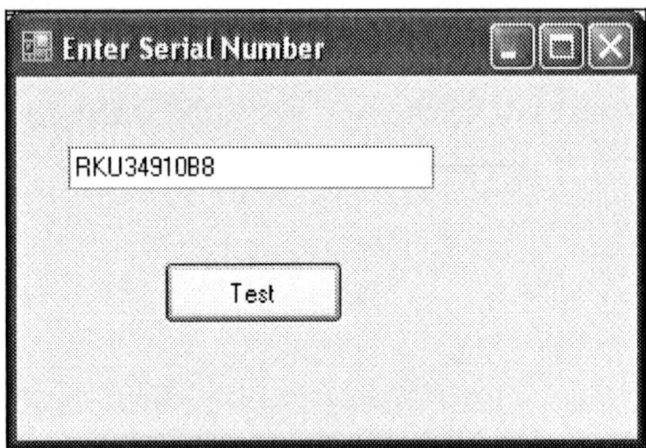

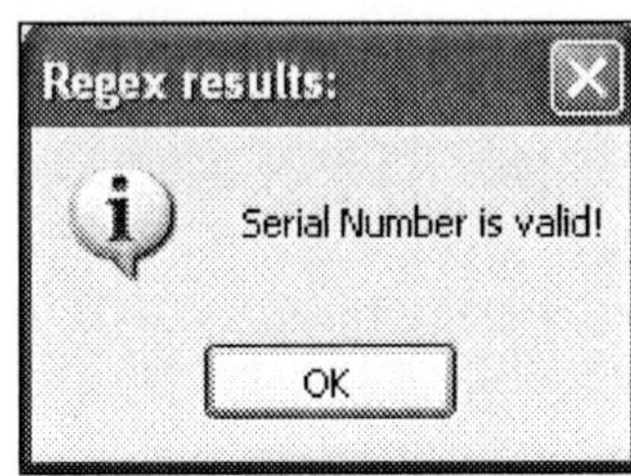

Now, experiment with altering the serial number slightly in the textbox and then press the button again. You should be able to see how certain strings are accepted and others are rejected based on the rules laid out in the Regex pattern `@"^[A-Z]{3}\d{4,7}[AB]\d$"`.

Let's see what serial numbers will be matched and what will not.

The serial numbers that match are:

- ABC1234A1
- XYZ1234567B1
- AAA1111A1

The serial numbers that don't match are (characters in underline show where the error is):

- AbC1234A1 (lowercase not allowed)
- ABC123A1 (not enough digits)
- ABC12345678C1 (too many digits and "C" is not allowed in this position)

Feel free to play around with entering different serial numbers until comfortable with what is allowed and what is not. It's a good idea to understand that before we look at the pattern in detail.

Our Regex Pattern in Detail

The pattern `@"^[A-Z]{3}\d{4,7}[AB]\d$"` looks very alien and complex, and at first glance seems to have little meaning. But the Regex system knows that this string has some very strict rules controlling it. Let's break it down into its component parts. Firstly we can discard the `@"` from the beginning and the final " from the end because they are just the normal parts of any C# string literal. So we are left with: `^[A-Z]{3}\d{4,7}[AB]\d$`.

Part	Meaning
`^`	Denotes the beginning of the string we are parsing.
`[A-Z]{3}`	The next 3 characters must be uppercase letters.
`\d{4,7}`	Between 4 and 7 numerical digits.
`[AB]`	Either "A" or "B", no other letter is acceptable.
`\d`	A single digit.
`$`	The end of the string.

Any deviation from this format pattern that is detected in the parsed string will result in rejection. But this is not to say that Regex is an all-or-nothing tool; on the contrary, it can be extremely useful in finding patterns that are similar to, or even not similar to a given format. It is literally unlimited in its capabilities as long as we can use it efficiently.

This is only a tiny subset of the overall power of Regex and it is a subject that is well worth looking into as it will definitely find a place in our arsenal of coding tools once we can appreciate its flexibility. However, it is an advanced topic and can be frustrating to learn without decent access to literature on the subject. Happily the Internet offers a huge amount of information on this subject, and there are some excellent books available on the subject.

Optimization and Coding Conventions

In this section we shall think about how to make our code easier and simpler. By looking at a large ungainly piece of code (maybe our own, maybe some code that was written by someone else) we should be able to spot some areas that could be cleaned up and clarified. Code that is easy to read and maintain is just as valuable as code that executes faster than the competition's code (if not more so).

We'll start by looking at a few common examples where habit has overtaken coding efficiency. In the tables below on the left we have the code in question and on the right, a suggested better alternative:

Bad code	Good code

`if(SomeBoolFunction())`
`  return true;`
`else`
`return false;`
	`return SomeBoolFunction();`

This situation is very common; it sometimes stems from when an originally more complex `if()` statement was gradually simplified until it was left like this. We can reduce four lines of code to just one. The compiled code will also decrease in size slightly as the branching logic is omitted in favor of a straight return value.

"Bad" Code	"Good" code

a=0;
b=0;
c=0;
d=0;
	a=b=c=d=0;

This is rather a matter of personal taste; it harks back to the days of C, and C++ programming. Instead of setting several variables to the same value one by one, we can do it in a 'cascade' on a single line. The code on the right executes from right to left; first `d` is set to zero and then `c` is set to `d` and so on until all four variables contain zero. Many programmers like this method because it looks more elegant than the code on the left. It will not be suitable for all occasions but it is often easier to read because it takes up less screen space. Any coder who has experienced "code blindness" from hours of scrolling up and down cluttered code will say this is a good tactic.

"Bad" code	"Good" code

for(int i=0; i<1000000; i++)
  for (int j=0; j<10; j++)
  {
    //loop code here
  }
	int i, j;
	
	for (i=0; i<1000000; i++)
	  for (j=0; j<10; j++)
	  {
	    //loop code here
	  }

This is a trick for speed optimization and thankfully has little effect on the readability of the code. The difference is subtle but important; the loop counters have been declared outside the `for()` constructs. This is because in the left-hand code sample the `j` variable would be initialized, used and destroyed 1,000,000 times. In the code on the right, `j` is initialized and destroyed only once but it is used just as many times. It has not affected the algorithm at all apart from avoiding having to create a variable over and over again unnecessarily. An appreciable amount of run time can be saved in this manner.

Pascal Casing and Camel Casing are two naming conventions used by programmers to facilitate the code reading and understanding. In Pascal Casing convention the first character of each word is a capital letter (e.g. PascalCasing). The Camel Casing capitalizes the first character of each word excepting the first one (e.g. camelCasing).

Summary

In this chapter we have outlined a few topics that will improve the working relationship between our users and our software. We have detailed some frequently overlooked subjects such as consistency in appearance, and how to politely restrict a user's input options without making it obvious that we are doing so. We have seen some easy and quick ways to make our code more readable and therefore more maintainable and less prone to bugs.

13
The PieChart Control

Welcome to the last chapter of this book! This is a special chapter, which doesn't introduce you to any new theory. Instead, we'll create a fully functional custom control from scratch, covering much of the theory you learned in this book.

Many ideas crossed my mind when I started writing this chapter. What control should I develop in this chapter? Should this example be familiar? Should this example be a simple, or a complex one? The idea of a pie chart came up one night while I was eating a pizza. Building a pie chart control will be an interesting for both you and me, so let's get started!

The pie chart is a graphical representation of a two dimensional table. Every slice corresponds to one element. Often the sizes are expressed in percent. If not, these values are normalized so as to fit the pie. All slices of one pie will together correspond to one hundred percent. From all other graphical representations, the pie chart is the most intuitive one. Everybody has cut a pie or a pizza in slices, and the pie chart is very familiar.

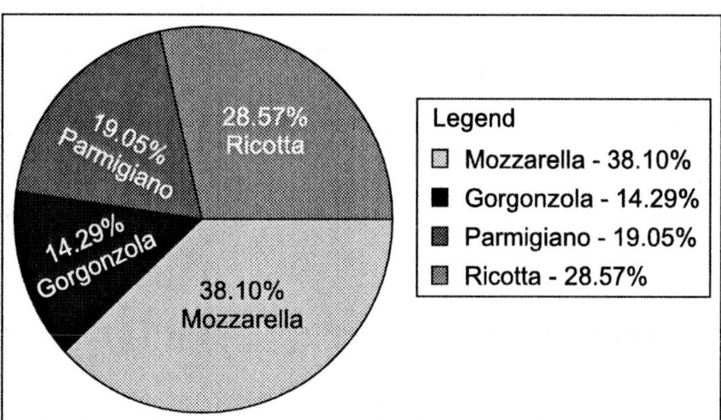

The `PieChart` control has one disadvantage: you can't use it successfully when you need to represent a large number of slices. However, it may be ideal to represent a graph having no more than five to ten slices.

This chapter divides your journey into multiple stages. Instead of following many steps that build the entire application, we'll be smarter and create bits of functionality one at a time.

Creating the PieChart Control

We'll start by creating the barebones `PieChart` control. To test this `PieChart` control you will create a typical Windows Application, and you'll add the `PieChart` UserCcontrol to the project. To render the pie and its slices you will use the `DrawEllipse()` and `FillPie()` GDI+ methods. The `PieChart` control will use another class, called `Slice`, that will store the name, the size, and the color of a slice. Let's get down to business.

Time for Action—Creating the PieChart Control

1. Create a typically Windows Application File | New | Project and name it PieChartApp.

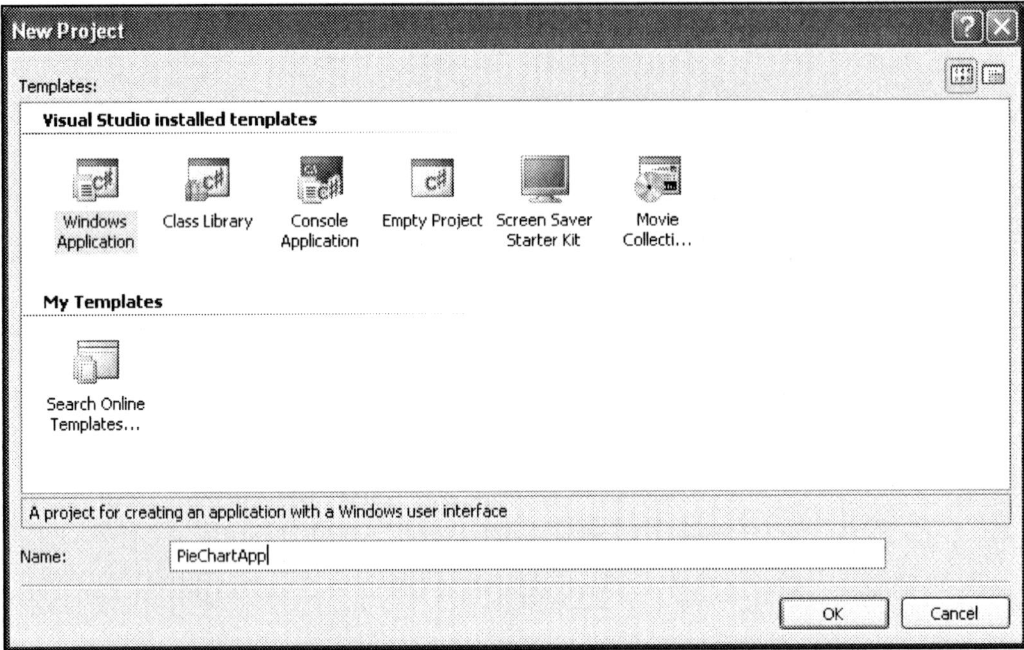

2. In the Solution Explorer tab, right-click the PieChartApp and select Add | UserControl.
3. Name this new control PieChart:

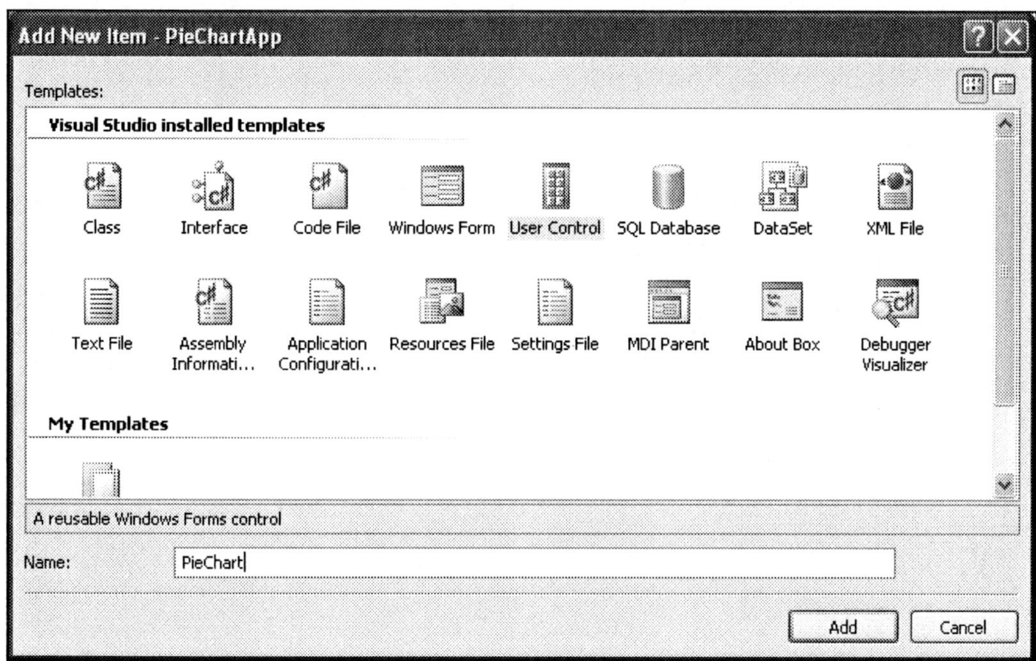

4. Right-click the PieChartApp in the Solution Explorer tab and select Add | Class. Name this new class `slice`.

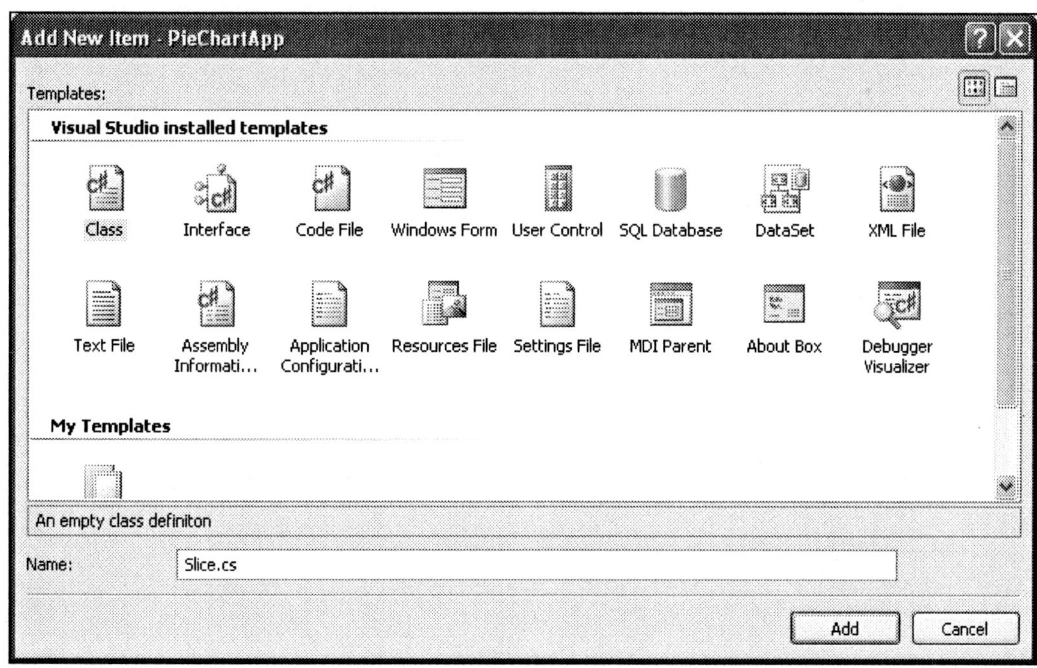

5. Add the following namespace references to `Slice.cs`:

```
using System.Collections;
using System.Drawing;
```

6. Make this class public by adding the public modifiers in `Slice.cs`

```
namespace PieChartApp
{
  public class Slice
  {
  }
}
```

7. Insert the member variables into the `Slice` class:

```
private string sliceName;
private int sliceRange;
private Color sliceColor;
```

8. Add two constructors to the class:

```
private Slice()
{
}
public Slice(string name, int range, Color color)
{
  sliceName = name;
  sliceRange = range;
  sliceColor = color;
}
```

9. Add the `Get` methods for the member variables:

```
public string GetSliceName()
{
  return sliceName;
}
public int GetSliceRange()
{
  return sliceRange;
}
public Color GetSliceColor()
{
  return sliceColor;
}
```

10. Now go back to `PieChart` control class. Add the following namespace reference:

```
using System.Collections;
```

11. Add the following member variables to the `PieChart` class:

```
int totalCount;
ArrayList mySlices;
```

12. Now it is time for the `SetArray()` property:

```
public ArrayList SetArray
{
  get
  {
    return mySlices;
  }
  set
  {
    if (mySlices != value)
      mySlices = value;
    Invalidate();
```

```
    }
  }
```

13. Set the value for each slice:

```
private void SetValues()
{
  totalCount = 0;
  if (mySlices != null)
  {
    foreach (Slice slice in mySlices)
      totalCount += slice.GetSliceRange();
  }
  // mySlicesPercent.Clear();
}
```

14. The two important functions of the `PieChart` control are the `add()` and `remove()` slice functions.

```
public bool AddSlice(Slice slice)
{
  bool isThisSlice = false;
  if(mySlices == null)
  {
    mySlices = new ArrayList();
    mySlices.Add(slice);
    return true;
  }
  foreach (Slice sliceTemp in mySlices)
  {
    if (sliceTemp.GetSliceName() == slice.GetSliceName())
      isThisSlice = true;
  }
  if (isThisSlice == false)
  {
    mySlices.Add(slice);
    Invalidate();
    return true;
  }
  return false;
}

public bool RemoveSlice(string sliceName)
{
  bool isThisSliceName = false;
  foreach (Slice sliceTemp in mySlices)
  {
    if (sliceName == sliceTemp.GetSliceName())
    {
      mySlices.Remove(sliceTemp);
      isThisSliceName = true;
      break;
    }
  }
  if (isThisSliceName)
    Invalidate();
  return isThisSliceName;
}
```

15. Right-click the `PieChart` in the designer and choose Properties. Select the Events tab and double-click the `Paint` event. This will bring you back to the `PieChart.cs` in the `OnPaint()` method.

```
private void PieChart_Paint(object sender, PaintEventArgs e)
{
  Pen penCircle = Pens.Black;
```

```
        Pen penLine = Pens.BlanchedAlmond;

        SetValues();
        e.Graphics.SmoothingMode = System.Drawing.Drawing2D.
                                   SmoothingMode.AntiAlias;
        e.Graphics.DrawEllipse(penCircle, new Rectangle(1, 1, this.Width -
                               2, this.Height - 2));
        if (mySlices != null)
        {
          int actualCount = 0;
          foreach (Slice slice in mySlices)
          {
            Pen penSlice = new Pen(slice.GetSliceColor());
            int actualRangeSlice = slice.GetSliceRange();
            int startAngle = (int)((actualCount /
                                   (double)totalCount) * 360);
            int widthAngle = (int)(((actualRangeSlice) /
                                   (double)totalCount) * 360);
            Brush br = new SolidBrush(slice.GetSliceColor());
            e.Graphics.FillPie(br, new Rectangle(1, 1, this.Width - 2,
                               this.Height - 2), startAngle, widthAngle);
            actualCount += slice.GetSliceRange();
          }
        }
      }
```

16. Drag a `PieChart` control from the Toolbox onto Form1. You will get a picture like this:

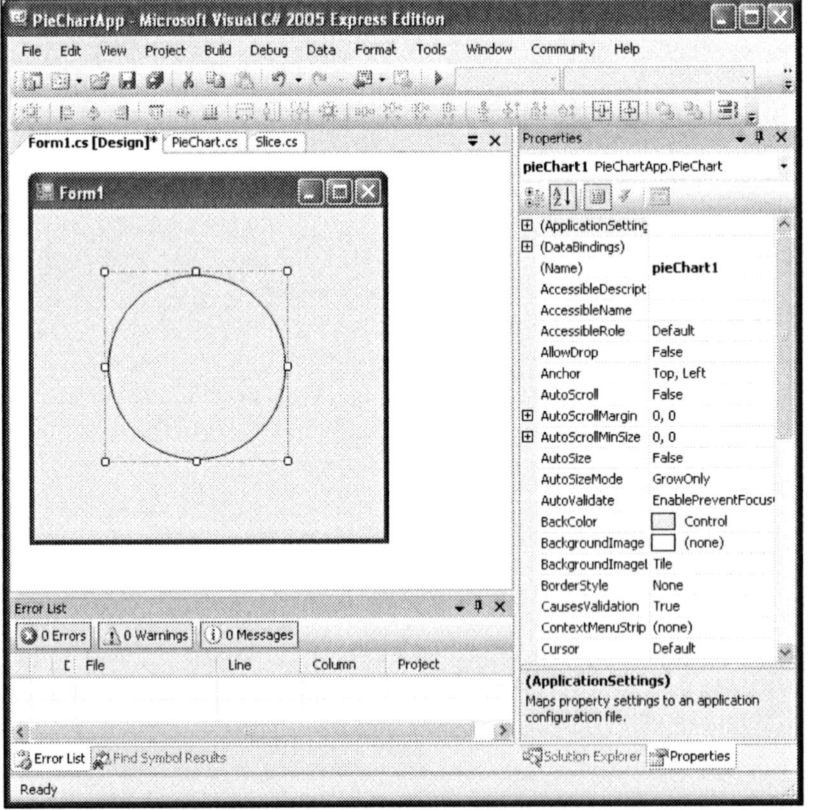

17. Now, double-click the form and you will automatically override the `pieChart1_Load()`method.

```
private void pieChart1_Load(object sender, EventArgs e)
{
  pieChart1.AddSlice(new Slice("Mozzarella", 55,
                               Color.FromArgb(255, 0, 0)));
  pieChart1.AddSlice(new Slice("Gorgonzola", 15,
                               Color.FromArgb(0, 255, 0)));
  pieChart1.AddSlice(new Slice("Parmigiano", 25,
                               Color.FromArgb(0, 0, 255)));
  pieChart1.AddSlice(new Slice("Ricotta", 25,
                               Color.FromArgb(255, 0, 255)));
  pieChart1.RemoveSlice("Ricotta");
  pieChart1.AddSlice(new Slice("Pecorino", 25,
                               Color.FromArgb(0, 255, 255)));
}
```

18. Build the application and run it.

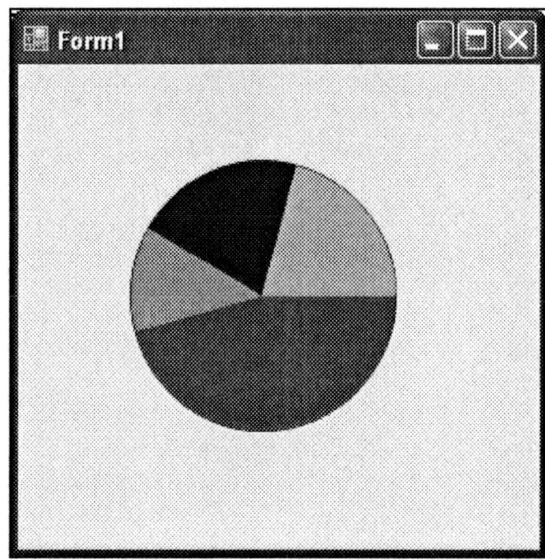

What Just Happened?

Congratulations on building the first version of `PieChart` control! The application also contains the `Slice` class, and the container form. The form doesn't do much; it just adds the four slices to your pie.

The smallest element so far is the slice itself. For this you have created a class that has three member variables: `sliceName`, `sliceRange`, and `sliceColor`. These variables describe the slice's properties: the name, the range, and the color. The class has one constructor without parameters, and one constructor that receives parameters used to initialize the class. Here you discover the first difficulty: the constructor doesn't test the input data (the received text could be null, or the range negative). Another issue is that you don't have a way to set the member variables other than using the constructor, so if you want to change the details of a slice, at this moment you will have to delete the slice and create a new one with a new text.

> In the next version of `PieChart` you will create `Set()` methods that are not yet implemented.

The custom control derives from UserControl and offers two possibilities to add slices. One is by directly using the `AddSlice()` method; the other one is by using the `SetArray` property. The following code snippets will have the same effect:

```
pieChart1.AddSlice(new Slice("Mozzarella", 55, Color.FromArgb(255, 0, 0)));
pieChart1.AddSlice(new Slice("Gorgonzola", 15, Color.FromArgb(0, 255, 0)));
pieChart1.AddSlice(new Slice("Parmigiano", 25, Color.FromArgb(0, 0, 255)));
pieChart1.AddSlice(new Slice("Ricotta", 25, Color.FromArgb(255, 0, 255)));

ArrayList al = new ArrayList();
al.Add(new Slice("Mozzarella", 55, Color.FromArgb(255, 0, 0))
al.Add(new Slice("Gorgonzola", 15, Color.FromArgb(0, 255, 0)));
al.Add(new Slice("Parmigiano", 25, Color.FromArgb(0, 0, 255)));
al.Add(new Slice("Ricotta", 25, Color.FromArgb(255, 0, 255)));
pieChart1.SetArray = al;
```

You can test the two blocks of code by inserting them in the `pieChart1_Load()` method. The `AddSlice()` method receives a `Slice` object as parameter, and in the code snippet we created four `Slice` objects on the fly. We also used the constructor with three parameters, which allowed us to add the four slices using a minimum of code.

Taking a look at the `PieChart` control picture in the application when running, you will notice it looks quite primitive and it doesn't have many features. For example, the slice names don't appear anywhere. How are you supposed to know which slice corresponds to Parmigiano, and which corresponds to the Ricotta cheese? Also, there are no delimiters between slices. You can create two slices having the same color and this way these slices are merged. The following picture contains two `PieChart` controls, each of them having four slices. However, in the pie on the right you can only see three, because two of them have the same color.

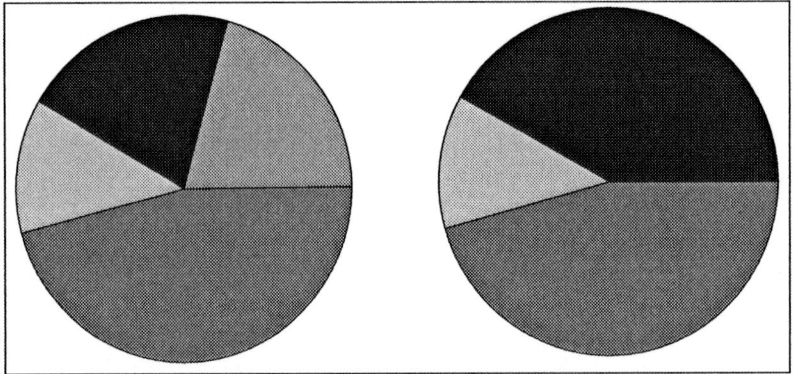

Adding Slice Names and Delimiters

In a second iteration through the project, we're solving bugs and adding new features to develop a great `PieChart` control. This is a normal process when developing software components. The situations when the developer knows from the beginning about all the potential problems he or she might meet are rare.

Let's improve the `PieChart` and generate a new version that implements the suggestions and observations so far. In this new version of the `PieChart` you want to:

- Test variables in the `Slice` class copy constructor
- Create `Set()` methods for the `Slice` class member variables
- Draw a slice outline in the `PieChart` control class
- Draw the name of the `Slice` in the `PieChart` control class

At the end your new `PieChart` will look like this:

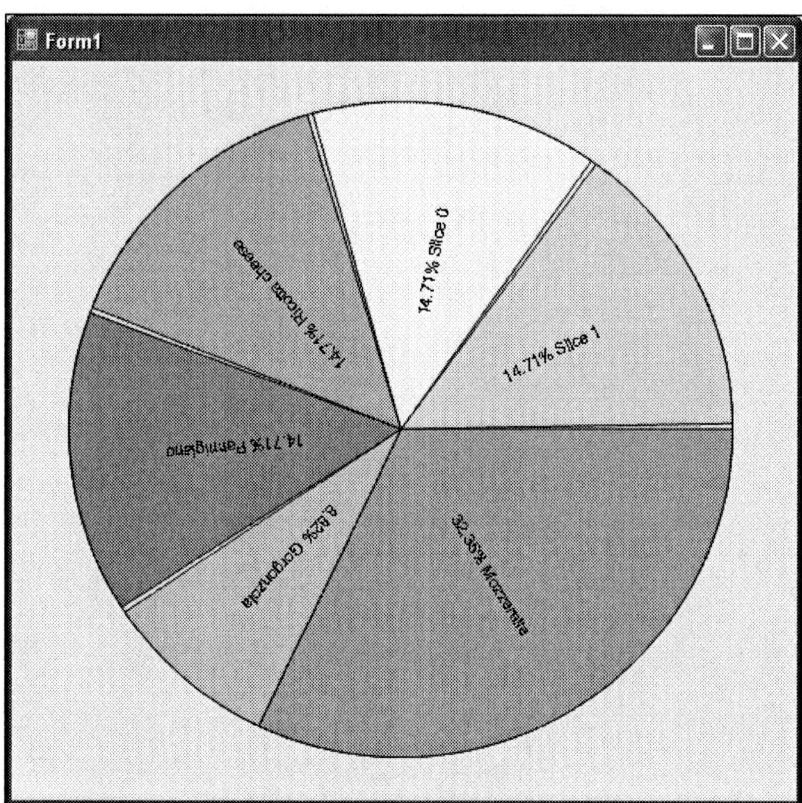

Time for Action—Improving the PieChart Control

1. Open the `PieChartApp` application used before.
2. Go to the `Slice` class in the `Slice.cs` file. Add a member variable to the class that will remember the number of unnamed slices.

```
// countNoName is static, so all instances of the
// Slice class will have access to the same value
private static int countNoName = 0;
```

3. Modify the constructor so it looks like:

```
public Slice(string name, int range, Color color)
{
  if (name == "")
  {
    sliceName = "Slice " + countNoName.ToString();
    countNoName++;
  }
  else
    sliceName = name;
  if (range < 0)
    range = 0;
  else
    sliceRange = range;
  sliceColor = color;
}
```

4. Add the `Set` methods to the `Slice` class. Using these methods you can set the name, range, and color for one slice object.

```
public void SetSliceName(string name)
{
  if (name == "")
  {
    sliceName = "Slice " + countNoName.ToString();
    countNoName++;
  }
  else
    sliceName = name;
}

public void SetSliceRange(int range)
{
  if (range < 0)
    range = 0;
  else
    sliceRange = range;
}

public void SetSliceColor(Color color)
{
  sliceColor = color;
}
```

5. Go to the `PieChart` class in `PieChart.cs` and add the `GetSlice()` method. This will return the slice with a given name.

```
public Slice GetSlice(string sliceName)
{
  foreach (Slice sliceTemp in mySlices)
  {
    if (sliceName == sliceTemp.GetSliceName())
    {
      return sliceTemp;
    }
  }
  // if there is no slice by a given name this function
  // will return a null text, zero range, white slice
  return new Slice("", 0, Color.FromArgb(255, 255, 255));
}
```

6. Modify the `PieChart_Paint()` method to draw the text in each slice, so that it looks like the following:

```
private void PieChart_Paint(object sender, PaintEventArgs e)
{
  Pen penCircle = Pens.Black;
  Pen penLine = Pens.BlanchedAlmond;
  SetValues();
  e.Graphics.SmoothingMode =
                  System.Drawing.Drawing2D.SmoothingMode.AntiAlias;
  e.Graphics.DrawEllipse(penCircle, new Rectangle(1, 1,
                        this.Width - 5,
                        this.Height - 5));
  if (mySlices != null)
  {
    int actualCount = 0;
    // draw each slice
    foreach (Slice slice in mySlices)
    {
      Pen penSlice = new Pen(slice.GetSliceColor());
      int actualRangeSlice = slice.GetSliceRange();
      int startAngle = (int)((actualCount / (double)totalCount) * 360);
      int widthAngle = (int)(((actualRangeSlice) / (double)totalCount) *
                  360);
      Brush br = new SolidBrush(slice.GetSliceColor());
      e.Graphics.FillPie(br, new Rectangle(1, 1, this.Width - 5,
                  this.Height - 5), startAngle, widthAngle);
      e.Graphics.DrawPie(penCircle, new Rectangle(1, 1, this.Width -
                  5, this.Height - 5), startAngle, widthAngle);
      actualCount += slice.GetSliceRange();
    }

    string stringName = "";
    Font fontName = new Font("SansSerif", 8);
    StringFormat formatName = new
                  StringFormat(StringFormatFlags.NoClip);
    formatName.Alignment = StringAlignment.Center;
    formatName.LineAlignment = StringAlignment.Center;
    Point pointName = new Point(this.Width / 4, 0);
    double actualAngle = 0;
    e.Graphics.TranslateTransform((float)(this.Width / 2.0),
                  (float)(this.Height / 2.0));
    // draw the text and percent for each slice
    foreach (Slice slice in mySlices)
    {
      Pen penSlice = new Pen(slice.GetSliceColor());
      double actualRangeSlice = slice.GetSliceRange();
      double rotateAngle = ((((actualRangeSlice) / (double)totalCount)
                  * 360)) / 2.0;
      Brush br = new SolidBrush(Color.FromArgb(0, 0, 0));
      e.Graphics.RotateTransform((float)(rotateAngle + actualAngle));
      stringName = "";
      stringName = string.Format("{0:f}",
                  (double)(slice.GetSliceRange() / (double)totalCount
                  * 100));
      stringName += "% " + slice.GetSliceName();
      e.Graphics.DrawString(stringName, fontName, br, pointName,
                  formatName);
      actualAngle = rotateAngle;
    }
  }
}
```

7. Now, modify the `pieChart1_Load()` method in the `form1` class so that we can take advantage of the new features:

```
private void pieChart1_Load(object sender, EventArgs e)
{
 pieChart1.AddSlice(new Slice("Mozzarella", 55, Color.FromArgb(255,
                  128, 128)));
 pieChart1.AddSlice(new Slice("Gorgonzola", 15, Color.FromArgb(128,
                  255, 128)));
 pieChart1.AddSlice(new Slice("Parmigiano", 25, Color.FromArgb(128,
                  128, 255)));
 pieChart1.AddSlice(new Slice("Ricotta", 25, Color.FromArgb(255, 128,
                  255)));
 // the first unnamed slice will be automatically named "Slice 0"
 pieChart1.AddSlice(new Slice("", 25, Color.FromArgb(255, 255, 128)));
 // the second unnamed slice will be automatically named "Slice 1"
 pieChart1.AddSlice(new Slice("", 25, Color.FromArgb(128, 255, 255)));
 // get the "Ricotta" slice
 Slice tempSlice =pieChart1.GetSlice("Ricotta");
 // if the slice exists i.e. has a name different from ""
 if(tempSlice.GetSliceName() != "")
  // and name it Ricotta cheese"
 tempSlice.SetSliceName("Ricotta cheese");
}
```

8. In the `Form1.cs` Design View resize the `PieChart` so that it will be bigger. By doing this we will see the slices and the text clearly. Now build and execute the application.

What Just Happened?

You just improved the `PieChart` by adding some extra functionality. At this moment you can get or set the slice name, text, and color. Moreover, each pie slice displays its percentage.

So this is it? Actually, this was just the beginning of writing a successful `PieChart` control. So what should you do next? First let's take a look at the resulting form and its custom control. The first thing that we see is the grey slices that have just appeared between the "real" slices. You will have to take care of this bug.

I would also add a map or a legend to the right of the control. This is not a difficult feature to add, but you will have to change the control's `OnPaint()` method, because the coordinates will be affected.

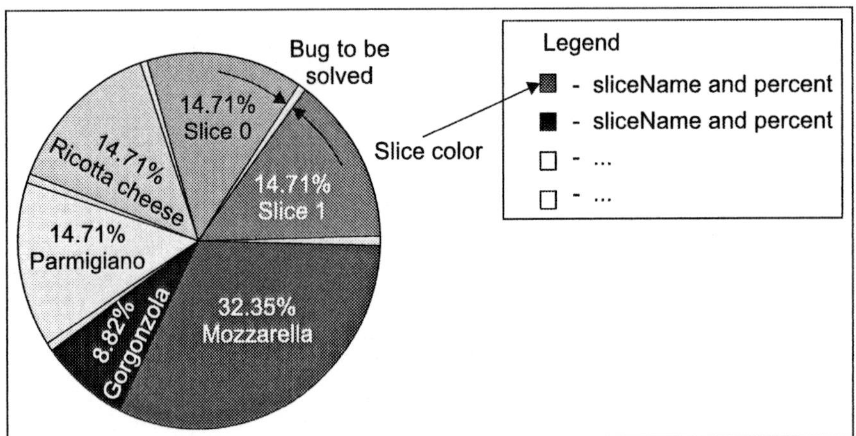

In the pie chart itself, the text on each slice could go outside the slice area if you shrink the control in the form. The workaround we'll implement is to draw the text only if it fits the given slice area.

Draw a legend outline, add a title and inside this area draw each item's name, and percent near the colored rectangle indicating the slice color, as shown in the previous figure. Also you must insert a condition to see the slice name only if it doesn't outrun the circle boundaries.

PieChart Legend

One of the most important parts of the `PieChart` control is the legend, which contains the slice names, sizes, and colors. When the user looks at the `PieChart`, he or she sees the slice color, and then looks up this color in the legend. Here, the user can read additional data about that slice, such as the text and the size in our case.

Let's focus on this simple mechanism and create the `PieChart` legend. To add this feature you will resize the control so that it will have a width double its height. In the right side of the control we will render the legend and in the left part we will place the pie. The size of the text in the legend will be calculated by a routine that will choose a text size that fits the legend.

Time for Action—Creating the PieChart Legend

1. Open the `PieChartApp` application developed so far.
2. Go to the `PieChart` control class and insert the new `PieChart_Paint()` method. Add the next piece of code so the method will look as follows:

```
private void PieChart_Paint(object sender, PaintEventArgs e)
{
  Pen penCircle = Pens.Black;
  Pen penLine = Pens.BlanchedAlmond;
  SetValues();
  e.Graphics.SmoothingMode =
                 System.Drawing.Drawing2D.SmoothingMode.AntiAlias;
  e.Graphics.DrawEllipse(penCircle, new Rectangle(1, 1, this.Width / 2
                      - 5, this.Width / 2 - 5));
  if (mySlices != null)
  {
    int actualCount = 0;
    // draw each slice
    foreach (Slice slice in mySlices)
    {
      Pen penSlice = new Pen(slice.GetSliceColor());
      int actualRangeSlice = slice.GetSliceRange();
      int startAngle = (int)((actualCount / (double)totalCount) * 360);
      int widthAngle = (int)(((actualRangeSlice) / (double)totalCount)
                      * 360) + 1;
      Brush br = new SolidBrush(slice.GetSliceColor());
      e.Graphics.FillPie(br, new Rectangle(1, 1, this.Width / 2 - 5,
                      this.Width / 2 - 5), startAngle, widthAngle);
      e.Graphics.DrawPie(penCircle, new Rectangle(1, 1, this.Width /2
                      - 5, this.Width / 2 - 5), startAngle,
                      widthAngle);
      actualCount += slice.GetSliceRange();
    }
    // draw the text within the legend
    string itemName;
```

```
int itemFontSize = 64;
Font itemFont = new Font("SansSerif", itemFontSize);
StringFormat itemFormatName = new
                          StringFormat(StringFormatFlags.NoClip);
itemFormatName.Alignment = StringAlignment.Near;
itemFormatName.LineAlignment = StringAlignment.Near;
int verticalPosition = 50;
// check if the text fits the legend
// if not -> modify the font
foreach (Slice slice in mySlices)
{
  itemName = "  ";
  itemName += slice.GetSliceName();
  itemName += " - " + string.Format("{0:f}",
              (double)(slice.GetSliceRange() / (double)totalCount
              * 100)) + "%";
  SizeF itemSize = e.Graphics.MeasureString(itemName, itemFont);
  Point position = new Point(this.Width / 2 + 40, verticalPosition);
  while((e.Graphics.MeasureString(itemName, itemFont).Width >
       (this.Width / 2 - 40)))
  {
    if (itemFontSize > 4)
      itemFont = new Font("SansSerif", itemFontSize--);
    else
      return;
  }
  while((50 + mySlices.Count*(e.Graphics.MeasureString(itemName,
       itemFont).Height+5)) > (this.Height))
  {
    if (itemFontSize > 4)
      itemFont = new Font("SansSerif", itemFontSize--);
    else
      return;
  }
}
verticalPosition = 50;
// draw the legend outline
Font legendTitleFont = new Font("SansSerif", itemFontSize + 5);
e.Graphics.DrawString("Legend", legendTitleFont, Brushes.Black,
                      new Point(this.Width / 2 + 20, 10));
int legendHeight = (int)(e.Graphics.MeasureString("Legend",
                    legendTitleFont).Height) * 2;
// draw item's text and colored rectangle
foreach (Slice slice in mySlices)
{
  itemName = "  ";
  itemName += slice.GetSliceName();
  itemName += " - " + string.Format("{0:f}",
             (double)(slice.GetSliceRange() / (double)totalCount *
                                               100)) + "%";
  SizeF itemSize = e.Graphics.MeasureString(itemName, itemFont);
  Point position = new Point(this.Width / 2 + 40,
                                      verticalPosition);
  e.Graphics.DrawRectangle(Pens.Black, new Rectangle(this.Width /
                           2 + 20, verticalPosition, 15,
                           (int)itemSize.Height));
  e.Graphics.FillRectangle(new SolidBrush(slice.GetSliceColor()),
                          new Rectangle(this.Width / 2 + 20,
                          verticalPosition, 15,
                          (int)itemSize.Height));
  e.Graphics.DrawString(itemName, itemFont, Brushes.Black,
                       position, itemFormatName);
  verticalPosition += (int)itemSize.Height + 5;
}
// draw the reactangle to include the legend
```

```
        e.Graphics.DrawRectangle(Pens.Black, new Rectangle(this.Width / 2
                          + 5, 5, this.Width / 2 - 10, verticalPosition));
        string stringName = "";
        Font fontName = new Font("SansSerif", 8);
        StringFormat formatName = new
                                StringFormat(StringFormatFlags.NoClip);
        formatName.Alignment = StringAlignment.Center;
        formatName.LineAlignment = StringAlignment.Center;
        Point pointName = new Point(this.Width / 8, 0);
        double actualAngle = 0;
        e.Graphics.TranslateTransform((float)(this.Width / 4.0),
                                (float)(this.Width / 4.0));
        // draw the text and percent for each slice
        foreach (Slice slice in mySlices)
        {
          Pen penSlice = new Pen(slice.GetSliceColor());
          double actualRangeSlice = slice.GetSliceRange();
          double rotateAngle = ((((actualRangeSlice) / (double)totalCount)
                              * 360)) / 2.0;
          Brush br = new SolidBrush(Color.FromArgb(0, 0, 0));
          e.Graphics.RotateTransform((float)(rotateAngle + actualAngle));
          stringName = "";
          stringName = string.Format("{0:f}",
                       (double)(slice.GetSliceRange() / (double)totalCount
                        * 100));
          stringName += "% " + slice.GetSliceName();
          if(e.Graphics.MeasureString(stringName, fontName).Width < (Width
                                                                     / 4))
            e.Graphics.DrawString(stringName, fontName, br, pointName,
                              formatName);
          actualAngle = rotateAngle;
        }
      }

      e.Graphics.Dispose();
    }
```

3. Resize the `PieChart` control in the form, build the project, and then run it. Repeat this step to see how the control redraws itself.

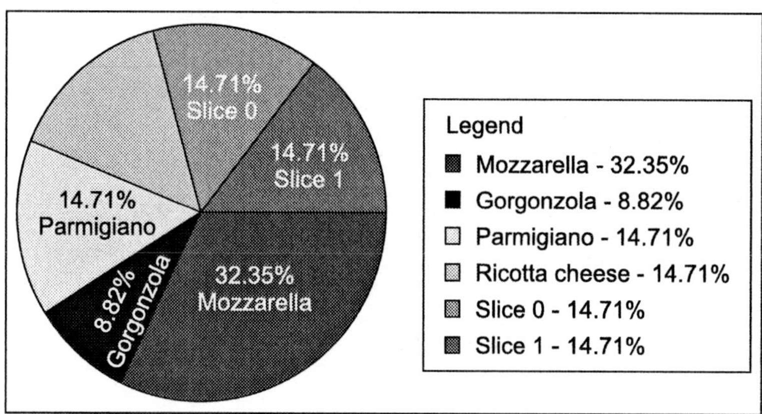

What Just Happened?

You have successfully created a resizable legend. Now the name of a slice will be drawn only if it fits the slice area.

You can test whether the string to display is larger than the pie radius with the help of the following code:

```
if(e.Graphics.MeasureString(stringName, fontName).Width < (Width / 4))
  e.Graphics.DrawString(stringName, fontName, br, pointName, formatName);
```

The bug that was causing the gray slices was solved by adding and extra degree when formatting the slice:

```
foreach (Slice slice in mySlices)
{
  Pen penSlice = new Pen(slice.GetSliceColor());
  int actualRangeSlice = slice.GetSliceRange();
  int startAngle = (int)((actualCount / (double)totalCount) * 360);
  int widthAngle = (int)(((actualRangeSlice) / (double)totalCount) * 360) + 1;
```

That bug occurred because the type-casting from double to integer used to cause some precision loss.

The control is resizable because when you modify the size, it redraws nicely.

The `itemFontSize` is computed in this block of code. In this loop, the size of the string, which occupies the place left in the control after drawing the pie, is tested. It starts with a font size of 64 and it decreases until the text fits the available width. After this block of code executes, the font size is stored in `itemFontSize`.

```
int itemFontSize = 64;
// check if the text horizontally enter the control if not -> modify the font
foreach (Slice slice in mySlices)
{
   itemName = "  ";
   itemName += slice.GetSliceName();
   itemName += " - " + string.Format("{0:F}", (double)(slice.GetSliceRange() /
                                 (double)totalCount * 100)) + "%";
   SizeF itemSize = e.Graphics.MeasureString(itemName, itemFont);
   Point position = new Point(this.Width / 2 + 40, verticalPosition);
   while((e.Graphics.MeasureString(itemName, itemFont).Width > (this.Width / 2
                                                                   - 40)))
   {
    itemFont = new Font("SansSerif", itemFontSize--);
   }
 }
```

The legend also contains a title that is five units larger than the font for the items. The legend title text is embedded in the code, so you cannot modify this from outside the control.

```
Font legendTitleFont = new Font("SansSerif", itemFontSize + 5);
e.Graphics.DrawString("Legend", legendTitleFont, Brushes.Black, new
                              Point(this.Width / 2 + 20, 10));
```

In the previous figure you saw that on one slice there was no text. This is because the text doesn't fit the pie radius. You can actually see in the legend that the slice name is the longest one of all.

Printing the PieChart

This control could use printing support. You could make a report and fill a table, and then represent that table in a graphical way using the `PieChart` control. If you want to print this chart, what do you do? Obviously, create custom control print functionality.

Because the control's width is greater than its height, we will print it in landscape mode. To make printing easier, we don't include functionality to print the control on more than one page, so if it doesn't fit in the page, the user will get a message box that tells him or her to resize the control before printing.

Time for Action—The Printable PieChart

1. Open the `PieChartApp` application. Open `PieChart.cs`, and insert the namespace:

```
using System.Drawing.Printing;
```

2. Add the next member variable to the `PieChart` class.

```
PrintDocument pieChartPrintDoc = null;
```

3. In the constructor add the following lines:

```
public PieChart()
{
  InitializeComponent();
  pieChartPrintDoc = new PrintDocument();
  pieChartPrintDoc.PrintPage += new
                  PrintPageEventHandler(_pieChartPrintDoc_PrintPage);
}
```

4. Before effectively printing the chart, we open the Print dialog, then the Page Setup dialog. To see a print preview, you open a Print Preview dialog.

```
public void Print(bool hardcopy)
{
  // create a PrintDialog based on the PrintDocument
  PrintDialog pdlg = new PrintDialog();
  pdlg.Document = pieChartPrintDoc;
  // show the PrintDialog
  if (pdlg.ShowDialog() == DialogResult.OK)
  {
    // create a PageSetupDialog based on the PrintDocument and
    // PrintDialog
    PageSetupDialog psd = new PageSetupDialog();
    psd.EnableMetric = true; // Ensure all dialog measurements are in
                             // metric Units
    psd.Document = pdlg.Document;
    psd.PageSettings.Landscape = true; //Ensure landscape view
                                       // show the PageSetupDialog
    if (psd.ShowDialog() == DialogResult.OK)
    {
      // apply the settings of both dialogs
      pieChartPrintDoc.DefaultPageSettings = psd.PageSettings;
      // decide what action to take
      if (hardcopy)
      {
        // actually print hardcopy
        pieChartPrintDoc.Print();
      }
      else
      {
        // preview onscreen instead
        PrintPreviewDialog prvw = new PrintPreviewDialog();
        prvw.Document = pieChartPrintDoc;
        prvw.ShowDialog();
      }
    }
  }
}
```

5. When the `Print` event is triggered you will get into the `_pieChartPrintDoc_PrintPage()` method. Here, the `PieChart` document will be printed.

```
private void _pieChartPrintDoc_PrintPage(object sender,
                                          PrintPageEventArgs e)
{
  Pen penCircle = Pens.Black;
  Pen penLine = Pens.BlanchedAlmond;
  e.Graphics.Clip = new Region(e.MarginBounds);
  Single x = e.MarginBounds.Left;
  Single y = e.MarginBounds.Top;
  int leftMargin = (int)x;
  int topMargin = (int)y;

  RectangleF mainTextArea = RectangleF.FromLTRB(x, y,
                        e.MarginBounds.Right, e.MarginBounds.Bottom);
  e.HasMorePages = false;
  if ((this.Height > mainTextArea.Height) || (this.Width >
                                          mainTextArea.Width))
  {
    MessageBox.Show("The control doesn't fit in the page. Resize the
                    control then try again printing");
    return;
  }
  Pen contourPen = new Pen(Color.FromArgb(0, 0, 0), 2);
  e.Graphics.DrawRectangle(contourPen, leftMargin, topMargin,
                           this.Width, this.Height);
  e.Graphics.SmoothingMode =
                    System.Drawing.Drawing2D.SmoothingMode.AntiAlias;
  e.Graphics.DrawEllipse(penCircle, new Rectangle(leftMargin + 1,
                        topMargin + 1, this.Width / 2 - 5, this.Width
                                                       / 2 - 5));
  if (mySlices != null)
  {
    int actualCount = 0;
    // draw each slice
    foreach (Slice slice in mySlices)
    {
      Pen penSlice = new Pen(slice.GetSliceColor());
      int actualRangeSlice = slice.GetSliceRange();
      int startAngle = (int)((actualCount / (double)totalCount) * 360);
      int widthAngle = (int)(((actualRangeSlice) / (double)totalCount)
                                                    * 360) + 1;
      Brush br = new SolidBrush(slice.GetSliceColor());
      e.Graphics.FillPie(br, new Rectangle(leftMargin + 1, topMargin +
                        1, this.Width / 2 - 5, this.Width / 2 - 5),
                        startAngle, widthAngle);
      e.Graphics.DrawPie(penCircle, new Rectangle(leftMargin + 1,
                        topMargin + 1, this.Width / 2 - 5, this.Width
                        / 2 - 5), startAngle, widthAngle);
      actualCount += slice.GetSliceRange();
    }
    // draw the text within the legend
    string itemName;
    int itemFontSize = 64;
    Font itemFont = new Font("SansSerif", itemFontSize);
    StringFormat itemFormatName = new
                          StringFormat(StringFormatFlags.NoClip);
    itemFormatName.Alignment = StringAlignment.Near;
    itemFormatName.LineAlignment = StringAlignment.Near;
    int verticalPosition = 50;
    // check if the text fits the legend
    // if not -> modify the font
    foreach (Slice slice in mySlices)
    {
```

```
    itemName = "  ";
    itemName += slice.GetSliceName();
    itemName += " - " + string.Format("{0:f}",
              (double)(slice.GetSliceRange() / (double)totalCount *
                                                   100)) + "%";
    SizeF itemSize = e.Graphics.MeasureString(itemName, itemFont);
    Point position = new Point(this.Width / 2 + 40 + leftMargin,
                     verticalPosition + topMargin);
    while ((e.Graphics.MeasureString(itemName, itemFont).Width >
          (this.Width / 2 - 40)))
    {
      if (itemFontSize > 4)
        itemFont = new Font("SansSerif", itemFontSize--);
      else
        return;
    }
    while ((50 + mySlices.Count *
          (e.Graphics.MeasureString(itemName, itemFont).Height + 5))
          > (this.Height))
    {
      if (itemFontSize > 4)
        itemFont = new Font("SansSerif", itemFontSize--);
      else
        return;
    }
  }
  verticalPosition = 50;
  // draw the legend title
  Font legendTitleFont = new Font("SansSerif", itemFontSize + 5);
  e.Graphics.DrawString("Legend", legendTitleFont, Brushes.Black,
                     new Point(leftMargin + this.Width / 2 + 20,
                               topMargin + 10));
  int legendHeight = (int)(e.Graphics.MeasureString("Legend",
                     legendTitleFont).Height) * 2 + topMargin;
  // draw items text and colored rectangle
  foreach (Slice slice in mySlices)
  {
    itemName = "  ";
    itemName += slice.GetSliceName();
    itemName += " - " + string.Format("{0:f}",
                                  (double)(slice.GetSliceRange()
                                  / (double)totalCount * 100)) +
                                  "%";
    SizeF itemSize = e.Graphics.MeasureString(itemName, itemFont);
    Point position = new Point(leftMargin + this.Width / 2 + 40,
                     topMargin + verticalPosition);
    e.Graphics.DrawRectangle(Pens.Black, new Rectangle(leftMargin +
                           this.Width / 2 + 20, topMargin +
                           verticalPosition, 15,
                           (int)itemSize.Height));
    e.Graphics.FillRectangle(new SolidBrush(slice.GetSliceColor()),
                           new Rectangle(leftMargin + this.Width /
                           2 + 20, topMargin + verticalPosition,
                           15, (int)itemSize.Height));
    e.Graphics.DrawString(itemName, itemFont, Brushes.Black,
                      position, itemFormatName);
    verticalPosition += (int)itemSize.Height + 5;
  }
  // draw the legend outline
  e.Graphics.DrawRectangle(Pens.Black, new Rectangle(leftMargin +
                        this.Width / 2 + 5, topMargin + 5,
                        this.Width / 2 - 10, verticalPosition));
```

```
        string stringName = "";
        Font fontName = new Font("SansSerif", 8);
        StringFormat formatName = new
                          StringFormat(StringFormatFlags.NoClip);
        formatName.Alignment = StringAlignment.Center;
        formatName.LineAlignment = StringAlignment.Center;
        Point pointName = new Point(this.Width / 8, 0);
        double actualAngle = 0;
        e.Graphics.TranslateTransform((float)(this.Width / 4.0 +
                             leftMargin), (float)(this.Width / 4.0
                             + topMargin));
        // draw the text and percent for each slice
        foreach (Slice slice in mySlices)
        {
          Pen penSlice = new Pen(slice.GetSliceColor());
          double actualRangeSlice = slice.GetSliceRange();
          double rotateAngle = ((((actualRangeSlice) / (double)totalCount)
                        * 360)) / 2.0;
          Brush br = new SolidBrush(Color.FromArgb(0, 0, 0));
          e.Graphics.RotateTransform((float)(rotateAngle + actualAngle));
          stringName = "";
          stringName = string.Format("{0:f}",
                       (double)(slice.GetSliceRange() / (double)totalCount
                       * 100));
          stringName += "% " + slice.GetSliceName();
          if (e.Graphics.MeasureString(stringName, fontName).Width <
                              (Width / 4))
            e.Graphics.DrawString(stringName, fontName, br, pointName,
                           formatName);
          actualAngle = rotateAngle;
        }
      }
    }
```

6. Drag a Button onto the form, set its text to Print, and double-click it. This will automatically generate the `button1_Click()` method.

```
    private void button1_Click(object sender, EventArgs e)
    {
      pieChart1.Print(false);
    }
```

7. Run the application. Click the Print button. You will get a preview similar to the one shown opposite:

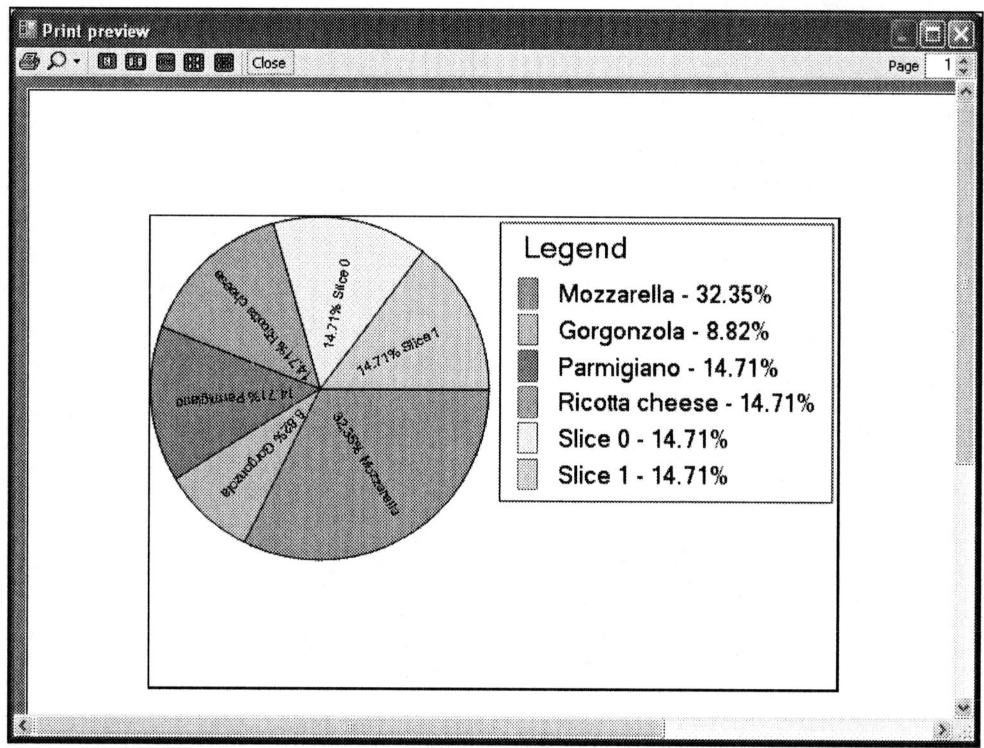

What Just Happened?

At this point your chart knows how to print itself. The print functionality starts with the `Print` event as declared in the control's constructor. Here you have instantiated the `PrintDocument` `pieChartPrintDoc` object that represents the printable document. The `Print` event will be handled in the `_pieChartPrintDoc_PrintPage()` method.

```
pieChartPrintDoc.PrintPage += new
                        PrintPageEventHandler(_pieChartPrintDoc_PrintPage);
```

The `Print()` method, which triggers the printing process, is public; so it's accessible for programs that use the control and want to print its contents. This method implies that a Print dialog, a Page Setup dialog, and a Print Preview dialog are shown before printing. All these dialogs are common dialogs so we will not focus on them. Once the settings are made, if you accept the print preview, the `_pieChartPrintDoc_PrintPage()` printing handler method will be called. This is a big function, implying a lot of code. Don't worry since there is little new here.

This is somewhat similar to the `PieChart_Paint()` method from *Time for Action—Creating the PieChart Legend*. We draw all the `PieChart` items found on your screen onto the printer but at a different position. When drawing onto paper printers usually don't draw on the whole paper, but they leave top, bottom, left, and right margins. If you draw at the (0, 0) position as you do on the screen, you will get a broken `PieChart` on paper. To eliminate this inconvenience we must translate the whole control surface with the left margin and top margin distances.

```
Single x = e.MarginBounds.Left;
Single y = e.MarginBounds.Top;
int leftMargin = (int)x;
int topMargin = (int)y;
```

The `leftMargin` and `topMargin` variables will be used to increment the coordinates of the printing items.

To simplify the printing process we only print charts that fit into one page:

```
e.HasMorePages = false;
```

For the same reason, the function will return if the control cannot be printed on one page.

```
if ((this.Height > mainTextArea.Height) || (this.Width >
   mainTextArea.Width))
{
  MessageBox.Show("The control doesn't fit in the page. Resize the
                  control then try again printing");
  return;
}
```

See, it was simple to draw your custom control onto the printer. To summarize the ideas, here are the three steps that you followed:

1. Start by copying the code in the `OnPaint()` method to the `Print()` method, and then customize `Print()` according to your needs. You may want, for example, to add headers and footers to the print version of a document.
2. Give your user options by showing the Print, Page Setup, and Print Preview dialogs.
3. Handle the printing of more than one page by breaking the control into one or more page printable pieces, if you decide to support this feature.

Adding and Removing Slices

All right, until now you have created the control, but you haven't done much to expose functionality that would allow external applications to work with this control. The basic operations you should support are those for programmatically adding and removing slices. Adding a slice will be based on a unique name, a slice size, and a color. Removing a slice is done using the unique name of the slice, which allows finding the slice in the collection of slices and deleting it from there.

Time for Action—Add Application Support for PieChart Slice Add/Remove Operations

1. In the `PieChartApp` form, called Form1, drag and drop onto the form a GroupBox control and set its text to Add Slice.
2. Drag two text boxes and name them addSliceNameTextBox and addSliceSizeTextBox.
3. Drag two buttons, set their names to addSliceColorButton and addSliceButton, and set their text to Set Color and Add Slice respectively. At this point, after inserting some intuitive text labels, the Add Slice GroupBox should look like the following figure:

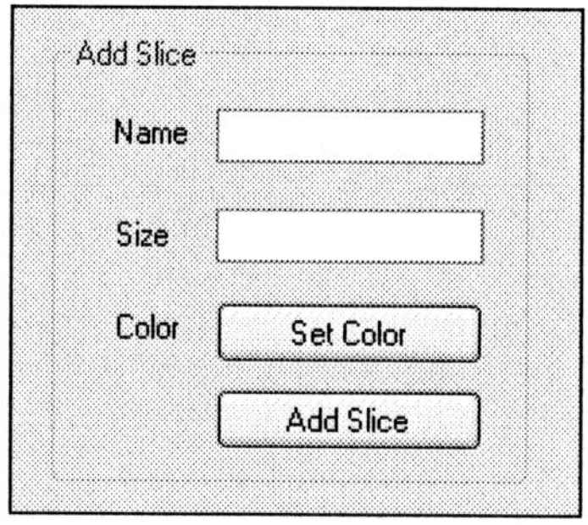

4. Drag another GroupBox and set its text to Remove Slice.
5. Drag a TextBox into this new GroupBox container and name it removeSliceNameTextBox.
6. Also add a button named removeSliceButton and set its text to Remove Slice.
7. Add a label next to the textbox and set the text to Name. Now your GroupBox should look like the following figure:

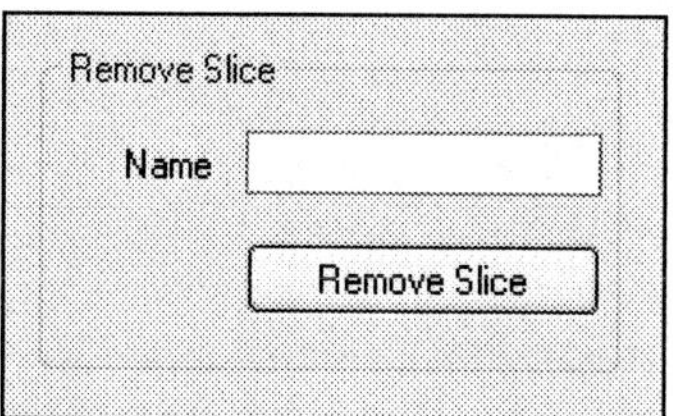

8. Drag a ColorDialog from the Toolbox onto the form. This will be automatically named `colorDialog1`.
9. In the `Form1` class add the next three member variables that will be used for temporary operations when adding and removing slices.

```
Color tempSliceColor;
string tempSliceName;
int tempSliceSize;
```

10. Delete all the code in the `pieChart1_Load` method. It must look like this:

```
private void pieChart1_Load(object sender, EventArgs e)
{
}
```

11. In the design view double-click the Set Color button. This will bring you to the button-click event-handler method:

```
private void addSliceColorButton_Click(object sender, EventArgs e)
{
  colorDialog1.ShowDialog();
  tempSliceColor = colorDialog1.Color;
  addSliceColorButton.BackColor = tempSliceColor;
}
```

12. Double-click the Add Slice button. Insert the new piece of code so that it looks like:

```
private void addSliceButton_Click_1(object sender, EventArgs e)
{
  if (addSliceNameTextBox.Text.Length <= 20)
  {
    tempSliceName = addSliceNameTextBox.Text;
  }
  else
  {
    MessageBox.Show("The entered name is not un up to 20 char
                     string");
    return;
  }
  if (ParseNumber(addSliceSizeTextBox.Text))
  {
    if(addSliceSizeTextBox.Text != "")
      tempSliceSize = Int32.Parse(addSliceSizeTextBox.Text);
    if (tempSliceSize == 0)
      return;
  }
  else
  {
    MessageBox.Show("The entered size is not an up to 8 digit
                     number!");
    return;
  }
  if (tempSliceColor.A == 0)
    tempSliceColor = Color.FromArgb(255, 255, 255, 255);
  pieChart1.AddSlice(new Slice(tempSliceName, tempSliceSize,
                     tempSliceColor));
  pieChart1.Invalidate();
  // clean name, size and color
  addSliceNameTextBox.Text = "";
  addSliceSizeTextBox.Text = "";
  tempSliceName = "";
  tempSliceColor = Color.FromArgb(255, 255, 255);
  tempSliceSize = 0;
  colorDialog1.Color = Color.FromArgb(255, 255, 255, 255);
  addSliceColorButton.BackColor = Color.FromArgb(236, 233, 216);
}
```

13. Once again, do that double-click operation on the Remove Slice button, and modify the newly added method:

```
private void removeSliceButton_Click(object sender, EventArgs e)
{
  tempSliceName = removeSliceNameTextBox.Text;
  pieChart1.RemoveSlice(tempSliceName);
}
```

14. Add a new method to the `Form1` class:

```
private bool ParseNumber(string userNumber)
{
  //create our parser that will do all our work for us
  Regex parser = new Regex(@"^\d{0,8}$");
  //return the bool result of parser's findings
  return parser.IsMatch(userNumber);
}
```

15. For the last added method to work, insert the following line of code in the beginning of the `Form1.cs`:

```
using System.Text.RegularExpressions;
```

16. Build the application, execute, and enjoy using the `PieChart` control.

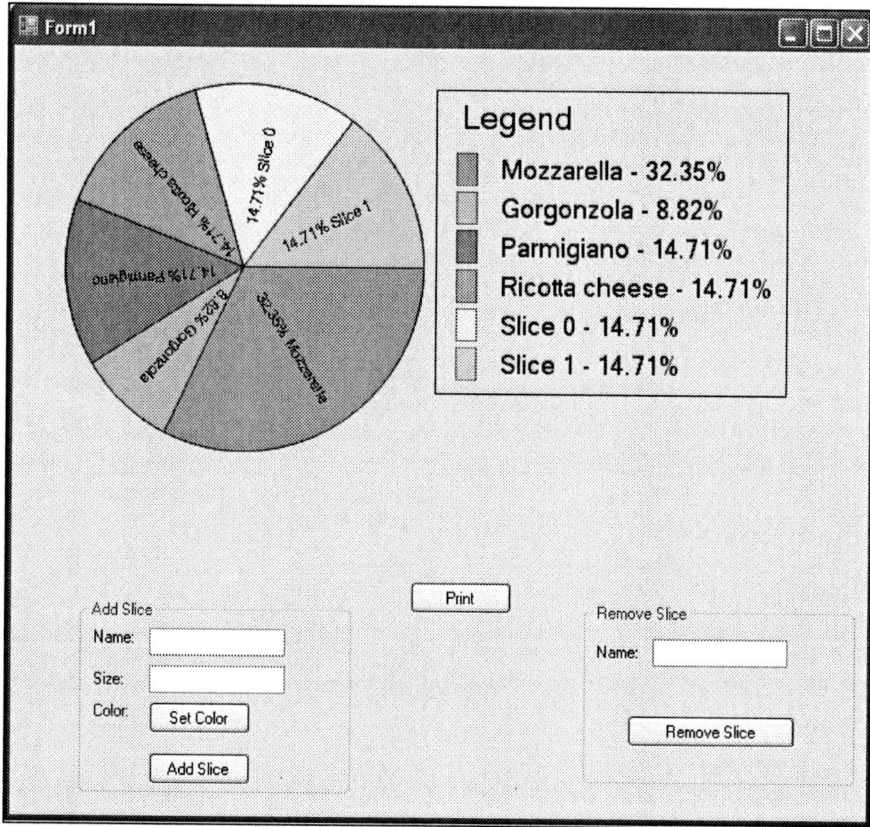

What Just Happened?

You have inserted two GroupBoxes with Add Slice and Remove Slice functionality. You can add slices by providing the name, the size, and the slice color. When you hit the Set Color button, a dialog will show up letting you choose the color. After choosing a color, it will be kept in the `tempSliceColor` object; also you will change the background of the button to give your user a visual confirmation.

```
tempSliceColor = colorDialog1.Color;
addSliceColorButton.BackColor = tempSliceColor;
```

When the user enters the data for a new slice and hits the Add Slice button, first you'll process the input data. The size will be cast to an integer, and a message box will display if it doesn't pass a validation test.

```
if (ParseNumber(addSliceSizeTextBox.Text))
{
  if(addSliceSizeTextBox.Text != "")
    tempSliceSize = Int32.Parse(addSliceSizeTextBox.Text);
  if (tempSliceSize == 0)
    return;
```

```
}
else
{
  MessageBox.Show("The entered size is not an up to 8 digit number!");
  return;
}
```

The `ParseNumber()` method uses a regular expression that verifies that the input string is a number of maximum 8 digits.

```
private bool ParseNumber(string userNumber)
{
  //create our parser that will do all our work for us
  Regex parser = new Regex(@"^\d{0,8}$");
  //return the bool result of parser's findings
  return parser.IsMatch(userNumber);
}
```

An alternative would have been to use the `Int32.TryParse()` method, which returns `True` if the input string can successfully cast to an integer. It also returns the integer version of the string in the form of an out parameter. In this case, you would have called this method like this:

```
if (!Int32.TryParse(addSliceSizeTextBox.Text, out tempSliceSize) ||
    tempSliceSize <= 0)
{
  MessageBox.Show("The entered size is not a positive integer!");
  return;
}
```

If no color is selected, the default color, which is a fully transparent one, will be used. In practice, the default color will look white.

```
if (tempSliceColor.A == 0)
  tempSliceColor = Color.FromArgb(255, 255, 255, 255);
```

If the user doesn't type a slice name, the `PieChart` control will automatically generate names such as Slice 0, Slice 1, and so on. The validation rule we implement is to make sure the entered name isn't larger than 20 characters.

```
if (addSliceNameTextBox.Text.Length <= 20)
{
  tempSliceName = addSliceNameTextBox.Text;
}
else
{
  MessageBox.Show("The entered name is not un up to 20 char string");
  return;
}
```

After validating the input data, the `AddSlice()` method of the control is called to create a new slice:

```
pieChart1.AddSlice(new Slice(tempSliceName, tempSliceSize,
                   tempSliceColor));
pieChart1.Invalidate();
```

To remove slices, we simply call the control's `RemoveSlice` method, passing as parameter the text entered by the user:

```
private void removeSliceButton_Click(object sender, EventArgs e)
{
  tempSliceName = removeSliceNameTextBox.Text;
  pieChart1.RemoveSlice(tempSliceName);
}
```

Summary

In this chapter you created a fully functional control from scratch. You created the control in multiple stages, implementing one feature at a time, facing challenges with each iteration. In the end, you succeeded, and ended up with quite a functional control, that can be easily customized for use in real-world projects.

While you may not be able to sell this control as it is (but who knows!), you're on the right track to make the most out of what you've learned in this book. With a few design skills and well-stated specifications, you can create fully functional and attractive custom controls, and use them to improve your current projects.

Always have your user in mind when developing not only custom controls, but also any other kind of software that has a user interface. Try to identify the user needs, pay attention to user ideas, and see where the troubles come from. This way serious ideas are born, and successful software is written.

Good luck!

Distributing Custom Controls

All the examples in this book were created, implemented, and tested in Windows Application projects. This made it easier to start building custom controls, and the method is guaranteed to work with any version of Visual Studio, including Visual C# Express. Of course all the custom controls will finally be inserted into Windows Forms, but you can create custom controls without making the projects dependent on a form.

When you want to distribute one or more custom controls you don't send the user the whole application containing the custom control. The custom controls can be packed, held, and distributed using a library.

This compiled library is actually a DLL file. **DLL** stands for dynamic link library, a set of program components that can be called from external programs. For example, your Windows operating system uses `Gdiplus.dll`, which holds graphical components used to render graphical objects.

Why do we use DLL files? The answer is simple! Let's assume you want to call a function that has a large body in several software components. You can include the function's code in all your software components or you can create a DLL containing this function and reference the DLL from all of your software components. You can even create your own library that contains several of your own custom controls.

Visual Studio offers two project types you could use to create custom controls: Windows Control Library projects and Class Library projects. Both versions hold classes and both generate DLL files when compiled. Visual C# Express not only provides the Class Library template but it also knows how to load a Windows Control Library project. The two project templates mentioned above differ in the code that is automatically created for you when you start the project. The Class Library project template is generic, and when a project is created you get a new class called Class1. When creating a Windows Control Library project, the environment creates a new custom control class named UserControl1.

In the end, both project templates are very similar, and both can be used to start creating custom controls. In the rest of this appendix, we'll cover both project templates, and we'll show you then how to use such an independent control compiled as a DLL file. Then you'll learn how to import the DLL file and use it in your projects.

Creating a Control Library Using Visual Studio 2005

To create a Windows Control Library using Visual Studio 2005 you need to follow a few simple steps. We'll explain this with an example:

1. First, you need to start a new Windows Control Library project. We're calling it CustomControls_WindowsControlLibrary here.

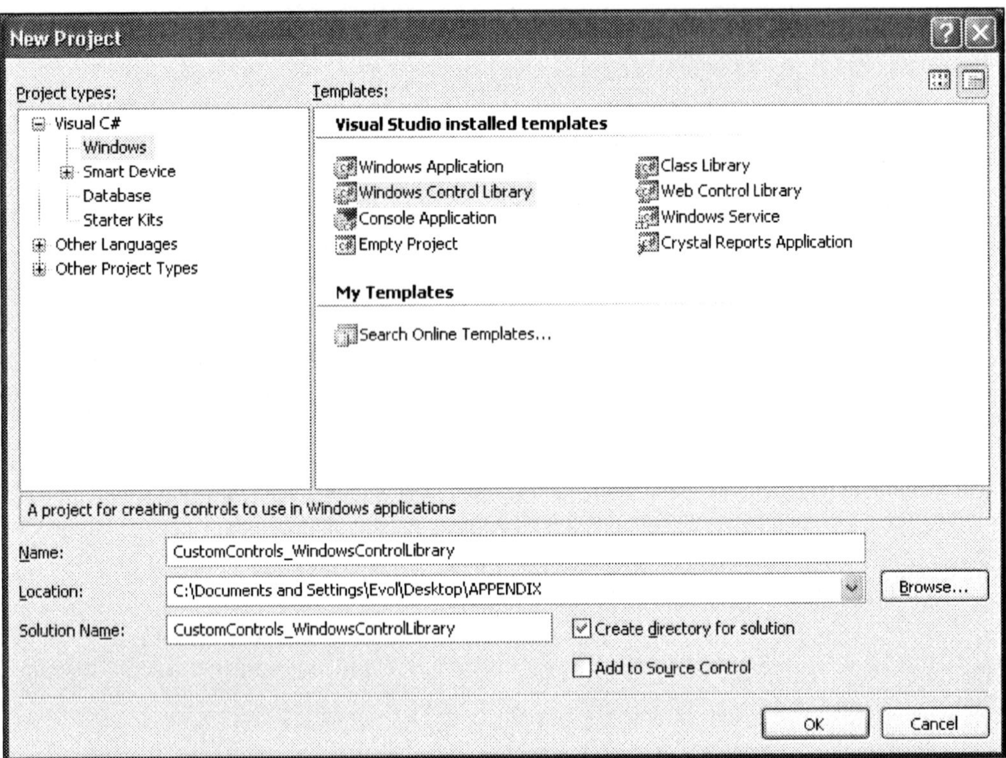

2. When creating this Windows Control Library, a User Control named UserControl1 will be automatically created and added to this project.

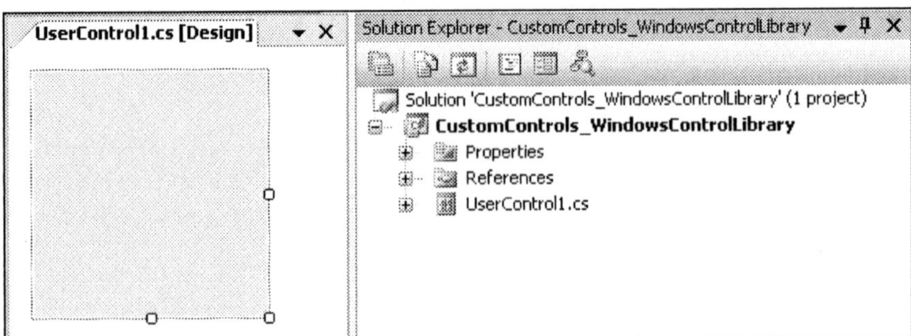

3. To change the default name, you need to right-click the UserControl1 and rename it as FirstControl. You will be asked if you want the change to propagate to all files, classes, and references. You'd normally choose "Yes".
4. Let's add some code to our fictional control. Right-click the `FirstControl` in Design View and choose View Code. In the `FirstControl` class add this member method:

```
protected override void OnPaint(PaintEventArgs e)
{
  e.Graphics.DrawEllipse(Pens.Black, ClientRectangle);
  Font stringFont = new Font("Arial", 12);
  e.Graphics.DrawString(
               "First custom control in the Windows Control Library",
               stringFont, Brushes.Blue, ClientRectangle);
  base.OnPaint(e);
}
```

5. Let's add another control to the project now. Right-click CustomControls_WindowsControlLibrary in Solution Explorer and choose Add | User Control. Change the name to SecondControl.

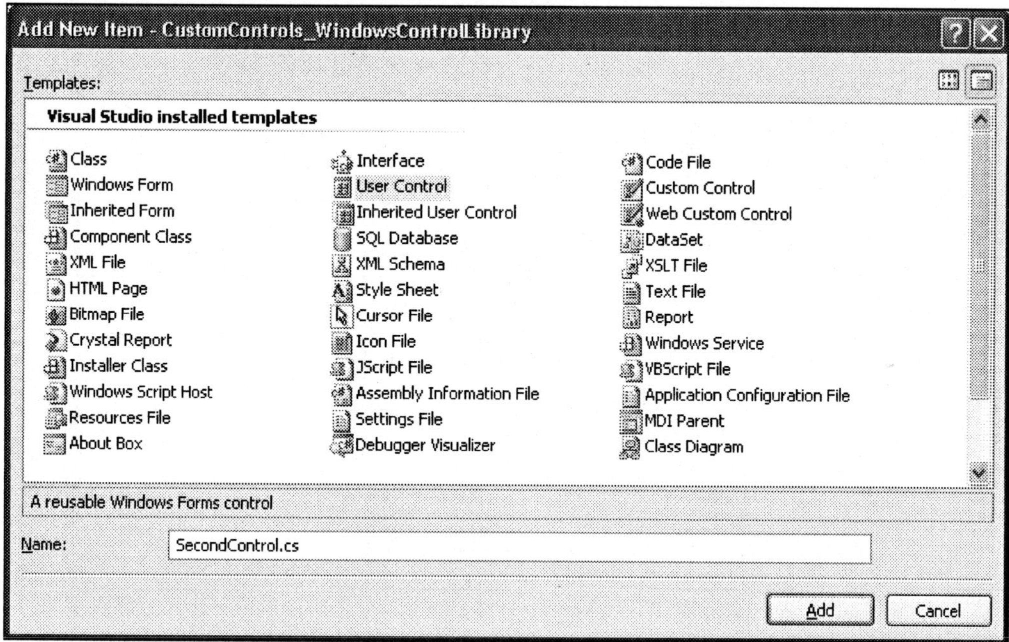

6. Go to the newly added class `UserControl2`, by choosing to view code in the right-click menu. Add the following method:

```
protected override void OnPaint(PaintEventArgs e)
{
  e.Graphics.DrawEllipse(Pens.Red, ClientRectangle);
  Font stringFont = new Font("Arial", 12);
  e.Graphics.DrawString(
               "Second custom control in the Windows Control Library",
               stringFont, Brushes.LightPink, ClientRectangle);
  base.OnPaint(e);
}
```

7. Now rebuild your project. The library will be built and a DLL file called `CustomControls_WindowsControlLibrary.dll` will be generated. This will be the file that you will distribute.

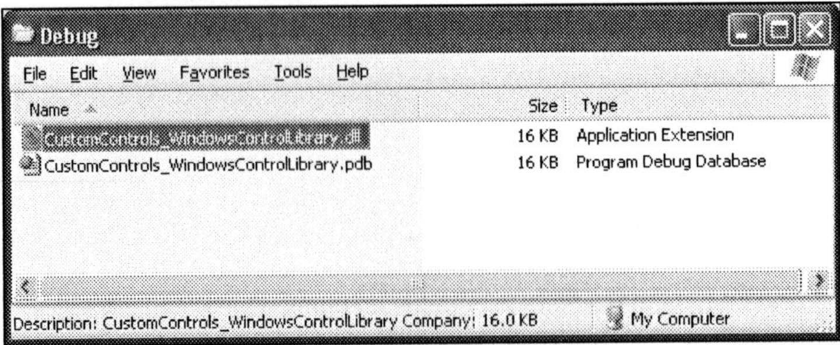

A DLL was created. This file is actually the Custom Controls Library. This was a very simple creation process. Start your own Windows Control Library project. Add some custom controls and implement their functionality. Build the project and feel free to do whatever you want with your DLL file; it is your first Custom Control Library. The custom control's functionality was kept to minimum, because it was not the important thing in this example.

Creating a Control Library Using Visual C# Express 2005

To create a control library using Visual C# Express, the steps are similar. Here's an example of how things would go:

1. Start a new Class Library project. Name it CustomControls_ClassLibrary.

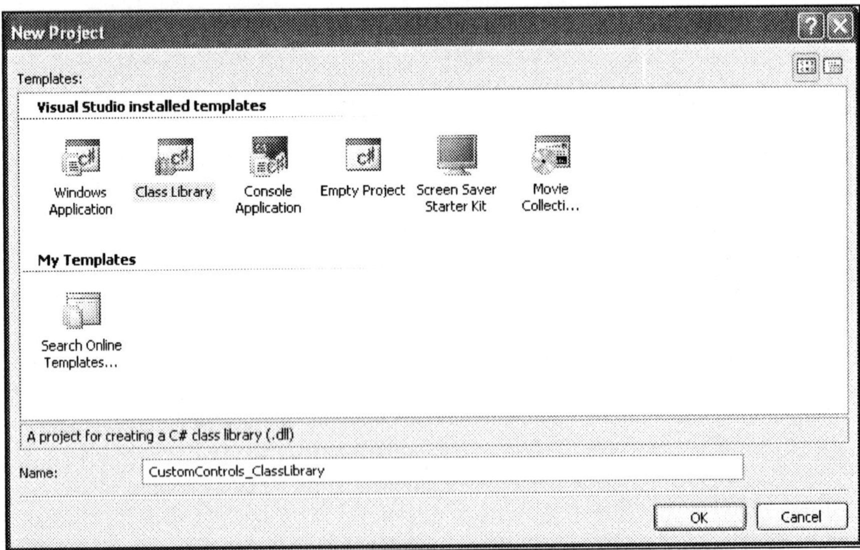

2. When creating a Class Library project, a new class named `Class1` will be automatically created and added to the project. Delete this class.

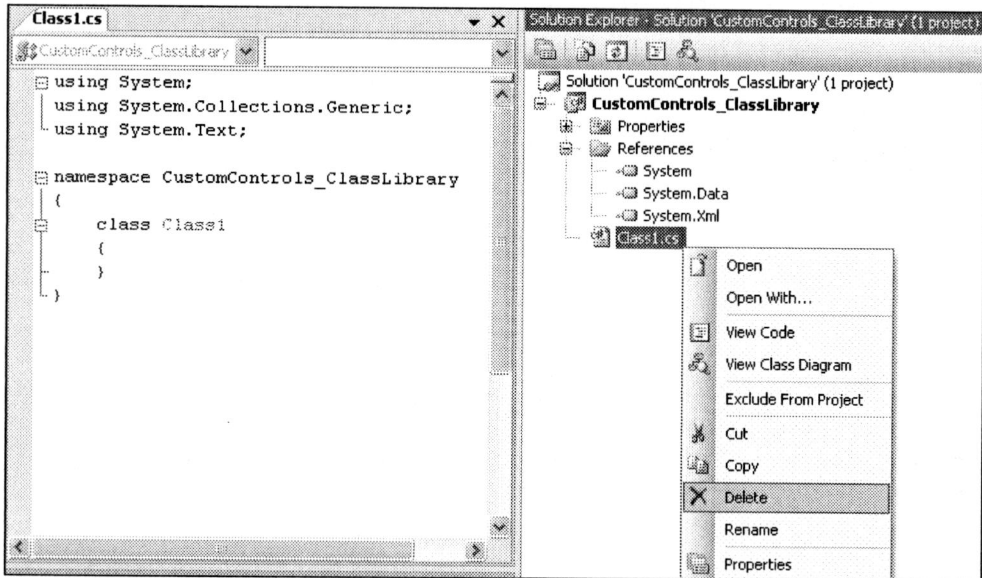

3. Add a new UserControl by right-clicking CustomControls_ClassLibrary and choosing Add | User Control. Name it ThirdControl.
4. Add the following method to the class:

```
protected override void OnPaint(PaintEventArgs e)
{
  e.Graphics.DrawEllipse(Pens.Green, ClientRectangle);
  Font stringFont = new Font("Arial", 12);
  e.Graphics.DrawString("First custom control in the Class Library. It
            is named ThirdControl for this example, but is actually
            the first one in the CustomControls_Class Library.",
            stringFont, Brushes.GreenYellow, ClientRectangle);
  base.OnPaint(e);
}
```

5. Build. A DLL file called `CustomControls_ClassLibrary.dll` will be generated as output.

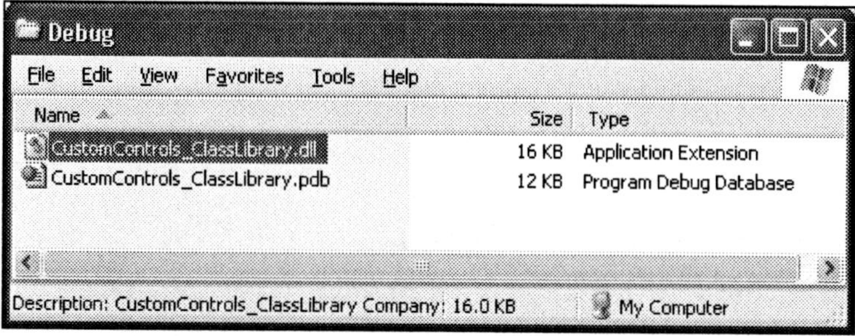

You have created a Class Library containing a custom control. This library was compiled as a DLL file and can be loaded in other projects where you want to use it. When creating Class Library projects, you'll usually delete the `class1` automatically inserted by the Class Library template and manually add your custom controls.

Using a Custom Control Library

You have now learned how to create a Custom Control Library. There are more ways to do the job, but all have the same result. You end up with a DLL file containing some custom controls that you (or your clients) want to use. The steps for using such a DLL file are identical in Visual C# Express and Visual Studio 2005:

1. Start a new Windows Application project, naming it LibraryTester.
2. First you will need to add a reference to the custom controls library. Right-click References in the Solution Explorer and click on Add Reference.

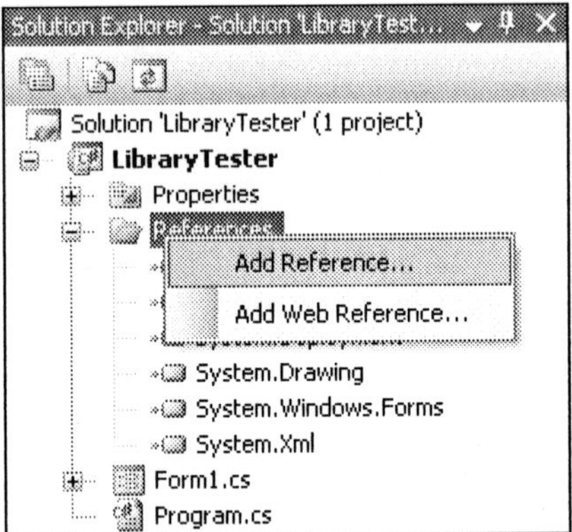

3. Select the Browse tab and find the DLL that you are looking for: CustomControls_WindowsControlLibrary or CustomControls_ClassLibrary (the following screenshot is for CustomControls_ClassLibrary):

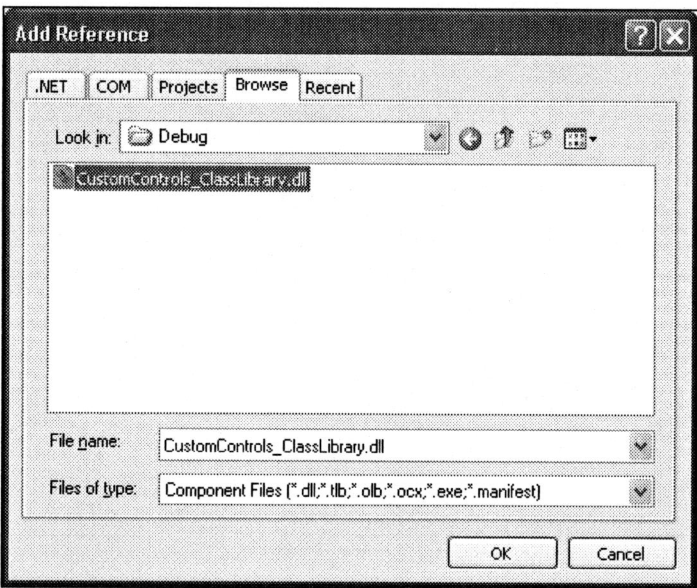

4. Add a new tab in the Toolbox, named My controls. To create a new tab you just need to right-click the Toolbox and select Add Tab.
5. Right-click this new tab and select Choose Items. Click Browse to browse to your new control library entry and open it. This will select the controls of the library for you.

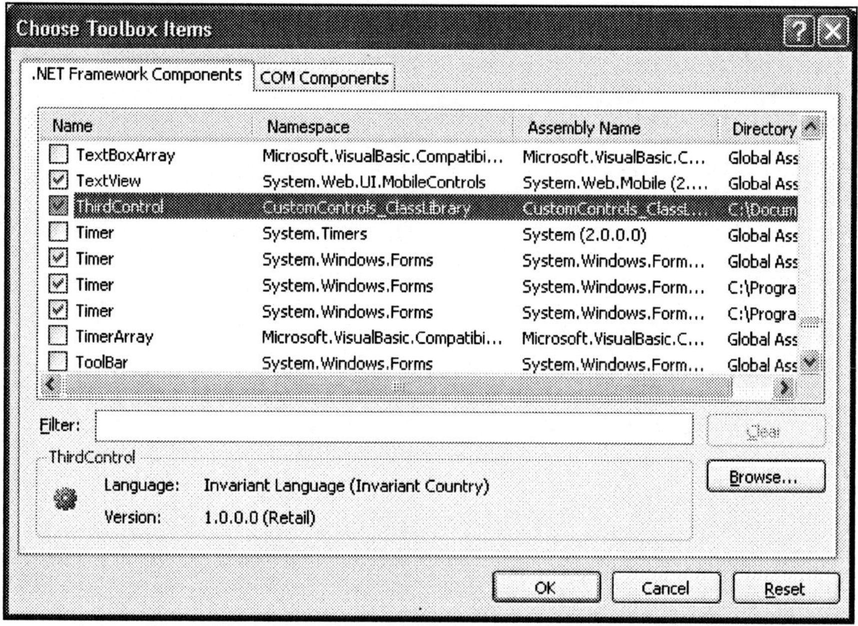

6. Choose OK. In the My Controls tab in the Toolbox, the recently added controls will be seen.

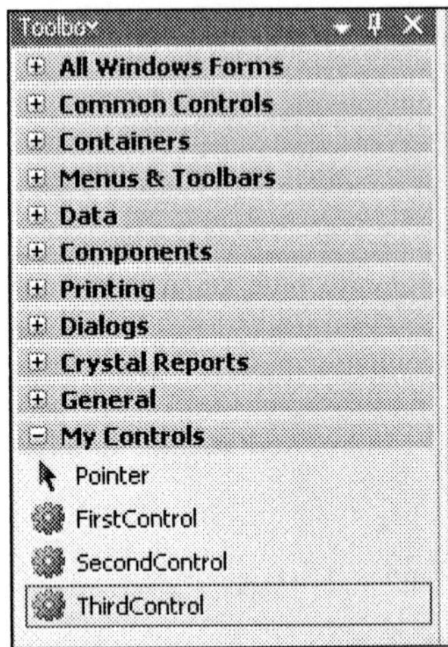

> If you add just the `CustomControls_ClassLibrary` DLL file you will have just the ThirdControl in the My Controls tab. The FirstControl and the SecondControl controls are part of `CustomControls_WindowsControlLibrary`.

7. Drag the new controls to your form, to ensure they really work.
8. Double-click the form to add the `Load` event handler. Assuming you've references to both libraries and have added all the three controls to your form, you could complete the event handler like this:

```
private void Form1_Load(object sender, EventArgs e)
{
  // if you have added the FistControl and SecondControl
  firstControl1.BackColor = Color.LightCoral;
  secondControl1.BackColor = Color.DarkGoldenrod;
  // if you have added the ThirdControl
  thirdControl1.BackColor = Color.Brown;
}
```

9. Building and executing the application will have the referenced controls working for you:

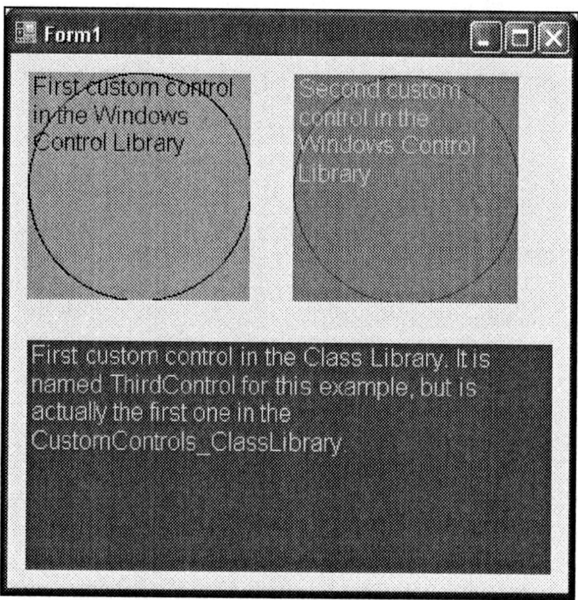

To use the Custom Control Library you mainly need to follow two steps: the first is to add a new reference to this DLL, and the second is to add the controls to the toolbox so you can easily access them.

> When you use custom controls this way, by referencing their DLL files, you need to rebuild the DLLs every time you need to implement a change in the controls.

Index

A

B

C

D

E

F

G

H

I

M

N

O

P

R

S

T

U

V

W

PACKT PUBLISHING

Thank you for buying Web Content Building Custom Controls with Visual C# 2005

About Packt Publishing

Packt, pronounced 'packed', published its first book "*Mastering phpMyAdmin for Effective MySQL Management*" in April 2004 and subsequently continued to specialize in publishing highly focused books on specific technologies and solutions.

Our books and publications share the experiences of your fellow IT professionals in adapting and customizing today's systems, applications, and frameworks. Our solution-based books give you the knowledge and power to customize the software and technologies you're using to get the job done. Packt books are more specific and less general than the IT books you have seen in the past. Our unique business model allows us to bring you more focused information, giving you more of what you need to know, and less of what you don't.

Packt is a modern, yet unique publishing company, which focuses on producing quality, cutting-edge books for communities of developers, administrators, and newbies alike. For more information, please visit our website: `www.packtpub.com`.

Writing for Packt

We welcome all inquiries from people who are interested in authoring. Book proposals should be sent to `authors@packtpub.com`. If your book idea is still at an early stage and you would like to discuss it first before writing a formal book proposal, contact us; one of our commissioning editors will get in touch with you.

We're not just looking for published authors; if you have strong technical skills but no writing experience, our experienced editors can help you develop a writing career, or simply get some additional reward for your expertise.

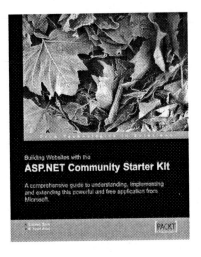

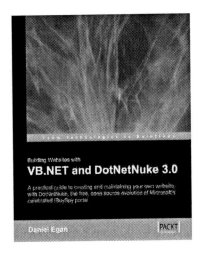

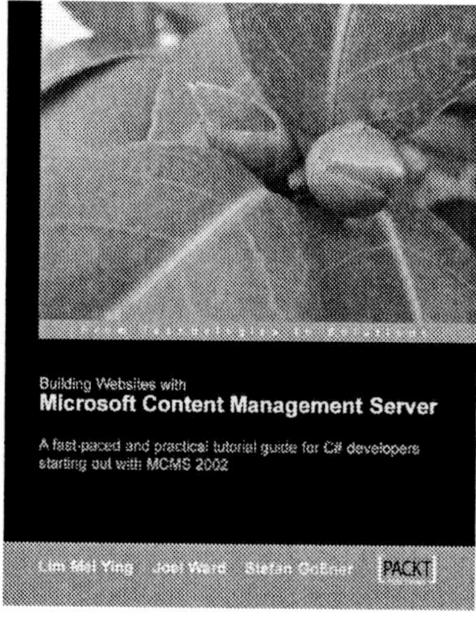

Building Websites with Microsoft Content Management Server

ISBN: 1904811167 Paperback: 638 pages

A fast-paced and practical tutorial guide for C# developers starting out with MCMS 2002

1. Learn directly from recognized community experts
2. Rapid developer-level tutorials built logically throughout the book
3. Develops a feature-rich custom site incrementally
4. Tips and Tricks from developer newsgroups and online communities

---

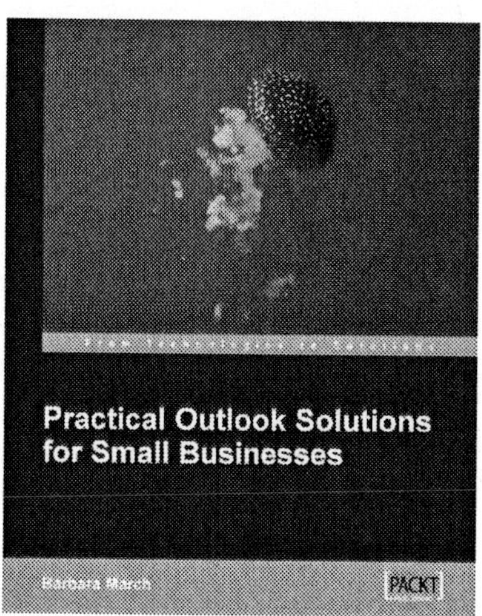

The Microsoft Outlook Ideas Book

ISBN: 1904811701 Paperback: 150 pages

How to organise and manage yourself, your team, and your activities with Outlook and Exchange

1. Packed with ideas of how all Outlook users can create useful solutions you never thought possible
2. Step-by-step instructions for storing and extracting information from the Calendar, Contacts and Tasks folders to create integrated business solutions
3. Great ideas for business, personal, educational and home users

Please check **www.PacktPub.com** for information on our titles

Printed in the United Kingdom
by Lightning Source UK Ltd.
113603UKS00002BB/2

9 781904 811602